The Logic of Culture

B

NEW PERSPECTIVES ON THE PAST

General Editor
Constantin Fasolt, University of Chicago

Advisory Editors
Michael Burns, Mount Holyoke College
Pamela Kyle Crossley, Dartmouth College
R. I. Moore, University of Newcastle upon Tyne
Ian Morris, Stanford University
Patrick Wormald, Christ Church, Oxford
Heide Wunder, Universität-Gesamthochschule Kassel

PUBLISHED

IN PREPARATION

* now out of print

The Logic of Culture

Authority and Identity in the Modern Era

William Ray

BLACKWELL
Publishers

First published 2001

2 4 6 8 10 9 7 5 3 1

Blackwell Publishers Ltd
108 Cowley Road
Oxford OX4 1JF
UK

Blackwell Publishers Inc.
350 Main Street
Malden, Massachusetts 02148
USA

British Library Cataloguing in Publication Data
A CIP catalogue record for this book is available from the British Library.

Library of Congress Cataloging-in-Publication Data
Ray, William, 1944–
    The logic of culture : authority and identity in the Modern Era /
William Ray.
        p.   cm. — (New perspectives on the past)
Includes bibliographical references and index.
    ISBN 0–631–21343–0 (alk. paper) — ISBN 0–631–21344–9 (pbk. : alk. paper)
    1. Culture.   2. Group identity.   3. History, Modern.   I. Title.
II. New perspectives on the past (Blackwell Publishers)
    HM621 .R39   2001
    306 — dc21
                                        2001000759

Typeset in 11 on 13pt Sabon
by SetSystems Ltd, Saffron Walden, Essex
Printed in Great Britain by Antony Rowe Ltd, Chippenham, Wilts.

This book is printed on acid-free paper.

Contents

Series Editor's Preface

History is one of many fields of knowledge. Like other fields it has two elements: boundaries and contents. The boundaries of history first acquired their modern shape in early modern Europe. They include, among other things, such basic principles as the assumption that time is divisible into past, present, and future; that the past can be known by means of records and remainders surviving to the present; that culture can be distinguished from nature; that anachronism can be avoided; that subjects are different from objects; that human beings are capable of taking action; and that action is shaped by circumstance. Above all else, of course, they include the assumption that history does actually constitute a separate field of knowledge that is in fact divided from neighbouring fields – not merely a hitherto neglected corner of some other field whose rightful owners ought ideally, and are expected eventually, to reclaim it from the squatters now dwelling there without authorization and cultivate it properly with the tools of, say, an improved theology or a more subtle natural science.

A prodigious harvest has been gathered from the field bounded by those assumptions. Making a tentative beginning with the humanist discovery of antiquity, gaining confidence with the Enlightenment critique of religion, and blossoming into full professionalization in the nineteenth century, modern historians have managed to turn their produce into an elementary ingredient in democratic education and a staple of cultural consumption. They have extracted mountains of evidence from archives and turned it into books whose truth can be assayed by anyone who cares to follow their instructions. They have dismantled ancient legends that had been handed down through the ages and laid them to rest in modern libraries. They have emancipated the study of the past from prophecy, apocalypticism, and other providential explications of the future. Pronouncements on the past no longer command respect unless they have been authenticated by reference to documents. Myths and superstitions have given way to knowledge of unprecedented depth, precision, and extent. Compared with what we read in older books, the books of history today are veritable miracles of comprehension, exactitude, and impartiality.

Success, however, has its price. None of the assumptions defining the modern practices of history are self-evidently true. The more they are obeyed, the less it seems they can be trusted. Having probed the realm of culture to its frontiers, we cannot find the boundary by which it is supposed to be divided from the empire of nature. Having raised our standards of objectivity to glorious heights, we are afflicted with vertiginous attacks of relativity. Having mined the archives to rock bottom, we find that the ores turn out to yield no meaning without amalgamation. And having religiously observed the boundary between the present and the past, we find that the past does not live in the records but in our own imagination. The boundaries of history have been worn down; the field is lying open to erosion.

The books in this series are meant to point a way out of that predicament. The authors come from different disciplines, all of them specialists in one subject or another. They do not proceed alike. Some deal with subjects straddling familiar boundaries – chronological, geographical, and conceptual. Some focus on the boundaries themselves. Some bring new subjects into view. Some view old subjects from a new perspective. But all of them share a concern that our present understanding of history needs to be reconfigured if it is not to turn into a mere product of the past that it is seeking to explain. They are convinced that the past does have a meaning for the present that transcends the interest of specialists. And they are determined to keep that meaning within reach by writing good short books for non-specialists and specialists alike.

Constantin Fasolt
University of Chicago

Preface

Yes, another book on culture. It takes a certain amount of foolhardiness even to use the word in a title these days, much less to use it in the way I intend to. For unlike the many excellent accounts of culture that have been published in the past half century, and especially in the past decade, I do not intend to catalogue the meanings of the word or analyze its affiliation with a discipline or particular social class, much less lay bare its pernicious complicity with structures of domination. Most of the works that have been written on culture from the perspective of the humane – as opposed to the social – sciences, have been concerned with either the genesis of the term, or the various ways in which it has been used by individuals, political movements, ideologies, or historical periods, especially in the British tradition. My goal here is both humbler and more ambitious. I intend to explain what I think culture means for all of us at the level of a foundational logic of thought. Rather than looking at the different ways in which particular parties have invoked or used the term, I want to uncover what they all have in common, what the shared way of thinking might be that justifies their – and our – collective reliance on a term which manifestly means very different things for different people. The chapters that follow constitute a speculative essay, not a scholarly inquiry in particular traditions. What I am after might be called the "deep structure" or "grammar" of culture: the implicit conceptual syntax it provides for our thinking about individual and social identity, and historical progress.

As a category of thought and conceptualization, culture exercises extraordinary leverage. In the contemporary era it has acquired the status of a universal given, "a manifest truth unsullied by historical contingency," as Christopher Herbert aptly put it in his inquiry into the genesis of the anthropological concept of culture.[1] Yet the rule of culture is a historical phenomenon in all of its dimensions, not merely as a category of analysis, or signifier of social identity, but also as an ethic of self-realization, a model of moral progress, a form of authority, and a set of institutions. Only in the last two centuries have these various notions merged under one category and achieved widespread assent as a framework for understanding how individuals and collectives relate to each other, themselves, social practice, and history. It is the goal of this essay to shed some light on that merger, from its origins in the early modern revaluation of discursive authority, through its crystallization at the end of the Enlightenment in the word "culture," to its legacy in our contemporary practices of critique.

This would be an overly ambitious menu for a scholarly investigation. Like many other master tropes of our age, culture is too invested with conflicting values and meanings to be simply "understood." I shall therefore make no pretense of accounting for all the uses of the term in specific contexts. My concern is with excavating the underlying logic or grammar of thought which the "cultural way of thinking" purveys and charting the historical antecedents of that logic.

Even thus limited, the topic would be too vast were I to attempt accounting for national differences. While the paradigms and trends I outline are more or less applicable to most Western European and American traditions, I have focused on the articulation of culture as it occurred in Revolutionary France, with secondary emphasis on German and British thinkers. One could chart similar developments in most other developed European nations, but France makes an especially useful example for two reasons: it had set the paradigms of cultivated life during the preceding century; and the Revolutionary theoreticians who set out to create a new polity and citizenry were particularly explicit and methodological in their elaboration of culture as an instrument of social formation. Using specific case studies to complement the theoretical and historical overviews, I will examine the ideals of behavior, analytic strategies, ethical postures, cognitive agendas, and ideologies out of which the concept or logic of culture emerged, and which it has been used to underwrite.

It is a consequence of its brevity that this essay can do little justice to many of the complex historical developments it alludes to in the course of the argument, much less attend to the tremendous amount of excellent secondary literature that has in recent years undertaken the reevaluation of specific cultural phenomena or polemics. Many of the developments I chart are embedded in multiple systems of determination and can be understood from a number of different perspectives more attentive to material, political, spiritual and social dimensions. However, this is a book about the emergence of a very broad framework of analysis, the full account of which has required neglecting these many other factors. I would simply refer the reader to the numerous detailed studies of how "culture" functions with relation to specific political, economic, and ideological systems in various periods and countries.

Similarly, the more general philosophical and historical developments that I invoke as a framework of analysis have received extensive treatment elsewhere. It is not my intention to discount their particularities or downplay the many ways in which they are unrelated. However, at the risk of running counter to the post-Foucauldian infatuation with ruptures and discontinuities, I seek to uncover the ways in which these various periods and practices might be united by a subterranean logic or shared analytic framework that has become so universal, so deeply embedded in our thought that we take it for granted.

Many people and many discussions are behind this book. I have come to understand what I mean by culture in the course of a decade of vigorous debate, with colleagues, friends, and students. In a sense this essay is a way of explaining to all those who were generous enough to spend their time trying to enlighten me, that which I could never quite get across in the course of a conversation, namely, just what I mean by culture. Were it not for their interest this essay would never have seen the day. Needless to say, none of them should be held responsible for the defects in what follows.

The idea of this book came from Constantin Fasolt, who should receive any credit it accrues. Under his encouragement, it took shape in a number of discussions with him and the other Fellows of the National Humanities Center in 1996–7, to all of whom I am indebted, but especially David Armitage, Don Lopez, and Chris Waters. I also received valuable feedback on my ideas on reading from the French History Seminar sponsored by the

Center, and am grateful to Philip Stewart, Steven Vincent, and the other members of that group for inviting me. I could not even begin to calculate the contribution of Keith Luria, with whom I have shared many a lively discussion over lunch in Paris, or Mary Sheriff, who has been a source of stimulation and support for years. It has been my great fortune to teach for many years at an institution that actually still has a distinct "culture" and the kind of "community" that theoreticians of culture generally evoke only with nostalgia. My debts, intellectual and otherwise, to the following friends and colleagues are so great and varied that I can only express them alphabetically: thank you, Doris Berkvam, Samuel Danon, Nathalia King, Lisa Steinman and Christopher Zinn, for years of intellectual stimulation and friendship. I am especially grateful to Elizabeth Drumm and Hugh Hochman for their careful reading of early drafts, and to Géraldine Deries, who took on the task of reading the final draft of the entire work in spite of pressing time constraints of her own. And finally I must thank my best reader and friend, Kathleen Nicholson, for her indefatigable support and perceptive critique, from the start of this project to the end.

This project was made possible by the generous support of the Reed College Faculty Paid Leave Awards Program, and the Levine Fund, as well as by the National Humanities Center and the National Endowment for the Humanities, to all of whom I express my gratitude.

Introduction:
The Paradox of Culture

In 1791, during an impassioned plea for the founding of new monuments, a French administrator named Armand-Guy Kersaint evokes a "new religion that considers people in their relationships with one another." Kersaint christens this new religion the "cult of laws" because its immediate objects of worship are the laws emanating from the national assembly and in particular the new constitution.[1] However, the deity behind these laws, the entity that gives them their authority and guarantees that they are just, is none other than the collective will and identity of the people – what the Revolutionaries called "the public thing." In that sense, what the people are to venerate, the entity to which they are to pledge their obedience, is simply an abstract projection of themselves, considered as members of a coherent collective. The French people understand themselves as both the subject and the object of their "new religion" – and in two different capacities: as individuals lending their will to the legislative process and legitimating its decrees with their free consent and obedience; and as a collective entity whose identity transcends the sum of its parts and can only be inferred from the rules it leaves in its wake – the decrees, laws and shared practices which express and constrain it.

Such ideas would have been unthinkable in France a few centuries earlier, as in most other parts of Europe. The law was embodied not in the people, but in the church and the monarch; the human community did not reflect collective will, but divine design. One of the purposes of this book is to understand what made it possible to think the way Kersaint does, and to seek the answer in the new forms of discursive behavior that developed from the early modern period up through the nineteenth century.

It is fitting that Kersaint makes his observation in the course of an argument about monuments and art, and how they relate to the nation's collective identity. For his "new religion" outlines a dialectic model of self-expression and law formation that would subsequently be generalized to all human communities under the rubric of "culture." Like the cult of the law, which aimed at securing the coincidence of law and individual belief "in the heart of the virtuous person," the idea of "culture" welds rational autonomy and the expression of individual will to the disclosure and production of a framework of rules, values, beliefs, and practices. These situate, legitimate, and give meaning to specific acts, as well as a distinctive identity to the community; the complex whole which they form is what social scientists denote with their use of the term "culture."

But just as in Kersaint's model the new religion is both the ground of individual initiative and its result, so too there is another side of culture that consists of the free acts of self-expression that produce the historical legacy of the collective. This is Culture with an uppercase, and it designates the endeavors of self-realization we undertake within the constraints of our culture and, by extension, the products of those endeavors. Culture, like the "public thing" is both the origin of individual action and its result. It is both the abstract term we use to characterize a communal heritage and the acts of assessment and interpretation individuals engage in as a means of improving that heritage – and asserting themselves as both different from, yet members of, their community.

These various meanings resonate unevenly in the expressions that have proliferated in the last half century around the term "culture." "Cultural Revolution," "cultural evolution," "culture shock," "culture wars," "cultural capital," "corporate culture," "counter culture," "working-class culture," "popular culture," "high culture," "the culture of personality," "cultural literacy," "the Culture Industry," "multiculturalism," "cultural diversity," "cultural opportunity," "cultural studies" – the proliferation of concepts like these testify not only to protean character of "culture," but also to its value as an ideological category and political trump card. Few terms are as persistent and ubiquitous in modern western intellectual discourse, and few combine so many contradictory meanings. Wielded by the Left and the Right alike, from

Matthew Arnold to Maxim Gorky, from advocates of cultural diversity to those who decry it, "culture" resists reduction to any simple meaning.

In our general usage, we use the term to designate the shared traditions, values, and relationships, the *unconscious* cognitive and social reflexes which members of a community share and collectively embody. Paradoxically, though, we use the same term to denote the *self-conscious* intellectual and artistic efforts of individuals to express, enrich, and distinguish themselves, as well as the works such efforts produce and the institutions that foster them. In the first case "culture" names the beliefs and practices we *share* with all members of our society; in the second "Culture" marks our efforts to fashion ourselves into *particulars*, that we might acquire a measure of distinction within that society.

"Culture" thus articulates the tension between two antithetical concepts of identity: it tells us to think of ourselves as being who we are because of what we have in common with all the other members of our society or community, but it also says we develop a distinctive particular identity by virtue of our efforts to know and fashion ourselves as individuals. In abstract terms, culture simultaneously connotes sameness and difference, shared habit and idiosyncratic style, collective reflex and particular endeavor, unconsciously assimilated beliefs and consciously won convictions, the effortlessly inherited residue of social existence, and the expression of a striving for individuality.

To these conflicting semantic vectors of "culture" correspond two modalities of being and two visions of how we acquire our identity. Culture as communal identity tells us we become who we are in spite of ourselves, effortlessly and inexorably, as we unconsciously internalize our community's habits of thought, values, and forms of behavior. Culture as self-improvement contradicts this message by encouraging us to think of our selves as something we construct through a strenuous, deliberate, self-conscious pursuit of individual perfection. Culture thus locates authenticity simultaneously in our most reflective, institutionally mediated strivings and in our immediate social reflexes which elude awareness precisely because they set its parameters. Paradoxically, although we cultivate ourselves in order to realize our unique potential against the pressures to conform, we measure our level of cultivation in the degree to which we have assimilated norms and rules: canons, bodies of knowledge, artistic traditions, rhetorical skills.

"Culture"'s alternate celebration of the conscious and the unconscious complicates its ethical valuation as well. Identifying a practice as "culturally constructed" has become shorthand in recent years for disqualifying it as inauthentic or at least open to examination and revision.[2] At the same time, however, cultural heritage is regularly invoked as a sacred domain of identity so authentic that to contest or attempt to regulate its content, especially in the case of minority communities, is tantamount to obliterating the identity and dignity of its subjects. A similar contradiction is visible in the cultivated classes' nostalgia for undivided, "organic" life, which is always enunciated from within a high Cultural enterprise. Celebrations of the blissful cultural embeddedness of others almost always occur as part of a project of critical self-distancing from the reflexes and practices of one's own society.

The most visible paradox of culture in the postmodern era is of course the fact that the imperative to "distinguish oneself" has become universal. What we all have in common is our uniqueness. We are all taught to think for ourselves; and the badge of our self-awareness is our ability to question the cultural values we take pride in understanding. The compulsion to overcome cultural reflex has become our distinguishing cultural reflex.

If our common usage of the term "culture" is fraught with contradictions, so too are the formal models of knowledge and truth that have been elaborated in its name. The idea of culture as rational self-perfection assumes knowledge can be achieved through systematic inquiry, self-discipline and social self-aware-ness – the kind of programs which educational institutions prom-ulgate in the name of civilization, progress, and self-fulfillment. Yet since before the Enlightenment, the idea that truth is the product of disciplined rational inquiry has competed with a view that sees all claims to "truth" as transcriptions of cultural preju-dice and preconception, as accounts biased by local contingencies, internalized through habit and ritual, and operating at a subcon-scious level.

This conviction that our culture contaminates what and how we know leads not only to skepticism of received truths, but to an instinctive enthusiasm for forms and practices that subvert tradition. Contesting one's culture thus comes to compete with assimilating that culture as the surest course toward intellectual and moral autonomy: it is the only certain means of avoiding determination by collective habits. Of course, both intellectual skepticism and the taste for the subversive can themselves be thought of as culturally determined tendencies: wanting to get free of culture is a cultural trait.

Culture's predication of both rational reflection and unreflective bias yields conflicting frameworks for moral judgment. One of these sees rational analysis of the high Cultural kind as leading to universal values. This places the onus of ethical behavior on the self-aware individual and the community made up of such individuals, arguing that people should know the difference between right and wrong, and if they do not, they can learn it. However, if moral value is culturally relative, the product of inherited value systems and habits of thought that no person or community can ever fully overcome or impartially judge, there can exist no such absolute right. Even if people are educated to know the difference between right and wrong, the terms of that difference are always ultimately determined by a cultural system which attenuates the individual's responsibility.

The ambivalences of culture have found little resolution in recent efforts to understand what it is and does, not just on the part of anthropologists and students of the arts, but also in the work of literary scholars and proponents of Cultural Studies. Norbert Elias's early study of culture and civilization and Raymond Williams's oft-cited analysis of the word's history have been supplemented with a number of astute studies focusing on the historical developments tied in with its appearance, the various ways it has been used in the recent past, the long-term fortunes and misfortunes of the ideals it conveys, and the ideological projects which have relied on it.[3]

Understandably, most of these attempts, like most of their predecessors in the nineteenth century, assume that intuitively we know what culture is; they thus elucidate its complexity – and they do so very well – by examining specific instances of its deployment by various individuals, periods, or theories.[4] This has been the rule, historically: one defines culture by opposition or comparison to competing or related terms or historical formations. Thus as a philosophical concept, it has been alternately opposed to nature and to civilization, to anarchy and philistinism, to the passivity of the masses and the more authentic venues of subjectivity that preceded the industrial revolution. As social practice, it is alternately identified with the pursuit of artistic value, with the articulation of moral law, with the subordination of the poor by the affluent, with the natural formation of elites, with the interpellation of the citizen by the state, with the development of disciplinary discourse, and with concrete activities ranging from museum-going to the hunting and gathering techniques of early peoples. As a set of objects, it is identified with everything from potsherds to cantatas, pyramids to pornography. As a political force it is associated with deliberate strategies of state formation, but also with the assertion of minority identity, and with the development and perpetuation of an oppressive class hegemony. As the bedrock of tradition, it is seen by almost every generation as declining, on the verge of fragmentation or suffering fatal dilution. As the excrescence of a dominant society it is vilified as a malignant force of repression that relentlessly expunges dissident identities. Yet when invoked by those minorities, the same homogenizing powers are seen as a valuable form of resistance against just such oppression. Culture here is exalted as a redemptive force, a principle of identity whose menaced status confers upon it an indisputable positive value.

Culture can assume so many different guises in part because of our tendency to confuse the fundamental framework of thought which we designate by that name with the particular scenarios of social and political order that are elaborated with its assistance. For reasons that shall become clear, the idea of culture lends itself to ideology. My concern in this essay is, however, not to catalogue the various reconfigurations of the social world or polity which have been proposed in the name of – or in opposition to – culture, but to excavate the fundamental logic or grammar of thought on which they all draw.

Even at this level of a fundamental paradigm of thought, however, culture is not a coherent concept. It is far more a strategy for understanding in dialectical terms, and thus legitimating as reciprocals of each other, the competing imperatives of social order and individual freedom, hierarchy and mobility, continuity and change, law and choice. As a kind of underlying logic that persists through all of its ideological reductions, culture embodies both the play between these imperatives and the acknowledgment *of* that play which allows us to imagine and strive for – or against – alternative modes of social organization, values, practices, and expressions of identity. If it accommodates so many competing accounts, it is because it frames truth, law, and identity not as stable structures or unvarying doctrines, but as the constantly changing products of *a dialectic between individual initiatives of understanding and the rules and traditions which undergird them – and are continually being revised by them.* Most simply put, the cultural way of thinking always imagines autonomy and individuation in terms of the mastery and internalization of customary ritual and law, while at the same time understanding law and customary ritual to be precipitates of individual judgment and action.

One way of grasping this transaction might be to understand culture as a process and structure of accommodation – of the sort Freud had in mind when he noted that "a good part of the struggles of mankind centre around the single task of finding an expedient accommodation – one, that is, that will bring happiness – between this claim of the individual and the cultural claims of the group."[5] In fact, culture has long been at some level intuited as a way to "imagine and reconstruct a lost wholeness" as Geoffrey Hartman puts it.[6] From Matthew Arnold through Ortega y Gasset and F. R. Leavis to E. D. Hirsch, culture is seen as a way of resolving what Hartman calls "the antinomy between culture as a social or collective process and culture as the province of individual and often rebellious creation." It thus becomes synonymous with the recovery of a fullness that would overcome the alienation of modern mediated subjectivity.

However, I would suggest that the idea of culture is as much the origin of this ideal as its recovery. Envisioning identity and social order in terms of a dialectic that knows no end, but locks us into historical becoming, culture precipitates the ideal of wholeness and closure as its logical obverse. It is this vision which lures us into the project of self-definition central to culture's logic of social consolidation. By simultaneously insisting that our identity is a projection of shared categories *and* that we must be the authors of that identity, culture draws us into the project of articulating our social inscription – of specifying and making the object of our critical assessment the rules, values, and practices that we have inherited from our community.

It is tempting to understand these divergent scenarios of determination as cleaving subjectivity into two conflicting tasks: on the one hand, conformity to a unified community and its traditions; on the other, the rational assertion of independent judgment and personal freedom. However, what makes culture so powerful – and difficult to conceptualize – is the fact that it construes each of these tasks as the dialectical reciprocal of the other. It specifies cognitive autonomy, social status, and ethical distinction to be the logical correlate of our assimilation, mastery, and display of collective norms and rules. We can only express our distinction and get beyond cultural determination by articulating our cultural determination explicitly, thus making it the *product*, as well as the origin, of our act of free judgment. Of course we can never get the upper hand on culture, since as an impersonal set of norms and rules it by definition exceeds the compass of the individual acts through which it accrues and is continually reiterated and reinscribed as collective law.

In other words, the cultural way of thinking imagines the social in terms of a permanent dialectic between autonomy and community, the coherence of the group and the self-realization of its members. And the ethic inscribed in this way of thinking makes the subject responsible for overcoming this tension. It insists that we re-cognize the law of social practice in our own terms, thus internalizing its imperative and making its observance a matter of personal desire. The logic of culture predicates autonomy to be an effect of observing the law, self-assertion to consist in the effortless mastery of collective norms.

We have all long since been assimilated into this way of thinking, which saturates modernity and has produced our world and our understanding of it. It operates at the subterranean level of a framework of analysis so self-evident and ubiquitous it seems simply logical. And it makes otherwise paradoxical notions seem logical as well – such as the idea that we are all unique, yet similar, in control of our destiny and thoughts, yet governed by a web of collective usage and tradition we never fully comprehend.

I will argue in the following chapters that this logic develops independently of the word "culture," to which it is associated only once it has matured into an explicit and commonly held set of assumptions and thus become available for ideological deployment. The logic of culture crystallizes gradually over several centuries, insinuating itself into the void of authority left in the early modern period by the collapse of the unified power structure of the church and the prince. It develops in conjunction with the growing conviction that the forces structuring human lives in their materiality derive from the practices, customs, and tacit rules of the social economy, rather than from nature or God. In conjunction with a number of other complex categories we now take for granted – the individual, society, reason, public opinion, the state, the aesthetic, ideology, to name just the most obvious – culture emerges to help us make sense out of a world that could no longer be accounted for by existing ways of thought.

A key feature of my argument will be that the logic of culture is inculcated in the public imagination first and foremost by discursive institutions and practices. The new forms and sites of discourse that proliferated from the early modern period through the eighteenth century instituted a dialectic between social and individual identity and insinuated it into the folds of collective thought well before it received explicit theoretical articulation in the philosophical literature. The voyage, the café, the novel, the press, the rhetoric of revolution, and the museum have as much to do with the implantation and refinement of cultural logic as do the theories of Herder, Fichte, and Schiller.

In the first chapter of this book I seek the roots of the shifts that concern us in the reassessment of authority that occurs in the early modern period under pressure of contact with new peoples and the development of the print economy and print communities. There is a growing awareness that social practice and shared discourse constitute a body of truth and authority all the more formidable for its impersonal, systematic nature; and with this awareness comes the desire to harness systematic authority through the elaboration of disciplined forms of inquiry and discourse, the most celebrated of which were the New Science and Cartesian rationalism. These reconfigured truth, natural order and identity into logical correlates of a consciously systematic practice, and they paved the way for the subsequent formation of more generalized communities and disciplines of discursive authority such as the "philosophical" critique that proliferates during the Enlightenment.

The second chapter will examine how the grounding of identity and authority in discourse was generalized to society at large during the eighteenth century. I will examine the role of both private institutions of public discourse and state enterprises of citizen formation in the dissemination of the logic of culture as a general framework for understanding social and political agency. The eighteenth century proposes critical analysis and historical interpretation as the nucleus of an ethic of self-realization that it extends to all citizens, not just a privileged minority. This occurs under the aegis of endowing every citizen with cognitive and ethical autonomy, but the politicians who set out to equip every citizen with analytic capabilities also discover in analysis a powerful new mechanism of indoctrination capable of forming a truly self-regulating subject. To illustrate the mechanisms of this process, I will look in detail at the periodical press during the French Revolution, as well as the theories of education that proliferated during the same period. Interspersed with these analyses, a theoretical account will trace the conceptual speculations about identity that lead to the explicit emergence of the term "culture" at the end of the eighteenth century.

The third chapter will examine how Culture was successfully universalized as an ethic of self-realization and implemented at an institutional level. An important part of my argument will be that while the aesthetic theory of the late eighteenth century played a major role in the theorization of high Culture, its mechanisms of subject formation were being constructed in the public consciousness well before, by the discursive protocols of the century's most prominent new genre: the novel. It is traditional to credit aesthetic theory with the central achievement of modern state formation, on the basis of its reformulation of freedom as the expression of the law, individuality as the internalization of a collective will. I will argue, though, that the logic of aesthetic evaluation circulated by the novel had as much to do with the formation of social hierarchy as with state formation.

A close examination of the genre's new reading protocols will show how fiction provided an instrument of social coalescence and triage that enlisted readers in their own social classification. Like most subsequent aesthetic institutions, the novel provided a means for its readers to find and express their proper place in the social hierarchy on the basis of their capabilities and inclinations, rather than their birth or fortune. It not only argued for social distribution on the basis of virtue and intellectual capacity in an age when rank and wealth were increasingly discredited, but induced its readers to take an active role in the disclosure of their own inclinations and abilities, and hence to specify their own position in society.

In the final part of this chapter, after a theoretical examination of aesthetic experience as theorized by Schiller, I will contrast the subject-forming procedures of the novel with those of a more explicit high Cultural institution that emerged at the close of the eighteenth century: the art museum. The latter, I will argue, establishes the paradigm for formal Cultural enterprises of aesthetic criticism by sponsoring two divergent models of subjectivity, agency and identity, the interplay between which recruits the individual into collaborating in the construction of a collective legacy.

The final chapter of the book will consider how the identification of "culture" with various theories, institutions, and practices in the modern era reflects the need to appropriate its dialectical authority to specific ideologies. While all such ideologies acknowledge the primacy of culture, they also seek to reduce its dialectical complexity and harness its authority to their particular interests. Remarkably, though, in spite of their divergent agendas, all remain deeply committed to historical critique and the transcendence of local determination it seems to offer. To this extent, cultural logic functions as a "deep ideology" of our age.

The essay will close with a discussion of the way in the modern era the logic of culture is gradually extended to encompass economic behavior and the leisure practices of the social body, becoming a universal paradigm of identity formation and differentiation that is complicitous with, or parasitic upon (depending on one's point of view), the spread of capitalism. Inseparable from the practices of material production and consumption that accompany the globalization of the marketplace, a diluted form of self-cultivation seeks personal distinction in the consumption and acquisition of translinguistic, transnational symbols. The result is a generalized economy of self-conscious identity formation that penetrates every corner of the globe at the level of material practice, where it can operate the recruitment of individuals into social and economic norms under the guise of fostering their individuality. Culture thus continues to function as it always did: it involves people in their own distribution within the social order, disseminates and reinforces the law of collective practice by promoting its critique, and commits us to the formation of new norms of shared identity under the guise of self-differentiation.

1

The Roots of Cultural Logic

The term culture acquired its value as a way of conceptualizing individual and collective identity only subsequent to the Enlightenment. Not an especially charged term in previous centuries, it was used to designate any program for nurturing and regulating growth, most typically agricultural, but also occasionally with respect to child rearing or even intellectual and moral self-improvement. The disparate values it now carries – as a way of denoting the general progress of humanity, the collective identity of particular communities within that field, the aesthetic forms and institutions deployed by the community to express and maintain that identity, and the programs of personal self-improvement individuals pursue within those frameworks – coalesced gradually around the term from the end of the eighteenth century on.

These new concepts and the choice of "culture" as an overarching category to convey them reflect fundamental changes in the structure and exercise of authority, and in the way people thought about knowledge, truth, identity, and the purpose and shape of their lives. Many of these changes are consequences of the fragmentation of authority during the Reformation and early modern period, when the unified structure of ecclesiastical and secular power which had regulated the world since the Middle Ages was displaced by a heterogeneous economy of competing domains and discourses of authority. While the facts surrounding this crisis are well known, it is worth rehearsing the pertinence of certain key shifts to the emergence of the conceptual frameworks we associate with the word "culture."

Collective Practice and the Authority of Systems

First, during the early modern period there is a growing persuasion that what passes for true and natural in the world is as much the result of custom as of divine design. Contact with new peoples during the age of exploration had revealed that civilizations of equivalent levels of technological and economic development could have radically different belief systems and values. The presence of such differences brought into question the very notion of a universal standard of morality, a single Providential scheme, and "natural" behavior. As Bartolomé de las Casas noted in the middle of the sixteenth century à propos of the Amerindians, "there is no man or nation which is not considered barbarian by some other ... Just as we consider these peoples of the Indies barbarians, so they, since they do not understand us, also consider us barbarians and strangers."[1] A few years later in his famous essay on cannibals, Montaigne generalizes the point: "we seem to have no other criterion of truth and reason than the type and kind of opinions and customs current in the land where we live."[2] Prefiguring our own conflicted notions of culture, this statement is both a lamentation and a concession. To grant the primacy of custom is to acknowledge that one is subject to it; however, that gesture of self-awareness also inaugurates a movement of self-distancing calculated to provide us with some conceptual leverage over custom. This double movement of acknowledgment and resistance, embeddedness and awareness, forms the nucleus of all subsequent paradigms of the cultivated person.

That custom influenced collective beliefs was hardly a new idea. Still, the idea that it could naturalize practices as repugnant to the European mentality as cannibalism suggested that its authority was both more complex and less anodyne than classical treatments had suggested. Unable to reconcile the civilizations they encountered with the Scriptures, and incapable of acknowledging the validity of the "barbarians'" foundational myths, the Europeans attributed the behavior of the latter to the tacit rules of social life that had evolved over time to govern their community. The lesson of the travel narratives that proliferated during the age of exploration was that practice formed a kind of law in its own right that needed to be confronted.

There was both a negative and a positive dimension to this insight. On the one hand, the power of practice seemed to foreclose on any notion of self-determination. Its ability to shape one's perception of what was true and natural put into question the possibility of free will and hence of human finality. If other people's sense of the true and the natural was determined by their habits, what assurance could one have of the justness and viability of one's own beliefs – particularly when the traditional authority of the church had been undermined by the overwhelming evidence of practice itself? Clearly even the most fundamental human attributes, such as shame or the fear of death, were not universally ordained, but simply the deposit of shared tradition.

On the other hand, once the power of systematic practice to engender belief came under scrutiny, the notion of systematicity itself could be consciously developed as a means of regaining some measure of social and individual self-determination. Abstracting the idea of a governing system from its embodiment in troubling particulars, the early modern European mind found a solution to its own enclosure in system by making systematicity the ground of its knowledge: by rationalizing the mechanism of social habit into a theory of historically accrued systematic rule, one could bring its production under control.

One can see this in the meaning and use of the word "society" as it evolves between the sixteenth and the nineteenth century. Originally denoting companionable association or intercourse with other people, it comes to designate a structure of common interest defined by shared practice and laws, as well as the ordered community which that structure governs. Arising in tandem with the steady urbanization and industrialization of Europe, this new idea of society identifies collective life with the rules, standards, laws, and values that are deposited over time by communal practice. To conceptualize life in this way is not just to move away from a concept of divine ordination, but to take a first step towards criticizing and regulating those rules.[3]

Another way of understanding this process – which we will see repeated throughout the early modern and modern eras right up to the present – would be to say that the *identification* of an economy of authority (in this case social practice, in later eras religious belief, public opinion, forms of discourse, capitalism, or culture) as both inescapable and foundational, inaugurates the denaturalization of its workings and opens them to understanding and elision. This quite logically entails turning the mechanisms of authority back against itself. Having perceived the systematicity of social practice to constitute a formidable reservoir of authority, the early modern period sets about *systematizing* its cognitive efforts. And it deploys the knowledge such efforts produce as a countervailing body of authority to that of unconscious habit.

From the outset, then, the legislative power of systematic practice carries two contrary values. In the form of the habits, assumptions, and prejudices absorbed unconsciously, it is an adversary to be overcome before we can realize our full humanity. Increasingly deprecated under the aegis of "custom," "usage," "prejudice," or "superstition," this social residue is antithetical to the self-consciousness and free will that differentiate humanity from the beasts. One acknowledges the power of custom, but deplores it as well. As Pascal will lament in the mid-seventeenth century, regarding the lack of a firm ground for justice: "merely according to reason, nothing is just in itself, everything shifts with time. Custom is the whole of equity for the sole reason that it is accepted."[4] One hundred and fifty years later, by the time of the French Revolution, custom, prejudice and superstition will have became blanket terms for designating any form of social practice – such as respect for the clergy or the nobility – that seems to have no basis of authority other than that of tradition.

However, to the extent that the systems at work within the social body can be brought to light and analyzed, their power can be harnessed to rational projects of social improvement. This is the positive value of systematicity: it can be turned into a tool of knowledge and power. Society can liberate itself from the tyranny of custom and prejudice by conceptualizing them as mechanisms and making them the object of self-conscious rational inquiry. Montaigne's *Essays* are already an incipient gesture in this direction, with their deliberate inward turn, their dissection of habit, and their juxtaposition of personal tendency to social norm. In a roundabout way they show how the power and authority of social practice which enveloped the early modern period also furnished it with the principle of its liberation. If the systematicity of practice could be analyzed and regulated, self-determination would become a real possibility: by studying one's own habits, as Montaigne does in essays such as "On the custom of wearing clothes" or "On Experience," one could learn how to change them and shape one's future.

This is already in a sense the lesson of a very different, earlier work, Castiglione's 1528 *Book of the Courtier*. Although concerned only with a tiny subset of society, Castiglione's work makes clear by its form as well as its content that the systematization of practice and the conceptualization of one's embeddedness in it were seen as natural prerequisites to the rational exercise of authority and power. Correlatively, in a move we shall come back to in a moment, the *Book of the Courtier* makes personal identity and distinction within the community contingent on the self-conscious performance of collectively elaborated and constantly renegotiated conventions.

The aristocratic setting of *The Courtier* reminds us that within court society the authority of collective ritual and its importance to personal identity had long been recognized and systematically exploited. However to assume that this means nothing had changed is to miss the point. All of the structural mutations that lead to the gradual emergence of "culture" as a logic involve changes in orders of magnitude. In the early modern period, a strategy for securing authority and identity for oneself and one's community that had long been the prerogative of the elite began to spread to society at large. To fill the vacuum of authority left by the fragmentation of church authority, the mandate of social self-consciousness that was a tradition for the clergy and upper classes was steadily extended to all classes of the population across local, national, and even continental boundaries. Thomas More's *Utopia* (1516) is the clearest dramatization of this project: it envisions custom and social practice as rationally planned mechanisms for disseminating and enforcing enlightened doctrine throughout an *entire population*. What *Utopia* shows is that not just the elite ruling class, but all members of society could become self-conscious authors of their community's rules and values.

Of course ideas like this would not have made sense, much less taken hold, were it not for the printing press and the reconfiguration of authority it occasioned. Printing operated a quantum shift in the structure of authority, dispersing it in the circuits of shared discourse. Print discourse diffused the power that had been located in a single sacred text and a sacerdotal body of exegetes throughout a systematic economy of exchange, negotiation, interpretation, and representation. It this sense it did not just disseminate narratives of strange collective practices, it made a particular kind of shared practice – its own – the basis of truth and identity.

Discursive Authority and the Print Revolution

In the simplest terms, the print revolution spawned a generalized discursive economy that carried an authority of its own, and it made this authority available to a substantial portion of the population. That words could shape social reality was nothing new; nor was the knowledge that this power was contingent on their dissemination and persistence by means of inscription in some durable medium. The authority of the church was based on these evidences. However it was also based on the assumption that not all words – or readers – were equal and that the power of textual authority could be managed. Historically, this had been the case, since access to the inscribed word had been restricted by the cost and methods of production of manuscripts, and interpretation of the Scriptures had been controlled. Printing and the Reformation changed this by involving a broader spectrum of the population in the production and consumption of the written word and hence in the construction of the assumptions, beliefs and accounts that bound their communities together.

If collective practice in general deposited customary truth in its wake, print discourse constructed it deliberately, demonstrating that the belief systems of communities could be shaped by – indeed, grounded in – little more than shared accounts, the authority of which derived primarily from the extent of their diffusion, the persistence of their reiteration, the level of acceptance of their message.

Enabling a vast international system of exchange and discussion, the print economy reinvented power and agency in terms of the play between individual initiative and systematic practice. The propositions that individuals expressed in their writing were sanctioned or censored, lived or died, by the constantly evolving collective judgment of the community of readers and authors. The truths that emerged from such negotiations enjoyed leverage over the pronouncements of officials in sacred or judicial ceremonies precisely because they could not be pinned down to a particular moment or place. They were difficult to denigrate or neutralize, because while at one level they could be attributed to a specific author, they derived their force from the collective reception that underwrote and legitimated them. The writings of Luther are exemplary in this regard. Over 400 editions of his biblical translations were published between 1522–46, constituting nearly a third of all books published in German for that period.

Because this new form of truth got its validity from the very fact of its circulation and could no longer be considered the exclusive property of any one person, writers like Montaigne or Galileo who drew conclusions from their personal observations always hedged their gestures in appeals to shared knowledge and common sense. They knew their acts of autonomous cogitation short-circuited the traditional institutions of authority; however, they also knew their words were sanctioned by the shared criteria, procedures, and codes that were conveyed by and embodied in the text itself. Hence their repeated appeals to universal standards and procedures such as human nature, reason, common sense, and mathematical measurement.

The print revolution also reconfigured the parameters of identity, and this at the level of the collectivity as well as the individual. When the attention and concerns of thousands of people are aligned by multiple copies of an identical text, whether it be a religious tract or a newspaper story, an implicit consensus is formed, a shared version of events. A new kind of community and community identity emerge.

A useful term for understanding this (and one that is, incidentally, profoundly "cultural" in its logic) is Benedict Anderson's notion of the "imagined community," which grounds the identity of the community not in the lived proximity or familiarity of its members, but in the way they imagine their communality.[5] The material dissemination of identical texts engenders such a phenomenon necessarily: people who imagine their world through the same shared texts, narratives, vocabulary, phrases, and categories inevitably come to constitute a community. The consensus they form is achieved not through geographical or social proximity but rather through reading, discussion, and correspondence around a common locus of attention (the standardized text) and according to collectively negotiated rules of interpretation and expression. In the 1620s, a century after Luther nailed his theses to the door at Wittenberg, Bacon could justly observe "by the Art of Printing, a thing unknown to antiquity, the discoveries and thoughts of individuals are now spread abroad like a flash of lightning."[6]

It is important to stress that print community formation does not require that everyone evaluate accounts, propositions, or thoughts similarly. It is enough that they agree on what they are talking about. Even in the case of controversy, a tacit accord as to the terms of disagreement emerges. This is the discursive community. It cannot be located in any place; rather, it originates like customary law in normative practices: those disseminated by and embodied in standardized texts, languages, and interpretive protocols.

The early modern period is characterized by such discursive communities, ranging from the Protestant sects that coalesced around the writings of people like Luther and Calvin, or the proponents of the new science, who found their common ground in the commitment to a disciplined methodology, to the Humanists who sought to revive the traditions of inquiry and eloquence of antiquity. Beyond their emphasis on self-consciously articulated collective practice, what all these movements have in common is their belief that *truth, virtue, and identity are contingent on the mastery of an impersonal system.*

Nowhere is this more evident than in the Humanist programs of education. These explicitly aligned self-realization, wisdom, and virtue with the mastery of codified usage. If scholars like Erasmus, More, and Colet devoted their lives to retrieving, standardizing, and publishing the texts of antiquity, it was because they felt the assimilation of those systems of thought to be prerequisite to an authentic life. The immediate objective was to provide people desirous of refining themselves – mostly members of the aristocracy and the wealthy merchant class – with a consistent set of models and system of rules according to which they might fashion their own written and verbal expression. But by insisting on a universal language (Latin) and a single field of reference (antiquity), the Humanists also sought to construct a new transnational community around shared modes of thought and expression and a consciously bounded field of reference.

What is involved goes far beyond a roughly delineated set of practices. In his *De copia (On the Foundations of the Abundant*

Style) – widely adopted as a textbook of rhetoric and continually expanded throughout his life – Erasmus not only identifies the best models of writing in antiquity, but exhaustively lists the figures of speech to be used, as well as the acceptable styles, lexical fields, techniques for achieving variety, ways of linking different topics, forms of transition, means of expanding or condensing a subject – in all several hundred different topics, covering nearly seven hundred pages in the modern edition, and including thousands of citations by means of illustration. And this is just one part of his program. In *On the method of study*, he carefully delineates the structure of an education, and the exact steps to be taken by both student and teacher. In his wildly successful 1508 *Adages*, he provided volumes of sentential adages which one might incorporate into one's writing, while his 1518 *Colloquies* furnished short, pithy moral vignettes designed both to edify the reader and to provide a model for composition. *On the Writing of Letters*, *On the education of children*, *On Manners and Civility in small boys*, *On the Education of a Christian Prince* provide further rules for a humanistic education. These and the hundreds of other texts Erasmus published testify to the link in the consciousness of the age between individual distinction and the mastery of an impersonal grammar of practice. This assumption will lay the groundwork for the ideology of self-cultivation and universal education that will be exhaustively debated at the end of the eighteenth century.

Discursive Identity and Distinction

We take the Humanist notion of education for granted today, but its fundamental assumption – that one acquired one's status and authority by mastering a bounded canon of material and the traditions it embodied – went against the natural association of authority and power with rank. What Humanism showed was that individual distinction and influence could be detached from birth and reconfigured in terms of one's mastery of a conventionally designated body of practice. Erasmus himself demonstrates the viability of this logic: in spite of modest (probably illegitimate) origins he was – indeed, remains – the most celebrated intellectual figure of the age, endowed with a distinctive identity and an undeniable authority. His works may celebrate antiquity and argue for universal norms, but they also proclaim his domination of European thought.

It is traditional to understand Erasmus's promotion of antiquity as a recovery of what Matthew Arnold might call "the best that has been known and thought in the world," but his focus on traditions and languages specifically designated as lost underscores the fact that the pertinence of the canon derives less from its treatment of contemporary problems than from the fact that it is a closed system. The languages, figures, adages, and colloquies he demands his pupils assimilate are not selected on the basis of their relevance to contemporary situations; they draw their authority rather from the fact that they are part of a bounded corpus of works pertaining to a single category (antiquity). Because Erasmus is the compiler of this system and the self-designated guide to its value, all of its merit accrues to him. His observations on the use of synecdoche are *his* observations, elevated to the level of law by his familiarity with, and unconditional allegiance to, a corpus of classical expression that he himself has defined and appraised. Individual distinction, Erasmus shows us, comes with the *appropriation* of systematic authority.

The case of Erasmus is a dramatic and extreme example of the extent to which authority, social distinction and power could all be won by identifying oneself with a system of thought. However, in the broadest sense every instance of print discourse – in fact every piece of writing that was read by someone else – did this, by simultaneously deploying and reconfiguring, however minimally, the collective norms that enabled it. It is a self-evidence that ideas expressed in print can function only to the extent they are read, understood, accepted and recirculated by other people. In this sense engaging in collective discourse carried obligations that were imposed by the discursive economy itself, with its evolving rules of expression and presentation. These naturally governed spelling and grammar, but also format, vocabulary, rhetorical forms, and the choice of subject matter. The discursive fashioning of identity was thus structurally inseparable from conformity to an impersonal set of evolving practices and rules.

Consigning one's identity to the economy of the written word is a strategy for minimizing one's indenture to unconscious habit and custom. By consciously inhabiting a different set of codified, purely conventional strictures (the rules of good writing), one momentarily neutralizes the socially embedded determinations of habit. What is significant is that in this move one espouses a mediated subjectivity that finds identity and individuation in the *conscious adoption of norms*. Prior to the printing press, truth flowed from Scripture, the perfect wisdom of which was adjudicated and delivered by an elect group of exigetes, the clergy, who alone were qualified to translate the divine word into terms the average person could grasp. Truth was arbitrated by figures of authority and transmitted to the lowest levels of society by human agents: the local priests. Print discourse substitutes for this personal mediation the impersonal mediation of systematic practice, embodied in the standards and procedures for writing and reading, and the material mechanisms of print distribution. These self-consciously adopted norms link individual and community in a dialectic of particular initiative and collective law, which implicitly grounds the truthfulness or value of the secular printed text in the collective – and shifting – judgment of the (print) community.

The lesson which the practice of print discourse gradually inculcates – but which receives explicit formulation only once the notion of culture makes sense of it – is that personal expression and the identity it secures can succeed only if one self-consciously acknowledges the radically impersonal codes and protocols of acceptable expression – from grammar, vocabulary and rhetoric, or the sets of topics considered fit for discussion, to the format and marketing of the book. Under various guises – "standards," "good taste," "*bienséance*," "correct expression" – these broadly accepted procedures and norms are increasingly invoked as the foundation of successful communication and of the ideals of "individual" identity which such communication secures. They persist today undiminished in the categories of evaluation we use in letters of reference: "ability to express oneself in writing," "effectiveness of oral communication," "independence of thought," "ability to conduct independent research," and so forth.

If self-determination and individual identity could be wrested from the grip of practice by a conscious engagement with system, so too could truth, and the virtue that comes with truth. Beyond emanicipating one from the chains of social habit, systematicity also furnished an instrument for attaining a knowledge and moral sense untarnished by the contingencies of circumstance.

Truth and System

The cognitive technologies spawned by the print revolution exhibit the same recourse to system as the programs of self-emancipation and identity formation, but they are motivated by the search for objective truth and absolute certainty. They similarly seek to escape from the blinders of habit and traditional authority by situating themselves in a consciously elaborated, rigorously monitored system of inquiry, whose principles and past would be continually reassessed in accordance with the larger economy of which they partake. Two very different implementations of this logic can be found in the scientific method and Cartesian rationalism. In both, the legitimacy of truth was derived from adherence to strict methodologies and protocols. Truth came from systematicity and the rationalization of assumptions and procedures, even when it was envisioned as a way of approaching divine intention.

Bacon's call for a new science in his 1620 *Novum Organum* is one clear expression of this principle. His strategy for understanding the laws governing the natural world relied on an experimental practice that was itself resolutely systematic: the inductive method of controlled experiment. Bacon sought to purify his system of both existing traditions and human volition itself, by grounding it entirely in a methodology of incremental induction. He deliberately repositioned authority and truth in quantifiable relationships or systems by proposing "laws" that were not derived from the pronouncements of rulers or the injunctions of the church, but from the observable systematic mechanisms of phenomena in the natural world, such as the expansion of gases when heated. These natural laws operated in a predictable and self-sustaining fashion independently of human agency or intent, and they could accordingly be grasped only through procedures of rigorous observation, measurement, and calculation that purged understanding of customary bias and substituted for it the impersonal laws of mathematics.

The product of such discipline is knowledge – not knowledge of the kind one receives through revelation or faith, but knowledge as accumulating sets of interlocking propositions that are constantly evolving in the wake of experience. Knowledge, in short, that is structured like social practice, with the exception that it is elaborated self-consciously in writing.

For Bacon the greatest form of human service is to contribute to this growing body of knowledge. Our duty to God and our species is to increase our knowledge: "the human race should be steadily enriched with new works and powers," for "it is this glory of discovery that is the true ornament of mankind."[7] There is thus an implicit ethic or program of moral conduct built into his science. The first step in this program involves redefining knowledge itself as the fruit of an initiative that continually interrogates its foundations and procedures of inquiry. This self-conscious disciplinary ethic anticipates the programs of self-realization that dominate subsequent cultural theory – the ideal that finds the highest human purpose and identity in disciplined rational inquiry. Although Bacon is primarily interested in learning about the natural order, the imperative to learn which he articulates will be generalized during the Enlightenment to all members of society, thus fostering both the concept of civilization as an endless process towards knowledge and the ethic of individual self-perfection that goes with that ideal.

Descartes similarly appropriates the authority of systematicity. His celebrated formulation of rational analysis in his 1637 *Discourse on Method* clearly partakes of a similar ethic of self-perfection through inquiry: "I have formed a method by means of which, it seems to me, I have the ways to increase my knowledge by degrees and to raise it gradually to the highest point to which the mediocrity of my mind and the short span of my life can allow it to attain."[8] Reflecting the early modern wariness with respect to custom, his search for certainty grows directly out of a skepticism with respect to received truth, gained during his extensive prior studies and travels: "on realizing that many things, although they seemed very extravagant and ridiculous to us, did not cease being commonly accepted and approved by other great peoples, I learned to believe nothing very firmly concerning what I had been persuaded to believe only by example and custom."[9]

Descartes' desire "once and for all to get all the beliefs I had accepted from birth out of my mind" is, as Ernest Gellner points out, a systematic reaction to what we today would call "culture."[10] However, by purging his thought of personal experience, Descartes obtains a new measure of personal autonomy in the form of absolute certainty. For what emerges as the ground of certainty once all other forms of knowing have been excluded is the *cogito* or thinking mind. Paradoxically, it is the systematic disqualification of individual perceptions, sensations, and memories in favor of pure disembodied logic which allows the individual mind to assume its position of primacy.

Cases like Bacon and Descartes confirm that while the role of social practice in the production of truth was still in dispute by the seventeenth century, belief in systematicity *per se* as the foundation for knowledge and self-realization had become widespread. The concept of culture that emerged in the late eighteenth and early nineteenth centuries has its foundation in this primacy of system. Theoreticians of culture saw the entire collective practice of a community as a coherent system, the understanding of which (learning about one's culture) led to the acquisition of virtue and the realization of one's finality (becoming educated or "cultured").

Although fundamentally opposed to this redirection of understanding towards social practice, Descartes nonetheless shares one of its basic assumptions: that autonomous thought and certainty can only occur within the matrix of an impersonal system – in his case logic and mathematics, in others grammar, the natural order, law, the market. Early modern society increasingly saw itself as an array of individual agents who acknowledged the primacy of, and elaborated their individuality in, shared discourse, customs, traditions, usages, forms of dress, speech, commerce – in short, in all of the interlocking systems of practice and meaning we now lump together as culture.

As the examples of Erasmus, Bacon, and Descartes dramatize, within this perspective the individual is not the opposite but the obverse or logical correlate of the systematic: systematic principles govern individual cognitive initiatives, but they also find their articulation in such initiatives. It is the dialectic between personal formulation and impersonal system which produces truth, virtue and, in later formulations, history. This is why Descartes structures his essay not as universal recipe – although it clearly is one – but merely as the presentation of his life "as if in a picture, so that each person may judge it." Like all discourse, the *Discourse* is from one point of view "merely a history – or if you prefer a fable" – the account of one individual's endeavors.[11] Yet to the extent that such endeavors underwrite and make manifest for the community a larger impersonal grammar of truth, they establish the identity and the "author-ity" of the individual.

Universalizing Critique

There is an implicit ethic and teleology embedded in the systematic strategies of rationalism and the new science. Their identification of knowledge and truth with method, rather than individual genius or divine revelation, opens intellectual inquiry and the pursuit of truth to any person capable of mastering the method – not just those predestined to the truth by their birth or fortune. And because the truth brings with it a clearer perception of the divine plan and presence, this option is really a moral imperative: if we can become better people by improving our knowledge, we ought all devote some portion of our energies to this task.

This tacit moral imperative aligns self-betterment not with more intense piety, but more disciplined inquiry; it sees virtue in the effort to understand one's self and the world. This is of course a venerable classical ideal, but one that prior to the early modern period had not been applied universally to people of all classes. In the Enlightenment it will be. What allows this is the universalization of reason.

In the opening lines of the *Discourse on Method* Descartes roundly declares that "the power of judging rightly and of distinguishing the true from the false (which, properly speaking, is what people call good sense or reason) is naturally equal in all men."[12] Humanity at large is thus invested with the possibilities of rational inquiry, autonomous judgment, self-reflexivity, and self-perfection which in the past had been pursued as an ideal only by a minority.

This is a simple extension of the Humanist ideal of self-cultivation, but it has profound political and ethical consequences.

As Schiller will note at the close of the eighteenth century, to universalize reason is to broaden the political mandate:

> a question which was formerly answered only by the blind right of the stronger is now, it appears, being brought before the tribunal of reason, and anyone who is capable of putting himself in a central position, and raising himself from an individual into a representative of the specie, may regard himself as an assessor at this court of reason . . . judgment is to be given according to laws which he, as a rational spirit, is himself competent and entitled to dictate.[13]

Once it is identified as an intrinsic feature of being human and associated with the production and judgment of law, the exercise of reason ceases being an option. For individuals it becomes an imperative; for the state, a right and an activity that needs to be regulated.

Given its importance, it is not surprising that reason ultimately leads to an ethics of continual education, designed both to exercise and perfect it, and to deploy its power towards its rightful objects. For as Hobbes makes clear, reason is not something one merely possesses; it must also be *cultivated*: "Reason is not as Sense, and Memory, borne with us; nor gotten by Experience onely, as Prudence is; but attayned by Industry."[14] If for Descartes reason is something equal in all of us but requiring a firm method to attain the truth, for Hobbes it is a faculty honed by systematic application; for both, it is inseparable from method, and its ultimate end is the increase of science, or knowledge.

As this line of thought develops over the course of the next few centuries, the purpose of human life is increasingly identified with a process of continual self-conscious rational inquiry and critique, the object of which is not only the natural world, but increasingly society itself, with its political and economic struc-tures. The collaborative disciplinary logic of the new science, the analytic rationality of Descartes, are turned to understanding human institutions and practices, imparting order into the infinite diversity of social life. Just as Bacon had argued that man's purpose in this world included apprehending God's perfection through an understanding of the natural order he had created, the Enlightenment would seek higher principles for the laws of the social order and locate the natural finality of humanity in the critical understanding of its own history, institutions, and prejudices.

This specification of social life as process and object of inquiry could never have occurred without the prior constitution of the social and moral realms as domains of knowledge distinct from the political and theological. Reinhart Koselleck has convincingly argued that this occurred in conjunction with the generalized ethic of critique that emerged in the early modern period. What enabled this in the first instance was the separation of the moral and religious domains from the political, following the wars of religion. Concerned to effect a lasting peace in the face of irreconcilable differences of creed, people devised the notion of a secular sovereign to whom they would pledge allegiance independently of their religious beliefs. Separating the political from the religious and moral realms, they retained for themselves the right to determine matters of conscience and morality, while granting the sovereign absolute power in things political.[15]

Thus was born the absolute state, but also a third domain of law from the political and theological – the "philosophical" – within which normal people could exercise a form of social legislation in the judgments they leveled at their peers. Koselleck locates the key moment in this development near the end of the seventeenth century when, under the influence of authors such as Locke, the right of expressing one's private opinions, one's praise or blame, becomes a duty for the citizens, on the assumption that "it is only in their independent judgment that the power of society is constituted, and only in the constant exercise of moral censure will this censure prove to be a law."[16] Ultimately, this imperative to critique will expand its purview to include the morality of the political compact which spawned it, thus calling into question the validity of absolutism and precipitating Europe into a protracted crisis of authority.

The modern legacy of these developments is the pervasive ethic of critique which we associate with cultivated persons, whose familiarity with the traditions of their society entitles them to determine the meaning and value of its practices and expressions. Like the new science, which extracts natural laws from the rigorous observation of the natural world, social critique examines variations in social phenomena. And it similarly grounds its claim to truth in an analytic protocol that continually reassesses its own procedures and assumptions.

Critique presumes that by grasping and dissecting one's immersion in practice one can somehow gain exemption from its grip. This assumption funds the growing tendency during the period in question to associate the repudiation of custom and tradition with a higher form of subjectivity and virtue. Two centuries later this will have become the hallmark of the cultivated person, finding expression in the privileging of originality, dissent, resistance, the rupture of the modern, the marginal, and so forth. Already in Descartes and Bacon we can detect this move. While each defends his project in terms of its revelation of God or his works, what secures this access for them, and thus implicitly assures them of their moral rectitude, is their vaunted repudiation of the law of custom.

Bacon's aversion to custom is profound and blatant. "Inveterate prejudices [are] like the delusions of the insane," he declares bluntly, counseling that "the safest oracle for the future lies in the rejection of the past. Current theories, opinions, notions, should be brushed aside, so far as a disciplined firmness of mind may be able to achieve it; and the understanding must be brought into contact with facts in a straightforward unprejudiced way."[17] Born merely of time, repetition, and routine, prejudices are not merely by-products of history, but positive obstacles to truth, and hence to the discovery of the good. What people do without thinking, the things they accept without reflection, their unconscious habits and collective customs, the received opinions and reflexes of belief that permeate and regulate their world – these are increasingly thought of as manifestations of an authority all the more pernicious for its omnipresence and concealment in everyday life.

As one approaches the Enlightenment, belief that has not been tested in the crucible of rational analysis is increasingly denigrated as deleterious to the soul and spirit. Kant in fact defines enlightenment as the overcoming of prejudice and superstition, thus confirming the elevation of self-consciousness into the primordial virtue. Only if one acknowledges the extent to which shared practice affects one's beliefs and knowledge, can one gain some measure of exemption from the delusions of custom and habit, and thus some greater prize on the truth.

This epistemological edge in turn distinguishes one from one's socially embedded contemporaries, as Descartes shows us. To establish a rational basis for knowledge, his first move is to systematically rid himself of received ideas: "I could not do better than to try once and for all to get all the beliefs I had accepted from birth out of my mind, so that once I have reconciled them with reason I might again set up either other, better ones or even the same ones."[18] However, almost immediately he adds that "the single resolution to detach oneself from all the beliefs one has once accepted as true is not an example that everyone ought to follow."[19] As it turns out, most people are better advised following customary truth, either because they do not have the capacities they imagine, or conversely, because they cannot imagine themselves more capable than those from whom they receive instruction. What makes Descartes different is precisely his acute *awareness* of the customary basis of knowledge:

> having learned since my school days that one cannot imagine anything so strange or unbelievable that it has not been said by some philosopher, and since then, during my travels, having acknowledged that those who have feelings quite contrary to our own are not for that reason barbarians or savages, but that many of them use their reason as much as or more than we do . . . [and that] it is more custom and example that persuades us than certain knowledge, and for all that, the majority opinion is not a proof worth anything for truths that are a bit difficult to discover, since it is more likely that only one man has found them than a whole people: I could find no one whose opinions, it seemed to me, ought to be preferred over the other, and I found myself constrained to try to lead myself on my own.[20]

Descartes claims cognitive and moral autonomy on the basis of his theoretical conviction that received opinion undergirds most of what we take as truth, and that conviction is in turn based on his personal experience with other sets of collective practices – what we would call other cultures. In a gesture that will become paradigmatic for generations to come, he founds the right to develop his own procedures of inquiry on a logical sleight of hand: he acknowledges that truth is always hostage to the shared reflexes of custom and opinion, but exempts his own inquiry from that limitation on the grounds of that acknowledgment and its double appeal to self-awareness and broad experience with other customs.

Both Descartes' rationalism and the new science anticipate our modern ideologies of self-cultivation in that they see the understanding and rejection of unexamined tradition and custom as a prerequisite to cognitive autonomy. In the place of unconsciously acquired habits they deploy consciously observed procedures and standards, securing exemption from systematic habit through the elaboration of systematic knowledge.

When the ideology of self-cultivation matures at the close of the Enlightenment it will attribute a measure of this self-awareness and critical prerogative to everyone who deliberately engages discursive authority. But the roots of this move are visible well before it is formalized. If early modern writers consistently stress the importance of collective practice after the invention of printing, it is at least in part because they see self-conscious systematicity and the disciplined critique of one's assumptions as a means of suspending or defusing the tyranny of custom and acceding to virtue. Like custom, the consensual truth of discourse is produced in an economy of reiteration by an aggregate of individuals, whose authority in turn derives from the system that validates them. Like custom, conclusions that originate in a discursive community owe their power to their diffusion; and like custom, they can grow stronger or weaker over time. Unlike habit or custom, however, the consensual truth that print promulgates is formulated – and in the case of books, consumed – *self-consciously*. Individuals who choose to express themselves through print must acknowledge and consciously assimilate the collective law that regulates the print community and makes individual expression feasible.

In sum, well before the Enlightenment, the idea of the "individual" – of a mode of personal identity founded on self-conscious conformity to a disciplinary system and systematic critique as a means of overcoming the delusions of unconscious habit and customary prejudice – was already developing. Well before the idea of culture gives theoretical coherence to the notion that collective systems subtend and enable the individual acts that articulate them, discursive practice had already insinuated the logic underlying that idea into the structure of consciousness.

Whatever their differences concerning the value of social practice, all of the forms of discourse cited thus far share – and foster – an ethic of self-awareness and self-betterment through knowledge. The emergence of social practice as a mechanism of determination encompassing *all* people, and which all people felt the need to confront and transcend, made self-consciousness and the critique of one's habits of belief and inquiry a universal imperative.

Of course there is something superficially paradoxical about claiming that because one can conceptualize the system of strictures within which one works, one can somehow overcome their limitations, but that is the paradox that will ultimately grow into the theory of culture. Perhaps the political version of the paradox is the most intuitively accessible: one finds the greatest freedom in the world with the strongest laws or most powerful sovereign – one thinks of Hobbes, naturally, but also Machiavelli, More, or even Castiglione: "it should not be said that true freedom consists in living as one wishes but rather in living under good laws."[21] However, looking ahead, one notes that a version of the same paradox structures our modern appetite for culture: "cultured" people are those who seek distinction and individuality by making explicit the normative strictures of taste.

2

Inventing Culture

If the eighteenth century is generally accepted as the threshold of the modern era, this is because many of the conceptual nuclei of the modern age, such as universal Reason and Enlightenment, the Aesthetic, Democracy, and Liberalism, were explicitly articulated during this period into scenarios of human endeavor and moored in institutional projects that would develop subsequently, such as universal public schooling, representational government and suffrage, public political discourse, the free press, economic liberalism, and state-sponsored artistic and cultural encounters.

Likewise, the frameworks for fashioning individual and collective identity which we associate with Culture were theorized during this period and incorporated into strategies for constructing a stable state. These did not always use the term "culture"; however, they deployed bureaucracies for administering the ethic of self-awareness and self-development that we now associate with that concept. They thus played as great a role or greater than the theoretical work of philosophy in embedding cultural logic in the collective imagination.

Key to these developments was the generalization to all of humanity of the logic of systematic analysis as a means of securing truth, certainty and a sense of fulfillment. What Descartes and Bacon had to demonstrate and argue, is henceforth taken for granted, its ethical entailments applied to all people, not just philosophers. The Humanists had shown that one could ground identity, authority and a transnational community in shared discourse; the eighteenth-century *philosophes* and their intellectual heirs across Europe and America extended and enlarged this logic to encompass society at large. They redefined life as the pursuit of perfection and the realization of one's unique potential. As Fichte puts it near the end of the century: "there are many drives and aptitudes in man and it is the destiny of each individual to develop all of his aptitudes as far as he can."[1]

More specifically, the ethic of critique that had developed in the early modern period was universalized to all people. This happened gradually over the course of the century under the aegis of "enlightenment," which in the terms of this study could be defined as the moment when the conviction that systematic rational analysis of human practices is the way to truth and virtue becomes a self-evident universal axiom. Near the end of the century, this ethic is attached to the word Culture. Again, Fichte:

> The acquisition of this ability, which on the one hand seeks to extirpate and suppress our own erroneous inclinations which arose before the awakening of reason and the consciousness of our independent initiative, and on the other to modify external objects and change them according to our concepts, the acquisition of this ability, I say, is called *culture* [Cultur].[2]

The obligation to apply one's reason to the understanding of human endeavor, to engage in the systematic critique of one's developing assumptions as a means of attaining virtue, becomes a universal imperative.

What makes this universalization possible are the eighteenth century's innovative institutions of public print discourse. The ideal of a universal implementation of reason by the state received full theorization only near the end of the century, but it was inaugurated in the private domain at the level of material practice well before that time by the many institutions of public discourse comprising what Jürgen Habermas called the *public sphere*.[3]

The Public Sphere and Public Opinion

The periodical press, the coffee house and the café, the theater, learned societies, freemason lodges – and even to a lesser extent privately consumed literary forms like the novel and the essay – became permanent features of the urban landscape during the eighteenth century, bringing social self-awareness and the virtues of critique within the reach of an ever-increasing segment of the population. These institutions made discursive collaboration and self-expression activities in which any literate person could engage – although, as Habermas notes, it was primarily the bourgeois reading public that was involved. In any event, as more people sought to "express themselves" by contributing to the new collective body of customary belief known as public opinion, the mechanisms of discursive authority became more explicit, the scope of its authority more ambitious.

The contribution of these institutions to the consolidation of systematic authority lay not in their depiction of society as a rigidly organized system, but rather in their systematic production of discourse and their expansion of its scope to include all manner of subject. The seminal British periodicals the *Tatler* (1709–11) and the *Spectator* (1711–12) did not deliver a tightly knit account of a social system, but they did disseminate their accounts throughout the urban environment according to a regular schedule, making the shared discussion of contemporary social reality a predictable and accessible institution – one which could itself develop into the kind of habit it was interested in analyzing. It is this regularity of production and predictability of content that induces the citizenry to structure their life around and in shared discussion.

The new discursive economy greatly expanded the compass of critique. For instance, the *Tatler* and *Spectator*, calculated to "banish vice and ignorance" from Britain, assembled a heterogeneous blend of anecdote, moral polemic, political observation, and gossip. Taking current social practice as their object of analysis, they convert the aleatory succession of fashions and enthusiasms into the morally commendable stuff of critique, enabling people to get beyond their collective obsessions of the moment by making those obsessions an object of amusement, ridicule, or at the very least, social taxonomy. The *Tatler* and *Spectator* are exemplary in this regard, but so are a host of subsequent periodicals in the same tradition, as are other literary genres such as the satires of Voltaire, the social comedies of Marivaux or Beaumarchais, the novels of Fielding, or the urban portraits of Restif and Mercier.

The concept that emerges to describe both this ongoing process and structure of social critique and its recruitment of individual intention into a collective articulation of norms and behaviors is that of *public opinion*.

Public opinion – frequently simply "opinion" in the writing of the time – prefigures in its logic the more expansive anthropological concept of culture that the nineteenth century would devise. It is more limited in that it expresses primarily the political and social views of the people, as well as the moral force those views have by virtue of representing the people. The term was as ubiquitous in academic and public prose of the late eighteenth century as "culture" is today, and like culture, it was understood to be both a product and a norm of social life. Moreover, like Culture (in the sense of a program of self-perfection) it was invoked in opposition to the other habitual categories that unexamined practice had deposited over time as custom.

Public opinion opens to society in general the cognitive strategies of systematization we studied in the previous chapter. It was invoked and deliberately fashioned as a systematic corrective to the authority of habit and tradition. As the compilation of the literate public's conscious assessment of social life and the expression of their desires, it could claim to represent their collective will, thus paving the way for a form of government that would reflect the rational energies of the entire literate populace.

That public opinion should articulate itself around social practice at the outset, and only secondarily and by extension broach political issues, is from the perspective of this study a logical outgrowth of its origins in the Renaissance reassertion of social practice as a determining form of authority. It reflects as well the initial exclusion of the political from the field of philosophical critique. By the time of the French Revolution, public opinion had grown to encompass virtually every dimension of social and political reality, and become in fact a powerful legislative mechanism in its own right. Still, even when it demanded direct political action, it continued to speak in the name of truth, virtue, and progress, reflecting its origins and claim to disinterested truth. The identification of public opinion with morality and truth was grounded in its consensual discursive structure. Because it by definition represented a collective expression, the judgments it articulated were assured of legitimacy in the majority of the people's minds; the institutions it underwrote were to their minds just. As one of the French Revolution's less illustrious but most prolific theoreticians, François Xavier Lanthenas, would optimistically assert in the midst of the Revolution, "free and unlimited debates on all questions are the best assurance of the triumph of liberty as well as that of truth. . . . if we want to perfect the social institutions of humanity, we have no other means than to write, discuss, converse, convince, persuade."[4]

Public opinion could be depended on to represent the conscious will of the people because it was deliberately produced. Like its negative analogs, custom and prejudice, it represented collective dispositions accumulated over time. However, the dispositions of public opinion were produced at regular intervals and sites by formal mechanisms concerned explicitly with their articulation and critique and adhering to the disciplined protocols of scientific inquiry, literary criticism, philosophical discussion, or even satire. Unlike custom, public opinion transcribed the self-awareness of the people, and it did so systematically.

The concept of public opinion and its new institutions of the public discourse make possible an ideal polity governed not by divine law, but by conventions collectively articulated by rational discourse in opposition to systems of prejudice. This is in fact how Benjamin Constant would characterize his era at the dawn of the next century, noting, significantly, that "originally, institutions are nothing other than opinions put into practice."[5] However, putting opinions into practice requires substantial mediational mechanisms, and these have the effect of reconfiguring human agency in ways that are not unambiguously positive. We can illustrate the problems, and put some substance into this abstraction, by considering in more detail an exemplary drama of such mediation: the newspapers of the French Revolution.

The Subject of Revolutionary Journalism

The mechanisms of discursive authority as it was institutionalized in the eighteenth century are nowhere more evident than in the periodical press, and in particular in the intense journalistic frenzy that followed the lifting of censorship at the start of the French Revolution. There were hundreds of papers launched in the early years of the Revolution, representing every conceivable shade of the political and social spectrum.[6] These newspapers did not see themselves as merely reflecting the changing political and social reality of the period but as active agents in the construction of that reality. They accomplished this by putting into circulation new paradigms of subjectivity and homogenizing public attitudes.[7] The Revolutionary press forged a deliberately political function for itself by assembling the disparate events of the Revolution into intelligible form and recasting them as the expression of the public will.[8]

Many papers explicitly associate themselves with the project of invigorating critical autonomy and transforming the French people from "passive subjects to active citizens."[9] There was nothing discreet about this operation; it formed the keystone of a strategy of self-legitimization based on the claim that only newspapers could reach the whole population, mobilize their energies, and weld them into a responsible citizenry. The most basic way they achieved this was of course through the systematic, regular dissemination of information. In theory, at least, newspapers form citizens by informing them, providing all readers with uniform and accurate accounts of events. Brissot, for instance, advances the utility of his paper, *Le Patriote français*, in such terms:

> Written in the heart of the capitol, at the source of movement and light, circulating rapidly, this paper will inform all the provinces in the same instant about the latest fact . . . It will put all of them in contact with one another, will instruct one by means of the other, and will thus produce harmony in their plans and operations. . . .[10]

This is the logic of discursive authority fully implemented. However, newspapers did not just assure the material conditions of that authority, they actively articulated the analytic critique it required. Brissot for instance sees his paper providing the public with the instruction necessary to understand the machinery of politics. In his view, the newspaper provides a "unique means of instructing a populous nation, restricted in its abilities, unaccustomed to reading, but who desires to rise out of ignorance and slavery."[11] The prospectus to another paper reveals the range of this educational ambition. *L'Instruction publique, Journal d'instruction sociale*, promises nothing less than

> To secure for the people the uncertain meaning of the words of this language; to give them the means for discussing all questions usefully; to indicate to them an appropriate method for directing their reflection surely towards all the knowledge they need; to

explain to them the principles of natural law which form the foundation of morality and of civil and criminal law, and the principles of political law upon which are grounded the rights of the citizens and the understanding of their natural duties; to teach them political economy; to familiarize everyone with the national resources of the population, the products of the soil they inhabit, their artistic and commercial contributions; . . .[12]

This broad program procures impressive benefits, as the description of *L'Instruction publique* modestly concludes: "to do all this is to form a clear mind for them; to protect them from fraud and fanaticism; to restore to the public interest citizens whose ignorance and incapacity put them at the mercy of those who wish to seduce them; to open new sources of livelihood for them; to render them fit for all civil functions and smooth the way to all virtues for them."[13]

Yet in its rhetoric this announcement reveals the ambiguity of journalism's promise of autonomy. It addresses a reader presumed capable of mastering the intricacies of political theory (and long, encyclopedic sentences), yet who is also in the final analysis "ignorant," "incapable," and willing to be qualified as such, since the passage is part of a prospectus pitched at potential readers. The effect is one of schizoid interpellation, which simultaneously constitutes the reader as a culturally impoverished subordinate who needs to subscribe to the journal, and an enlightened overseer who already subscribes to its grounding ideology.

The Revolutionary newspaper, like the official Cultural institutions that were being invented during the same period, intermingles and invokes simultaneously the antithetical ideals of critical autonomy and submissive conformity. The incongruity in this contradictory characterization is dissembled by the use of the third person to differentiate the "ideal" readers – those needing education – from the reader of the prospectus, as if the "people" whose mind the paper would form were any other than the very readers whose subscriptions – and eventual readership – were being solicited by the prospectus. Our modern familiarity with this equivocation in the way newspapers address us should not blind us to its consequences.

In effect, newspapers operate like the law: although we react to them and feel their impact as individuals, they are by definition never addressed to us as individuals: we never think the stories in a newspaper are written to us personally, like a letter, any more than we believe that laws are written with us personally in mind. At the same time, however, as members of the public we are exactly the intended addressee. The result is that at all moments we can and do read newspaper accounts of the community as if we were two different people: those being talked to and those being talked about. And we can shuttle between these two subject positions through an infinity of intermediate postures. The *Instruction publique*'s prospectus lays bare the ambiguous subject positions embedded in public sphere discourse – and in most forms of high Cultural discourse that will be deployed subsequently. Such discourse always addresses its reader on at least two different registers, soliciting both the acquiescence of the reader to an implicitly shared account *and* the critical activity of that reader.

Journalism is more blatant than most forms of Culture in the way it uses these two registers to inflect critical initiative into acquiescence, but we shall find the same strategy in all Cultural institutions. It operates on the assumption that people really only retain the conclusions they have come to on their own, so their critical initiative must always be elicited – even if it is severely monitored. When we read newspapers we assert our autonomy as individuals, free to endorse or dispute the version of things presented by the journal, or to appropriate to our own arguments the strands of public discourse it spins out. However, we also absorb the categories of analysis proffered by the paper, and affiliate ourselves with the normative views it purveys, whether they represent a party, community, region, or nation. By demanding that its readers be at all times both authors and readers, lawgivers and subjects, the paper fulfills the conflicting demands of the nation and the individual. Its model of individuation as affiliation, here expressed in the political terms of individual and collective will, freedom and law, will be adapted by subsequent Cultural institutions to cover the entire spectrum of individual and social life.

The rhetoric of the newspaper also puts into motion a process of what one might call autotriage, by means of which the readers, in selecting one or more addressee positions made available by the piece, classify themselves according to its limited range of options. Through the way we read, we sort ourselves out, becoming aware of where we stand, but sensing that position as a consequence of our own cognitive decisions and feelings. One might say that the public discursive transaction enlists us in the process of our own social distribution. Again, this is prototypical of the way modern Cultural institutions recruit us into the process of social stratification.

Finally, and this is a third essential characteristic of Cultural instruments, newspapers make their readers *aware* of the fact that they (the readers) are engaging in acts of autonomous judgment and conformity at specific levels of complexity, and that the readers' participation at that level has resonance in the register of social status. Cultural instruments like newspapers are consumed or used by people in different ways; and just as their meaning (what they "represent") shifts with different readers and different readings, so can they be said to represent at all times both the world that produced them (what the article is "about") and the views and status of the person reading them.

That duplicity is what allows them to perform individuation and integration simultaneously. The protocols of reading the press disseminates, the attitudes towards "facts" it fosters, the postures of self-assertion it accommodates, all of these subsidize the divergent, yet interconnected imperatives of acquiescence and authorship without bringing them into open conflict. While the election of a particular politician does not necessarily say anything about me as an individual, what I read and how I read it *does*, and this function of the Cultural instrument or institution is coded into its rhetoric.

The full-blown implementation of this logic animates the properly Cultural institutions that will form the subject of the next chapter, some of which, such as the museum, the Revolution theorized and began to put in place. However, the Revolutionary papers already anticipate the complexity of the Cultural transaction in their understanding of their political instrumentality. With respect to the political events they relate, they claim both a *descriptive* or mimetic, and a *prescriptive* or instrumental relationship: they both recount how things happened and determine how they will turn out in the future, by shaping public opinion and policy.

The tension implicit in these two functions emerges graphically in the intermixing of the claim to represent events accurately (representation as mimesis) and the claim to represent the public opinion (representation as the implementation of the people's will). Many journalists see themselves functioning, in other words, as both the source of information upon which the public formulates its will and the expression or exercise of that informed will.

One particularly virulent journalist, Fréron, theorizes how this works. As he sees it, fair representation in the political sense of the term can only be achieved through accurate (mimetic) representation on the part of the papers. Representative government, he claims, is potentially flawed by the fact that its laws reflect only the will and judgment of a few people: "The essence of law is to be the expression of the general will, yet the necessary result of the representative system . . . is to make laws that are really only the expression of the reason and wishes of eight hundred members of a national assembly."[14] The remedy to this situation is a free press, which can mobilize the desires of the people and express them directly to the legislature:

> With freedom of the press, this defect disappears . . . while all citizens may not translate their thoughts into the laws, they impress them into the minds of the legislators. Through freedom of the press, the representatives and the represented tend ceaselessly to merge, and democracy exists in a nation of twenty-five million people.[15]

The press solves the problem of democratic representation through transparent mimesis: when it accurately represents to the legislator the will of the people and to the people the acts of the legislator, each can "take into account" the desires and actions of the other.

The slippery transitivity of this notion of representation – the way it simultaneously makes citizen and legislator the subject and object of representation, observer and observed – concisely conveys how the rhetoric of Revolutionary journalism works – and by extension that of most Cultural instruments.[16] The political subjectivity it constructs cannot be grasped in a univocal model of power. However, this complex subjectivity is intuitively available in – and can be disseminated through – the polysemy of metaphors such as *representation*, or *public opinion*, which enclose and define complex, multifaceted transactions and models of power in which individual initiative or freedom and normative constraint or social law continually intersect and fund each other. Public opinion, after all, is born of the individual convictions it expresses; yet by its very nature it bespeaks a collective will beyond the grasp of the individual.

Observing the Law

A key metaphor that recurs with remarkable regularity in the press, even to the present day, is that of *observation*. The trope of observation accommodates a complex of disparate ideas and behaviors, running from surveillance to analysis, celebration, and obedience: one observes the law as well as the results of an analytic experiment, or the behavior of one's peers, or a national holiday. The Revolutionary press methodically exploits this semantic disparity to express the antithetical postures of dispassionate analysis, critical vigilance, and unquestioning submission that are simultaneously demanded of the citizen.

One function frequently demanded of the citizen is that of the censor, sentinel, overseer, or surveillant. By and large, the journalists of the Revolutionary period do not think of themselves as spectators, but as observers in the strong, censorial, United Nations-peacekeeping sense of the word. Constant observation of the government by the public forms the nucleus of the belief in a free press. (Scopic and surveillant language still dominates the titles of our newspapers, from the relatively neutral *News and Observer*, *Daily Mirror*, *Spiegel*, or *Nouvel Observateur*, to the more aggressively regulatory *Monitor*, *Guardian*, or *Sentinel*, the ever judgmental *Tribune*, or the frankly nosy *Examiner* and *Inquirer*.)

Careful observation (today we would say "transparency") is a prerequisite to democracy. As one of the instigators of the storming of the Bastille, Camille Desmoulins, puts it, one can only be sure that the principles of the Revolution are being implemented "when the administration is public, the government under glass; when the machine is infinitely simple, its mainsprings and movements visible to all; when an immense audience oversees the National Assembly; when . . . the people of France in its entirety attends every session every day."[17]

To observe the legislative process is not simply to witness the Revolution, but to *oversee* the formulation of the law in the censorial sense of the word. Brissot chooses for the motto of his paper *Le Patriote Français*: "A free gazette is a sentinel that ceaselessly remains on watch for the people." Marat carries the surveillant function even further, promising to "unmask hypocrites, denounce traitors, remove from public affairs . . . the cowardly and the unsuited, incapable of serving the Fatherland, those suspect men in whom it can have no confidence."[18]

In keeping with the double rhetoric of journalism, this right – indeed, this obligation – to monitor the government and denounce those unfit to serve in it implicitly extends to the reader. Near the start of the Revolution Desmoulins declares *la délation*, or denunciation, to be the "most important of our new virtues,"[19] and he invites his readers to acquire this virtue by becoming extensions of his observing eye: "persons having interesting facts to publish, useful views to communicate, opinions, demands, denunciations or justifications to insert, in a word any public good to propose, are invited to have them sent to the address below."[20] Five years later, fueling the reaction to the Terror, the same rhetoric persists in Fréron's exhortation to his readers: "Citizens, put all these conspirators under surveillance yourselves."[21]

This language exemplifies the rhetorical duplicity of the newspaper: it puts the public under surveillance in the same instant it imposes on the public the task of surveillance. And by making journalistic discourse itself the medium of that surveillance, it engineers its own political authority: under the guise of representing the public, it shapes that public to its own strategies of representation, by filtering their perception of the social and political world through its particular language, rhetoric, and thematic priorities.

In a long tirade against Robespierre's faction, Fréron provides an excellent example of how the complex rhetoric of journalism can deliver multiple messages simultaneously:

People . . ., let the professional slanderers, terrified by the mirror of truth, treat my writings as slanderous libel! In reading me, listen only to your heart and your reason; reflect, compare, and judge for yourself; inform yourself about all the events, even those that appear unimportant at first glance, and you will have no difficulty, once courageous authors have put you on the right path, discovering the machinations, as dastardly as they are hypocritical, which Robespierre's heirs have never ceased using to deceive you, vilify you, enslave you, alarm you and cut your throat!"[22]

At one level this passage seems to invest its readers with substantial autonomy. It invites them to "reflect, compare, and judge" for themselves. Strikingly, though, Fréron's writing claims for itself the role of "mirror of truth," the source of facts upon which individual judgments depend. It encourages one to listen to one's own heart and reason, but only under the guidance of those "courageous authors [who] have put [us] on the right path" – among whom Fréron clearly counts himself.

Still more striking is the way in which the exhortation to assert oneself clashes with the rhetoric of victimization: to persuade its readers of their critical autonomy and political enfranchisement, Fréron chooses language that reminds them that their habitual lot is to be deceived, vilified, enslaved, terrified, and slaughtered. This insistence on the readers' subjugation is presumably designed to motivate them to claim the right to judge for themselves, but it also subliminally delivers the lesson of their perennial incapacity to see through deception. The very discourse that promotes itself as the vehicle of the citizen's elevation to informed political agency, repeatedly positions that reader as a dupe or victim, incapable of fathoming tyranny.

The same duplicity characterizes the relationship between the message and its grammatical mode of delivery. The message that one should "take command" comes, ironically, in the form of a string of commands. The familiar apostrophe and repeated imperatives ("People, let them treat my writing as libelous! . . . listen only to your heart and your reason; reflect, compare, and judge by yourself") make the readers into transitive objects of the journalistic discourse, rather than political subjects. One acquires political agency only by acquiescing to the demands of a disembodied authority.

This is typical of Fréron, whose strongest exhortations to take action are generally delivered in the preemptory tone of a military order ("Citizens, form a sacred battalion around the National Assembly!").[23] But it also characterizes his nemesis Robespierre. Like Fréron, Robespierre stresses the need for the citizens to judge for themselves, to become autonomous subjects. He explicitly "invites" his readers to "observe attentively all the moves [of the enemy coalition]" reminding them "to judge men and things only because you have witnessed them and heard them yourself."[24] But when it comes to making specific judgments, Robespierre guides his readers' observations with a firm hand, a series of commands, and a few helpful adjectives, pre-figuring for them the scenes and judgments that they are to envision "on their own":

> *Observe* with what distrust – I almost said with what terror – they still envision the most numerous group of citizens, and the most pure, their ignorance and pride notwithstanding. *Observe* this permanent tendency to link the idea of sedition and brigandage with the masses and poverty. *See*, on the one hand, how difficult it is for the law to get at the powerful conspirators, with what speed, on the other, it cuts off the heads of the hapless, who are weaker than they are guilty. *See* with what deadly obstinacy the traitors, surrounded by the privileges of the old regime, are excused, defended, protected.[25] (my italics)

As with Fréron, Robespierre's language coerces its readers into autonomy; even as it demands they assume the surveillant function, its vivid imagery co-opts their semiotic initiative, requiring that they legitimize his vision of the revolution.

There are also rhetorical strategies that elicit a posture of dispassionate analysis, stressing the accumulation of truth over the direct intervention in events. Robespierre provides an example of this appeal to detachment in his articulation of a different version of observation, one that is strangely at odds with his normally inflammatory rhetoric: "Citizens, . . . remain calm and immobile. Observe their guilty maneuvers in silence. Let them unmask themselves and destroy themselves by their own excess. . . . Enlighten yourselves, enlighten your fellow citizens as much as it is in your power; dissipate the deception upon which the reign of conspiracy is founded and it will be no more."[26]

Observation here has less to do with surveillance and denunciation than with calm, rational analysis; it construes the political subject as a dispassionate observer; and it is systematically associated in Revolutionary papers with enhanced authority and political eligibility. It is distinct from the notion of the public as

sentinel, in that it associates observation with a deliberate program of self-enlightenment and a self-distancing from the passion
of the crowd. However, it also covertly associates political effectiveness with skill in analytic inquiry, thus enabling an alternative
process of internalization through analysis.

The claim to "observe" reality analytically saturates papers of
all persuasions. The reactionary journalist Rivarol views the
masses as cannibals at heart and ineligible for enlightenment. Yet
he too, like Robespierre, claims the analysis of cause and effect as
his paper's hallmark: "we shall pause at this great historical
moment in order to explain its causes and calculate its effects."[27]
At the other end of the political spectrum, Robespierre promises
to provide an "accurate depiction of the operations of the
National Assembly" by exposing the "mainsprings of all the
great events that shall determine the destiny of France and the
world."[28] Prudhomme likewise emphasizes the importance of
determining causal patterns: "as the object which we propose is
to expose rapidly the principles of disorder . . . and not to walk
the reader through a portrait gallery or the labyrinth of intrigues,
we shall continue to observe with the same method the principal
motors and causes."[29] His assumption, shared by most papers of
the Left as of the Right, is that only if one observes and understands the hierarchies and motives underlying the national debates
can one craft a reasoned judgment worthy of representing the
public will.

The observation these newspapers promise – and demand
of – their reader is not simple oversight, much less passionate
involvement, but critical analysis. As the editor of *L'Observateur
François, ou le Publiciste Véridique* asserts, "to observe is not
to surprise the secrets of a party, to spy on deliberations, to
divulge mysterious anecdotes . . . it is to follow the course of
events, to find relationships between them, to apply to the
moment we are living the lessons of twenty years of studying
men, to see in an object that which eludes the multitude; it is to
speculate with the help of a few facts and draw from facts
themselves a kind of instruction which only the philosopher can
see in them."[30]

Such language reduces all phenomena to part and whole, cause
and effect; and it predicates the affective detachment of the reader
from the events themselves, the better to synthesize them within

an abstraction. Analysis becomes the sole means to grasp the mechanism of politics objectively, and as such, the prerequisite for political enfranchisement. Only informed analytic readers can understand political events and participate responsibly in politics, and only regular readers of newspapers can be informed.

It is on the basis of these widespread assumptions that another paper, *La Feuille villageoise* set out to educate the rural folk of France. The paper took as its objective to provide the country folk with "that easy, gradual and uniform instruction" which is necessary to overthrow "the long tyranny of antiquated prejudice" and reinvigorate the "enfeebled good sense of the people" with "the torch of Reason."[31] The paper's editor, Joseph Cerutti, is optimistic about the transformative powers of logical analysis:

> There is no political, moral, or artistic truth which cannot be reduced to simple good sense and brought within the reach of the most uneducated mind . . . if one's reasoning proceeds from known principle to unknown principle, from natural logic to a more subtle, abstracted logic. This art of popularizing ideas requires a mind that returns to *causes* and *observes effects*, which embraces the ensemble and separates the details.[32] (my italics)

Veering from the rhetoric of pedagogical revelation to that of observation as abstraction, such language links political enfranchisement to proficiency in the specialized enterprise of rational analysis. To be an effective citizen one must assimilate the procedures of logical inquisition. We remember from the prospectus of *L'Instruction publique* why this should be so. The cognitive purchase of abstract understanding is necessary because it alone can immunize the citizen against fraud and zeal.

Yet Revolutionary papers such as Cerutti's also indenture the populace to a mechanism of self-initiated conformity. That the continual analysis of the political scene benefits the press, upon whose continual supply of information the process depends, hardly needs demonstration. More important is the mechanism for procuring uniformity among the public which is concealed beneath the call for analysis.

Analysis and rearticulation in one's own terms secures the reader's commitment to an idea in a way that no passive learning can. As Talleyrand would remark in a debate on education to which we shall return, "one really knows, really sees clearly, only that which one discovers, which one invents in a sense on one's own."[33] Talleyrand's logic, which was widely shared, was that by allowing people to "participate as it were in the creation of the various pieces of knowledge with which we wish to enrich them, by helping them to share with respect to each the glory of its inventor" one could elicit "their ardent emulation."

Because journalism claims to deal with events and ideas at the level of brute factuality, it can provoke this assimilation at the apparently self-evident level of historical event. The citizen who grasps political events as a neat chain of cause and effect cannot help internalizing their necessity: one can hardly take exception to something which has entered one's belief system under the guise of a factual occurrence. The very mechanism purported to secure objective purchase on the political economy simultaneously makes dissent impossible.

Paradoxically, then – but this paradox is the keystone of those theories that look to Culture as a means of consolidating the state – the subject's internalization of political order proceeds most efficiently under the guise of detachment from that order and its systematic reduction to an object of critical analysis. Rational observation's promise of dispassionate cognitive mastery leads not to enfranchisement, but to absorption. To make the law an object of observation, to internalize its logic through analysis and re-expression in one's own terms, is to come under its dominion.

That this assumption informs Cerutti's benevolent educational program in the *Feuille villageoise* becomes increasingly clear as his paper strives to cope with news of peasant disorders. At one point he warns his readers "if you openly refuse to conform to established order; if by writing, or speech, or by actions, you dissuade your fellow citizens from submitting to new regulations . . . *you are troubling the public order established by the law*; you are forgetting that reason, religion, and the law demand your obedience."[34] Apparently for Cerutti the value of critical understanding lies not in the fact that it allows the subject to oversee or monitor the legislative process, but rather in the *obedience* to the law which it secures. "One really obeys only that which one understands," he declares, advising his readers straight out that "the right and the duty of each of you is to study your laws, so as to learn to obey them."[35] To observe the law in the analytic sense leads necessarily to observing it in the more fundamental sense of obeying it.

Thus the admonition that the peasants need to be taught two things, "to judge and to obey," is in fact redundant, for once one understands the law one will automatically have internalized its logic and be incapable of disobeying.[36] Through rational analysis and comprehension, political law is absorbed and naturalized, its imperatives assimilated to the individual's internal structure of selfhood. Instructed by the newspaper, each citizen can learn to "be truly free, that is, to live according to the laws, to know them, *to be saturated with their spirit*."[37] As Lanthenas puts it, in a speech quoted by *La Feuille Villageoise*, "men are governed/ govern themselves [se gouvernent] only by the ideas they have acquired."[38]

What the trope of observation in these early journals underscores is the ability of public sphere discourse to meld analysis, surveillance and obedience into a single logic of behavior and to associate that behavior with an ideal of civic integrity and self-realization. The press in this sense operates analogously, but on the level of the political, to state-sponsored institutions of Culture such as the school, which also cast the realization of individuality in terms of an assimilation of collective values. The similarity not only of their enterprises but also their tactics finds striking confirmation in the fact that eighty years later the English educator Matthew Arnold would single out observing, reading, and thinking as the constituent operations of Culture, the way to knowledge and religion, and the antidote to anarchy.[39]

Translating into practical political terms the consensus-forming procedures of public sphere discourse, the Revolutionary newspapers put into place a mechanism of citizen formation even as the Revolutionary commissions are theorizing about how this might be accomplished. The daily analysis of events modulates the reader's cognitive autonomy into civil obedience. To the extent the law's logic is grasped and its reason acknowledged in the process of analysis, it will appear to be the execution of the reader's initiative, just as the speeches on the floor of the Convention seem to express public opinion:

> Who makes the law? The legislator? No, he just proclaims it; the law has been composed long before the town crier announces it in the street . . . each person has made the law, put his ideas in it, his will, even his expression, and when it is proclaimed and printed up, it is only obeyed or respected to the extent it is sanctioned in advance by public opinion.[40]

To the extent the law reflects the public's judgment, obeying it is simply a matter of complying with one's own convictions. The newspaper readers are convinced that they are indeed contributing to the political process they observe – indeed, that they are contributing to it *by* observing it. To the extent they have overseen the genesis of the laws, they have sanctioned them, melding their decision to the legislative process.

In sum, by fostering the divergent impulses of critical intervention and political conformity, and uniting them in a single dynamic, the press transforms the expression of individuality into an instrument of political regulation. Fueling and satisfying the contradictory demands of private interest and public order, absolute freedom and total conformity, it defines and assumes that essential "mediate" function which it continues to fill even today.

Still, as the turbulence and factionalism of the French Revolution testify, the effectiveness of the early press in galvanizing the public will in political matters posed a limit to its ability to achieve social consensus at the broader level. This is because it dealt primarily with brute political reality and competing solutions and interests. The consensus it formed among one group or class had tangible consequences for opposing groups at the level of immediate material reality: who was fed or starved, guillotined or lionized, hinged on the shifts of public opinion.

To integrate individual autonomy and social coherence at the level of the nation as a whole (and ultimately of whole global regions) the productive dialectic of analysis and collective law needed to be reimagined within the less politically charged space of social practice and phrased in terms less inflammatory than those of domination and subordination. This is where the notion of Culture as such entered, transposing the dialectic of law and freedom into the field of history, meaning, and identity.

Identity and the Dialectic of Reason

In the latter part of the eighteenth century and no doubt as a consequence of institutions like the newspaper, the various processes of identity formation we have been discussing start to coalesce explicitly around the word "culture." The reliance in authors from Rousseau to Hegel on terms like *cultivation, cultivated, culture,* and the slightly different German term *Kultur,* as well as the appearance of new concepts associated with culture, such as *civilization, nation,* and the *aesthetic,* confirm the accreditation of a new logic of identity and a new economy of truth and authority.

The rhetoric of the press illustrates how this new logic is articulated. Paradigmatic of public sphere discourse more generally, it disseminates a notion of political subjectivity that refuses to settle for either autonomy or subservience, demanding rather that the inscription of the law in the hearts of the citizens occur as the result of the latter's own cognitive initiatives. Concepts like "observation," "public opinion," "representation," become ubiquitous in the discourse of the times not because they provide a tighter grip on a specific reality, but because they accommodate and lend a semblance of rationality to the diametrically opposed imperatives of obedience and freedom, conformity and individuality, passivity and activity, which have come to be associated with the realization of one's selfhood and identity – and which find their political expression in the emerging republican forms of government and the concept of the citizen.

Culture is another such term, and by far the most powerful, for it not only connotes two modalities of subjectivity (the subject being formed and the subject doing the forming) but the dialectic of individual and collective and the intersection of human endeavor with material reality. Even at this early stage of its formation, culture designates both a process (farming or self-perfection) and a product (crops or knowledge), both an endeavor and a science (agriculture), both an individual initiative (the attempt to foster growth in something) and a characteristic of a community (the things it grows, the level of its agricultural development), both a material result (food) and an abstract one (learning).

As the term metamorphoses over the next two centuries, it will acquire further semantic content, its implicit dialectic of production recast in terms of collective and individual, history and event, determination and freedom, tradition and innovation, reiteration and dissent, past and present. One of the most fundamental versions of this process constructs individual reason out of experience and vice versa. This is proposed by Herder, whose early and influential theorization of culture makes him a logical point of reference.

Herder's decisive move is to recast individual identity in terms of a dialectic and to generalize to all of human social life the play between systematic practice and individual truth that we saw inaugurated in more limited contexts by the new science and rationalism. In his work the play between impersonal system and individual identity that was insinuated into material practice by the discursive print economies in the early modern period is formalized as a universal process of identity formation and experience.

We get a glimpse of this transformation in his meditation "Ideas for a Philosophy of History." Here Herder recasts the formation of reason by experience (which we recall from Hobbes) in terms of a dialectic between an accumulating frame of understanding and the individual constructions of truth it grounds and results from. Reason is formed by experience in order to become in turn its guide and a means of fashioning our lives:

> reason, in both its theoretical and practical manifestations, is nothing more than something *formed by experience*, an acquired knowledge of the propositions and directions of the ideas and faculties, to which man is fashioned by his organization and mode of life. . . . Man's reason is the creation of *man*. From infancy, man compares the ideas and impressions, particularly those of his finer senses, according to the delicacy, accuracy and frequency of his sense perceptions, and in proportion to the speed with which he learns to combine these. The result of these combinations constitutes thought, a newly created unity. And the result of the various combinations of thoughts and perceptions constitutes the process of distinguishing the true from the false, the good from the bad, the beneficial from the harmful. This ongoing process, which fashions our lives as human beings, is reason.[41]

Formed by experience, reason forms us. It is a process that "fashions our lives" but also "an acquired knowledge" that is "formed by experience." It is both the process and the product of life. The accumulation of knowledge is conditioned by knowledge, each successive stage of our development being from one perspective the product or "conclusion" of the last and from another, an act of shaping the future. For Herder "Human nature, even at its best, is not an independent deity: it has to learn everything, develop through progress, keep on advancing through gradual struggle."[42]

Further, in the process of "distinguishing the true from the false" we are shaped by and in turn shape the values of the collective which we articulate as the expression of our identity. Because reason is formed according to the individual's "organization and mode of life," "each form of human perfection . . . is in a sense, national and time-bound . . . Nothing develops, without being occasioned by time, climate, necessity, by world events or the accidents of fate."[43] Individuals and communities are by definition unique and yet similar, by virtue of their identification with a system of determination – which can itself be embedded in larger systems.

A similar dialectic between distinctive endeavor and determining conditions at the level of the collective governs the difference and similarity, the unique and multiple identities, of "nations" or "peoples" or "cultures." Just as from one perspective each individual is unique, so too "every distinct community is a *nation*, having its own national culture as it has its own language."[44] Culture is not something that can ever be the "same." It is constantly changing within one community and necessarily different between different communities. As Herder explains, "no nation succeeding another, even inheriting all its adjuncts, ever becomes what the other was. All the rudiments of its culture might be the same, but the culture itself would not be so, lacking the original influences which had helped to shape its former nature."[45]

Yet from another perspective our common involvement in the historical dialectic of experience gives us all a semblance of identity at a higher level of abstraction: "in the last analysis [man] is connected with the whole chain of the human species, since some links of this chain inevitably come in contact with, and thus act upon, the development of his mental powers ... Consequently, we are not the product of merely local circumstances."[46]

A feature of this model upon which Herder does not insist will become significant in the modern era when culture is invoked as a deliberate principle of identity: it is possible to theorize and feel oneself penetrated with multiple communal identities. The Auvergnat priest is an individual within his provincial community, but also a Frenchman, a European, a clergyman.

Similarly, this model contains a potential mechanism of social stratification which will be developed and refined by the high Cultural institutions of the modern era: as the individuals within a given society reason out their existence, they naturally sort themselves into different classes and groups, at once bound together by the system of constraints and norms within which they strive, yet differentiated by their varying accommodations of those norms, their different perceptions of good and bad, which society acknowledges through status and class distinctions.

The most important feature of Herder's model, however, is its explicit postulation that both individual identity and the system of norms and procedures within which that identity elaborates itself are precipitates of human endeavor. This constitutes a theoretical ratification of the authority of social practice that had been imposing itself on the collective mind to varying degrees for the past three centuries. Henceforth, individual destiny and the shape of society may be nominally attributed to divine design, but they are also understood to accrue naturally and inevitably over time as a deposit of both deliberate intention and incidental event, both thought and habit. Herder's dialectical model thus understands the rules of practice, which systematic knowledge exists to elude, as permanently reconfiguring themselves to incorporate the results of that knowledge – as well as habit. Incidental social practice or unconsciously acquired habit can engender laws and norms, but so can individual initiative and collective enterprise.

Identity and its enabling grammar are thus refigured as the precipitates of history as well as its origin. They endure as identifiable forms (of thought, belief, behavior) and are identified with the collectives or individuals that produced them; hence the anthropological idea of culture, and, as well, the common identification of culture as a set of rules with culture as the artifacts produced by individuals according to those rules, as in Georg

Simmel's 1921 definition: "we speak of culture whenever life produces certain forms in which it expresses and realizes itself: works of art, religions, sciences, technologies, laws, and innumerable others."[47]

Herder's model has another important feature. It generalizes to all of human life the teleology of incremental rationalization that had been put into circulation during the early modern period by the new cognitive disciplines. As Fichte rewords it, the "ultimate objective of man is to bring under his submission everything that is lacking reason and dominate it freely and according to his own law."[48] In 1869 Matthew Arnold will amplify and extend this claim in his celebrated polemic, *Culture and Anarchy*: "it is in making endless additions to itself, in the endless expansion of its powers, in endless growth in wisdom and beauty, that the spirit of the human race finds its ideal."[49]

By redefining the accumulation of knowledge and power as a function of life in general, rather than a strategy pursued to specific ends, this way of thinking makes it possible to endow the practice of self-cultivation with an aura of material disinterest. This is an essential move in the formulation of high Cultural ideology.

Disinterested Mediations and Mediated Agency

Cultural institutions such as the school can effectively recruit significant numbers of the populace into projects of self-inscription – projects of the kind that journalistic analysis of political events demonstrated at the level of political affiliation – only if such endeavors seem to transcend particular material interest in the name of universal truth. The claim of transcendence would be definitively secured only under the aegis of aesthetic value; however, an incipient version of the high Cultural ethic of disinterested intellectual speculation is already in circulation in the protocols of public sphere critique.

We recall from the last chapter that the practice of critique grew out of the separation of the moral and religious domains from that of the political. Explicitly disavowing any political motives, the "philosophical" discourse of enlightened critique was directed only at unmasking irrational prejudices – which by definition were constructed collectively and unconsciously. And because the conclusions that critique reached were adjudicated in public discussion to which all, theoretically, could contribute, it had a plausible claim to being independent of particular material interest. The ideas or opinions expressed in the public realm – say in a periodical such as the *Spectator* or in a philosophical discussion in a salon – were by convention not supposed in the first instance to represent the material or political interests of the party expressing them (although by extension they ultimately might), so much as the impersonal cause of truth or social enlightenment – and, by analogy, the reputation or social identity of their author.

To take a celebrated instance, when in 1758 Rousseau violently attacks d'Alembert's views on public theaters in Geneva, he is not assumed to be opposing theaters primarily for personal gain. Neither his livelihood nor d'Alembert's depends on the presence or absence of a theater in Geneva, nor are their arguments assumed to be structured in order to court favor from a particular patron. Rather, and whatever the ultimate material and political consequences of the arguments (which were none too good, in the case of Rousseau), they are assumed to be arguing over what they believe to be the *truth*.

Readers steeped in the ethos of academic dispute and its (tenuous) claims of disinterested inquiry may find this point trivial. But academic dispute is precisely the heir and beneficiary of the discursive conventions which developed in the eighteenth century to allow the passionate expression of personal conviction with relative impunity by individuals of no particular rank. Provided they conformed to the rules of etiquette and proper expression, people could express their beliefs in the public realm because, strictly speaking, those opinions *did not matter*: the public sphere was a realm by definition separated from the corridors of power; the ideas expressed in it were not intended, nor taken, to reflect political or economic policy, but only the abstract, shared – and by that token diffused and anonymous – convictions of the people. What was expressed was expressed in the service of truth and truth alone, and delivered in the disinterested voice of the scholar.

Kant defines this kind of discourse as the *public use of reason* in his 1784 essay "What is Enlightenment." The public use of

reason is "the use which a person makes of it as a scholar before
the reading public," as opposed to the private use of reason one
engages in when carrying out one's duties as a civil servant,
officer, or citizen. The citizen cannot refuse to pay taxes duly
levied, according to Kant – for that would be breaking the law –
but he can very well express publicly "his thoughts on the
inappropriateness or even the injustice of these levies."[50]

The notion that such discourse is disinterested goes hand in
hand with the understanding that it is *mediated* by some institutional forms. It is compliance with the protocols of philosophical
speculation, for instance, that makes it impossible for a work of
philosophy to express only the individual's immediate world and
interests: there are many works which do just that, but they
do not qualify as philosophy. Similarly, any scientific work
accredited by the discipline as such, by definition embodies and
expresses the discipline's norms of inquiry and standards of
evidence.

The mediated nature of critique, or the public use of reason –
or intellectual discussion more generally as it develops under the
aegis of Culture over the next two hundred years – entails a
deferred notion of individual action and effect. It tacitly renounces
direct agency for the individual in favor of a mediated effect that
is both more and less effective. More in that it can ultimately
change shared practices in a way which physical intervention by
one person or even a small group might not; less, in that it can
never advance the cause of the individual immediately.

This kind of mediated effectivity could be defined as cultural
intervention, since it attempts to change the laws of practice by
shaping practice over time. In the place of direct intervention in
the legislative process, it operates by indirect influence on the
public will, using abstract arguments circulated in the public
sphere. Presumably, through the ideas they disseminate people
shape policy without necessarily confronting each other – an
important advantage when multiple and even conflicting projects
of individuation occur under the aegis of self-expression.

The effects of public sphere mediation extend to identity as
well, which it repositions decisively in the play between impersonal shared system and individual expression. This is perhaps
why the notion of reputation (and its converse, ridicule) were of
such paramount importance in the eighteenth century. For

Enlightenment society, the crucial interactions by means of which one established one's identity were not between people, but between discoursing subjects and the discursive economies that regulated their celebrity. One "made a name" for oneself through the ideas one articulated, rather than by arguing one's particular cause – whether those ideas took the form of witty social critique, a disquisition on taxes, or literary criticism.

Rousseau, to take a celebrated case, was well aware that his identity as the famous author and eccentric "Rousseau" was a construct cobbled together by an often uninformed public on the basis of their interpretation (and as he saw it, misinterpretation) of the ideas in his writings.[51] But as his example illustrates, indirect action on public opinion can have far-reaching effects. By the time of the revolution he helped inspire, the power of abstract public sphere discourse to change the world will be taken as self-evident. And the mediation of identity it imposes will be understood as a tremendous advantage, not just for those wishing to influence history, but for all those hoping to achieve a measure of autonomy. Expressing one's self within an impersonal economy of truths, norms, and values obviates the need to depend on any particular other. Thus one contributor to the Revolutionary debates on education blithely exhorts:

> may the student never depend on people, but only on things . . . depending on things means being obliged to conform to the laws which result from the general will of the society of which one is a member. Depending on things is a natural dependence, a necessary one which in no way injures one's vanity, nor freedom or equality. When one depends on things one has the internal satisfaction of depending only on oneself, of knowing one's destiny is in one's hands.[52]

It is generally acknowledged, then as today, that modern subjectivity is irrevocably and multiply mediated, and that the forms of mediation specifically associated with critique, science, and intellectual and Cultural discourse in general, stake their claim to freedom of expression and the right to pursue their course of inquiry on their commitment to impersonal truth. What remains a perennial issue of debate is whether this is a good thing or a bad – whether discursive mediations afford the subject more liberty and social leverage or to the contrary, foreclose on authentic social and political relations.

One issue is the political effectivity of critique or public sphere discourse. For Reinhart Koselleck, the scholarly transaction between thinker and shared law only claims to be apolitical the better to operate its powerful political effect: "the political secret of the Enlightenment lay in the fact that its concepts, analogous to the indirect assumption of power, were not seen as being political. The political anonymity of reason, morality, nature, and so on, defined their political character and effectiveness. Their political essence lay in being non-political."[53]

On the other hand, the subject that espouses this mediated authority seems blocked from not only any form of direct political action but any kind of self-presence. One's identity, like one's interests, can be advanced only through the filter of the community's codes and protocols; any self-interested move will involve assimilating community values. Thus the assertion of identity tends to hook back on itself to embed the individual more deeply in the norms of the community.

Kant's example of the disgruntled taxpayer is illustrative in this regard. As a general lesson, it seems to say that rather than arguing one's immediate interests – and refusing to pay one's taxes, for instance – the enlightened citizen should construct an abstract argument about why the tax system is inefficient or unfair. Presumably, once this argument has gained currency in the public sphere and helped precipitate a modification of the law, the individual will reap a personal benefit. However, to win acceptance the argument will have to comply with the discursive protocols of the moment and underwrite the dominant values and beliefs of the community and its leaders. In this sense it will hardly be the "individual" who wins. By contributing to the formation of public opinion, social norm, and even, ultimately, official policy, individuals may obtain material benefit similar to that which one might get by arguing one's case in court; but as in court, that victory comes at the price of self-assessed conformity to the laws – in this case the dominant ways of thinking and the rules governing public expression.

For those who rejoice in the prospect of a coherent, homogeneous society, this is a harbinger of progress. Others, less sanguine than Kant, will see in it not the spread of enlightenment, but the habituation of the population to a new administrative regime, one that induces people to internalize normative values of their own accord, that encourages them to discipline themselves, in the Foucauldian sense and in mine, by indenturing their identity and agency to the discursive categories and regimes of practice that regulate their society.

As the ideology of identity formation and self-realization achieves dominance in the modern period, these two divergent evaluations of the cultural transaction become progressively more pronounced. From one perspective, one can envision a community of individuals achieving their different potentials and attaining their particular form of happiness through a disciplined enterprise of self-fulfillment. From this perspective, the rules structuring that enterprise express nothing more than the expediency of normative usage in a collaborative project: norms and regulations guarantee a level playing field and insure that one's efforts will have meaning for the community. The identity one forges for oneself is the product of individual agency and energy, but it has meaning within the community by virtue of being constituted according to the rules of that community.

This scenario – to which both Left and Right at times appeal – undergirds the ideology of Cultural self-realization that developed in conjunction with the theoretical notions of the "aesthetic" and aesthetic education. This was called "Bildung" – literally "formation" or "education" – by its German theoreticians, and the name has been retained by theory to designate the program of education that operates the assimilation of norms and the reconciliation of individual to state through the cultivation of aesthetic experience in the various disciplines associated with the "arts." Access to the realm of the aesthetic entails the internalization of consensual values and normative interpretative practices, but because these practices are specified to pertain to the recuperation of timeless aesthetic values, rather than to advance the interests of a specific class or regime, the individual feels no sense of coercion or political capitulation.

There exists, however, a countervailing darker vision of the same transaction, that sees the high Cultural regime of indoctrination as co-opting authentic, immediate subjectivity. In this view, the ethic and values of Culture serve class interests, not the timeless and universal values of beauty. They mobilize analytic energy only to neutralize it, displacing the energies of the most cognitively empowered members of society into the politically sanitized domain of aesthetic interpretation, where the pursuit of meaning displaces that of justice or truth, and the advancement of one's particular material interest is by definition out of order.

From this perspective the work of art is an effective vehicle of authority, but one that works for the hegemony. The laws it promulgates are all the more pernicious because, like the laws of habitual practice or prejudice, they can by definition never be specified conclusively, linked definitively to a single material need, or located at any particular social site. Rather, as "meanings," they insinuate themselves through the procedures required for their extraction and appear to express the moment and priorities of the individuals articulating them as much as those of their author, or the author's tradition or discipline. Moreover, at the material level the public sphere's regimes of expression are dominated by an elite of intellectuals and wealthy patrons who control what gets published or exhibited and what styles find acceptance or are scorned. In that sense, the high Cultural ideal of self-improvement conceals but a further elite-formation mechanism, one which substitutes intellectual achievement, verbal proficiency, and disciplinary patronage for the old regime practices of the courtier and the financier.

These conflicting modern valuations of the Cultural transaction do not simply reflect antagonistic ideologies: Right and Left regularly invoke the specter of manipulation by elite interests, just as both regularly appeal to the ideal of self-realization within a regulated system. Rather, these two divergent visions reflect a fundamental ambivalence with respect to the ends and means of the cultural machine: is collective order or personal freedom more important? What takes precedence, tradition or innovation? Individual interest or collective interest? Self-fulfillment or social coherence?

The answer is of course: neither, or rather both at all times. Individual cognitive initiative always carries both a promise of conformity and a menace of dissent with respect to the orders within which it frames itself, just as those orders offer both a framework of rules for self-realization and a threat of coercion and alienation. In fact, each of these is the ground of the other, each is the measure of the other's effectiveness: the attempt to transcend, undo, or rewrite the laws of one's culture is as much a part of the ethos of cultivated self-expression as is their celebration. From the perspective of the community, much of the energy needed to hold a "culture" together, whether it be at the micro scale of a corporation or neighborhood or the macro scale of a continent like North America, comes from the ongoing attempt by the individual members of that culture to understand, modify, and elude the laws that define it.

The modern era is so imbued with this assumption that we take its paradoxical dynamic for granted. But for the early theoreticians of culture it was the occasion of abiding anxiety and vacillation. Much as individual cognitive freedom alternately appeared to them to threaten and guarantee public order, so too public opinion alternately appeared to be the ultimate tribunal of social justice and the tyranny of some portion of the people over the rest. The hesitation between these conflicting evaluations reaches near-hysterical proportions in the extensive and lively debates over universal public education during the French Revolution.

Constructing the Citizen: Revolutionary Theories of Education

Given the Enlightenment teleology of human life as incremental understanding, it is not surprising that one of the earliest priorities of the Revolution should have been developing a system of universal public instruction. The rising authority of rational discourse and the spread of the ethic of critique during the century had resulted in a general move through Europe toward literacy, although at different paces.[54] Universal education is the logical culmination of that trend, and a crucial component in the universalization of the ethos of systematic self-actualization. The very notion of a standard education bespeaks the ascendancy of Cultural logic. Only if all were inculcated with the same system of understanding and the same urge to continue exercising their reason could representative consensual law and a rational state displace blind prejudice and the despotism that thrived on it. One delegate to the Convention succinctly explains this:

The necessity for a good theory of teaching is based on these truths: that it is enlightenment that made the Revolution and broke the chains of the slaves; that man is capable of indefinite perfection; that his perfection depends on the enlightenment he receives; that the more people are educated and especially generally educated, the more their governments will improve and the more they will appreciate the value of freedom and know how to preserve it; that the more enlightenment is within reach of all, the more equality there will be between people.[55]

The Committee on Public Instruction, which deliberated under various incarnations for three years from October, 1792 through October, 1795, was explicitly concerned with forming identity, and with the strategies a state might elect to shape the minds and bodies of its citizens. The Committee drew on the notion that each nation had its own identity or culture, and that this was formed by the government and the educational system, among other things. Helvétius's evaluation of thirty years earlier, was largely taken for granted by this period: "every nation has its particular way of seeing and feeling which forms its character; and among all peoples this character either changes suddenly or evolves gradually according to the sudden or insensible changes that occur in the form of their government, and consequently in their public education."[56]

The Committee took as its task devising a system of universal schooling capable of producing *citizens*, that is, people equipped to participate in a new form of government – one that grounded its authority in the collective will of the people, as expressed in public opinion. Differences in philosophy notwithstanding, all members of the Committee shared the conviction that their political authority was ultimately based on public opinion; and all parties recognized that public opinion differed from previous forms of political power in being grounded in collective discourse.

One delegate, François Lanthenas, explains how this works. His ideal engine of political truth and consensus is quite simply the ongoing conversation of the people:

one must imagine a number of individuals who would enter into conversations and candidly compare their ideas to those of others; who would modestly expose their doubts, examine and combat with good faith their difficulties; who would, finally, carefully cultivate and perfect this means of spreading truth and making it germinate and become embedded in peoples' minds through the most intimate persuasion. Let us suppose that some men, prepared by these initial conversations subsequently fan out further in the world, that everywhere they go they begin to explain succinctly, simply, and in the way most likely to draw attention to themselves, the true principles of society. Let us suppose, finally, that their auditors are moved enough to repeat this small number of simple truths to others, to their family and their companions; thus we will have an idea of the way in which truth can be disseminated.[57]

Unfortunately, the discursive economy that propagated revolutionary "truth" could just as easily disseminate the reactionary opinions associated with despotism under the category of *préjugés* – which included all manner of prejudice, unexamined predisposition, or superstition. Even more than for earlier times, prejudice formed the passive dark side of collective law for the Revolutionaries. They especially decried the unexamined religious dogma and superstitions that were exploited by the monarchy and the church to control the populace. As Fourcroy exclaims at one point, "up to now prejudice and despotism alone have fashioned man."[58]

The problem with prejudices was that they were immune to traditional military or economic forms of governmental intervention. As Marie-Joseph Chénier puts it, "prejudices are chronic diseases . . . [they are] opinions; you can't fire a canon at them; you can kill people, but there is no way to kill opinion. . . . so a clever government raises philosophers, not armies."[59]

Only enlightened public discourse could eradicate prejudice, by drawing the populace into reasoned analysis and self-conscious debate. This is why Lanthenas reminds his fellow delegates that the first objective of the Committee should be to encourage active, vigorous subjects and discourage discursive passivity: "the great objective which we must propose, and which is essential, is to invigorate public opinion and avoid anything that might cause it to fall into apathy and indifference."[60]

Yet public opinion could also become overly vigorous and run amok, especially when manipulated by fine speakers. As another delegate cautions, "the art of speaking well has great advantages and fine prerogatives in a free country; but the deplorable abuse of it we see every day makes it a menace to reason and fatal for liberty."[61] This is why even as Lanthenas calls for the invigoration of public opinion, he proposes a system of universal censorship, lamenting the deplorable things that have befallen the Republic now that "every individual, according to his prejudices and passions, has been able to influence public opinion and morality with enough force and success to produce substantial disruptions."[62]

The dilemma was thus to invigorate and to contain public opinion at once, by forming subjects capable of adding their voice to the collective chorus and resisting manipulation, yet not so discursively adventuresome as to influence it unilaterally. All agreed that universal education was the obvious means to achieve this end, yet two very different approaches quickly emerged, each expressing a slightly different anxiety.

One group drew directly on the Enlightenment faith in critical inquiry. They proposed rendering public opinion impervious to manipulation by maximizing every citizen's critical faculties. The strategy was to strengthen the social consensus by strengthening individual identity, on the assumption that analytic initiative, discursive sophistication, and self-consciousness could be relied upon to fortify public opinion, once they were widely dispersed throughout the populace. To combat the passive internalization of prejudice, thinkers like Talleyrand, Condorcet, Ducos, and Romme envisioned a subject who would *appropriate* the law by rephrasing it in his own language. Their model prefigures the logic of high Cultural critique: it assumes that normative regimes are best internalized not through coercion, but through analysis and reconceptualization in one's own terms. The immediate objective is to train subjects to judge for themselves and thus make them resistant to demagoguery:

Shall not the first objective of public instruction be to arm less educated citizens against the crude tricks of oratory charlatanism, by tailoring to their minds some simple yet sure methods of distinguishing noisy sophism from modest reasoning. Citizens, the people will be truly free when they can judge their orators independently.[63]

But as we earlier glimpsed in our discussion of the papers, this "arming" of the citizen also enlists him. The complete explanation of how this occurs is given by Talleyrand, in one of the earliest proposals for a complete educational system. His assumption, which becomes a foundational assumption of all Cultural institutions deployed by the state, is that the subject internalizes propositions and principles not only by habit, but also through deliberate cognitive assimilation:

> it has been proven a thousand times that one really knows, one clearly sees, only that which one discovers, that which one invents oneself, in a sense. Ideas that come to us in other ways may penetrate our minds, but they do not belong to us; they are not part of us, but foreign plants that can never take root. What is thus to be done? Promote above all the use of *analysis* which reduces any object to its true components, and of *synthesis*, which recomposes it subsequently out of them. By means of this double operation ... one does not simply receive an idea, one acquires it.[64]

The same logic applies to moral education. "To saturate oneself with morality, which is the first requirement of all constitutions, one must not merely inscribe it in the heart by means of sentiment and conscience, but also teach it like a genuine science, the principles of which will be demonstrated to the reason of all men for all time."[65]

Talleyrand's confidence in the power of analysis to inculcate ideas is typical of his era, and it reveals how the procedures of analytic inquiry which the Enlightenment had generalized from rationalism and the new science were transformed from a strategy of resistance to unconscious collective practice into a mechanism for the assimilation of practices. The universalized ethic of personal development convened individual initiative and autonomous judgment in the name of standardization.

Other members of the Committee are even more extravagant in their faith with respect to analysis:

> a new day has dawned on the sciences that have adopted this method so wise and fertile in miracles, this *analysis* which keeps track of every step it takes but which never takes a false step backwards or to the side: it can bring the same simplicity of

language, the same clarity into every kind of idea . . . this method which alone can accomplish what Bacon and Locke demanded, which alone can recreate human understanding . . . will become the universal organ of all human knowledge and the language of all professors.[66]

For proponents of analysis, it is not through mindless habituation, but deliberate abstraction, reflection, and expression in one's own words that one internalizes republican values. In so doing, one not only assimilates the structures and values of the community, one gains a sense of critical autonomy and of an increment in knowledge: "analysis is to the sciences and to teaching what liberty is to political constitutions; the one and the other make people feel their dignity and contribute to their perfection.[67]

Such remarks illustrate the extent to which the construction of identity and the elaboration of systematic knowledge, already intertwined in the general protocols of discursive authority that evolved during the early modern period, merged into a single ethic of rational inquiry and community formation during the Enlightenment. Talleyrand invokes analytic discipline not primarily as a means of securing individual identity, but rather as a procedure of indoctrination by means of which citizens could be induced to absorb shared values and make them their own. The discursive discipline that the Enlightenment touted as a source and proof of critical autonomy was from the outset understood as a device for regularizing subjects – and this two centuries before Foucault.

Talleyrand's confidence in the interpellative potential of analytic thinking was not shared by his opponents, who saw in it only the potential for demagoguery. The Jacobins, for instance, seem driven by a visceral fear of critical initiative, which they saw as far more likely to foster discord and far less predictable than the evils of prejudice. Consequently, they proposed an alternative model of education based on the concept of straightforward indoctrination.

Convinced that imbuing the people with indelible values and habits of virtuous behavior was less risky than enlivening their analytic resources, they suggested that rather than *overcome* prejudice and habit, the nation should *engineer* habits – habits congenial to *its* philosophy. This it would accomplish by supervising every aspect and minute of the individual's childhood. As Jean Debry bluntly puts it:

> if you want your laws to be stable and the revolution to make of the people an immense body so tightly united that the impact of particular interests and little individual passions won't be able to unsettle it, give the people, in the form of habits, all those things which advance the objective of this revolution: festivals, morals, principles, the exercise of civil rights, all of that has to make up the civic life of the people in the way eating, drinking, dressing, and sleeping comprise their physical life. Do not leave the *citizen* anything that can remind him of the ways of the subject.[68]

Debry is of course using "subject" in the sense of a subject of the monarchy. But the best known proposal for implementing this strategy of habituation leaves little doubt that the subjectivity to be erased in the children was that which we associate with cognitive initiative and individuality. This was Le Peletier's controversial project to put all children in France in boarding houses under control of the state.

Le Peletier had a fairly simple goal: "it is a matter of giving children the physical and moral qualities, the habits and knowledge, which have a common utility for all."[69] To this end he envisions putting every child between the ages of five and twelve under continual observation: "constantly under the eye and hand of active surveillance, every hour will be marked for sleep, meals, work, exercise, relaxation; the entire regimen of life will be invariably regulated."[70]

While proponents of this approach frequently pay lip service to the citizen's autonomy, their working assumption is that the ideal subject is an undifferentiated creature of reflex, a creature whose behavior can be relied on never to deviate from the interests of the state precisely because it has been purged of semiotic initiative: it will make no determinations on its own, specify no meanings, draw no conclusions. While such a creature would seem strangely reminiscent of the ancien regime subject, this does not seem to cross their minds. Debry muses on the utopic world where the Convention would have at its command "the docile will of twenty-five million beings."[71] Le Peletier notes the advantages of his strategy in similar terms: "the entirety of the child's existence belongs to us; the raw material, if I might use that expression, never leaves the mold; no external object is going to come and disfigure the shape you give it. Prescribe, and execution is certain; imagine a good approach and it is instantly adopted."[72]

Indeed, what could be more stable than a state predicated on a public will incapable of change, in which every citizen is a semiotically inert embodiment of republican values, structured by habit, trained to reiterate, and disinclined to analysis? Le Peletier's children grow into adults whose virtue is effortless because it is habitual, rather than the result of personal decision or initiative. His mechanism of internalization prefigures in concrete terms our notion of culture as something unconscious, inescapable, absorbed since childhood, and in some sense natural – if not necessarily good – to those who embody it. It also suggests the Enlightenment distrust of custom and habit was not unwarranted.

It is striking that while Le Peletier's proposal and that of Talleyrand elect diametrically opposed strategies, both are concerned with endowing the citizenry with shared values. Their educational proposals, like the Committee's countless other innovations for cultivating the citizenry – museums, libraries, natural history collections, learned journals, a new decimal calendar, national festivals, a national observatory – all issue from an anxiety about social coherence and order. Culture as a formal enterprise and preoccupation of the state derives from an awareness of the discursive foundations of social order and a desire to intervene in that discourse and regulate it.

Yet it would be inaccurate to suggest that the Committee wanted to subordinate personal freedom to the welfare of the nation – as if the two were incompatible. In the wake of the Revolution, the opposition between despot and people, privilege and deprivation, is largely superseded by a model of reciprocal benefit which melds individual self-realization to the self-realization of the state. This idea would receive its fullest philosophical elaboration in the work of Hegel, for whom "law, morality, the State, and they alone, are the positive reality and satisfaction of freedom" rather than the "caprice of the individual" or the "license of particular desires."[73] But already in the work of Rousseau, in many respects the spiritual father of the Revolution, virtue, personal fulfillment, and happiness are posited to be contingent on how well individual programs of self-realization fit into and successfully exploit the possibilities of codified collective practice.

The members of the Committee were perhaps not fully convinced of this interdependence, or of their ability to harness its dynamic. Each faction seemed intent on demonizing and excluding from their scenarios the other's concept of the subject. Significantly though, the specter of that subject repeatedly creeps back into their models as a necessary side effect. It is as if their contrasting conceptualizations of the citizen as creature of habit and as analytic individual seem to call each other forth – as if they were already understood to be just two moments or aspects of a single complex dialectic.

For instance, along the same lines as Talleyrand, Condorcet proposes establishing regional centers of secondary and higher education where individuals could pursue their development regardless of their location or social status. His strategy is to make specialized training available to anyone with the inclination to study. Yet his plan in a sense represses individuality by forcing everyone to master the same cognitive strategy: that of analysis and classification. As one delegate envisions it: "analysis covers all branches of human knowledge; . . . so let us offer analysis everywhere, in the books designed for instruction, in the explanations that the teachers will give, and let us impart the habit of analysis to the young people; in this way you will have eliminated a large number of prejudices."[74]

The most deliberate strategy for nurturing individual expression inadvertently curbs it by insisting on a single paradigm of understanding, a single avenue of self-realization: "in all domains the formation of our ideas is the same, only the objects differ; . . . analysis, applied to all the varieties of ideas, in all the schools, will destroy the inequality of enlightenment."[75] The last phrase of this assertion confirms that the insistence on a single way of forming ideas was designed to undo the inequalities that were seen to exist between those skilled in thinking and arguing – and thus in influencing public opinion and legislation – and those who were unable to argue analytically.

Yet delegates of varied persuasions were quick to point out that intensified instruction in a single way of thought, mastered only by a minority, and which could therefore be only imperfectly disseminated, rather than fostering an egalitarian society of freely competing individuals, would simply precipitate a new disenfranchised underclass of the analytically less inclined. As one opponent of Condorcet's proposal, Masuyer, declares, "this system is subversive of every principle of liberty and freedom . . . it will have no other effect than creating two classes of people, *those who think and reason, and those who believe and obey.*"[76] Bancal echoes these sentiments: "the privilege of enlightenment is the most dangerous of all . . . I can see . . . the most cultivated citizens drawn together by an involuntary but inevitable sentiment . . . I see them forming a bundle of enlightenment, a coalition that can act in the national assemblies and become deadly for equality and liberty."[77] For him, the mechanism designed to create people capable of resisting tyrants could well end up disarming the majority and producing a tyrannical minority of indistinguishable clones.

Those who favor of Le Peletier's plan of total surveillance fare no better in excluding the object of their anxieties. They subscribe to benevolent indoctrination in the belief that however draconian it appears, it at least has the virtue of not dividing France into "a lot of reasoners and a lot of slaves."[78] Yet the apologists for indoctrination could hardly discount the necessity, even within their model, of a managerial elite, namely those who oversee the millions of interned children and write their scripts of habit. Clearly, a program of cultural management as ambitious as uniform education requires both notions of the subject – as critical thinker and as habit-bound member of the collective – just as a healthy public opinion entails both a persisting, stable set of truths and the constant interrogation and reformulation of those truths.

The strange vacillation in these debates between positive and negative visions of the autonomous thinker and the consensual majority, like the persistent concurrence of theories of self-formation with theories of indoctrination, underscores the extent to which the logic of individual identity formation and that of unconscious collective reflex (be it positively inflected as public opinion, or negatively, as prejudice and habit) are inseparably intertwined. They are connected both in the fact of their structural interdependence – it is in their interactions with public opinion and their struggles against prejudice that individuals forge their identity; it is within such transactions that public opinion and prejudice are shaped – and in their conflicted valuations of semiotic habit and initiative. Each of the two opposed visions of the people, as passive creatures of habit and authors of their own values, can appear as both a promise and a menace. And each can metamorphose into the other.

It is not just that the redemptive power of public opinion is grounded in the belief of custom's power, and vice versa (the awesome political power of public opinion is a permanent reminder of how quickly prejudice can form, and the dangers it can pose); or even that what makes the ideal of analytic autonomy so attractive – the capacity of one individual to sway millions – is also what makes it so fearsome. It is rather that the most careful theorizations of how to construct either conformity or individuality seem destined to swerve out of control, effecting the opposite result. Behind every idealization of a community of emancipated autonomous thinkers lurks the specter of internalized conformity. Every mechanism for constructing social equality brings with it the inevitability of a new elite. What one person sees as the means of inoculating the state against tyranny can be read by another as its very manifestation, "subversive of every principle of liberty and freedom." The mechanism of administered indoctrination that eliminates class differences will necessarily reintroduce them in the persons of the administrators.

Two centuries of political theory have accustomed us to these swerves of valuation: we are no longer surprised when a notion like hegemony, introduced as a potential revolutionary tactic by Gramsci, is reduced by the undergraduate mind to a vague signifier of conservative repression. Or when education, traditionally extolled as a means of liberation and enfranchisement by Left and Right alike, becomes associated in the thought of Althusser with the most insidious form of state control. But such reevaluations are not a function of our political sophistication; they inhere in the structure of the cultural way of thinking, which surfaces in these early institutions with particular clarity. Culture, we now intuitively know, mobilizes the energy of, and at all moments entertains, two competing ideals: individuality and conformity, semiotic initiative and semiotic uniformity, originality and legibility, self-expression and collective tradition, personal integrity and social solidarity.

The challenge the Revolutionaries faced was to acknowledge

and maintain the dynamic contest between these two benefits/ menaces, so as to stimulate simultaneously in every citizen both critical vigilance *and* obedience, both an innate awareness and respect for laws and norms *and* a wariness with respect to their genesis. Collectively their proposals for public schools reflect and address both of these imperatives, but seldom as two faces of a single dialectic. More often than not, the fear of rampant demagoguery or class domination disrupted the formation of consensus in their own ranks.

That they perceived these threats is instructive, however. The Revolutionary press and the debates over education confirm that the procedures of discursive self-realization which were deployed in the name of political or social consolidation were known from the outset to effect class differentiation and social hierarchization.

Self-realization and Social Triage

It is a pretense of our contemporary writing to expose the connivance of Culture with class interests – typically those of the bourgeoisie. But already in the eighteenth century this revelation was a commonplace. The inscription of self-realization within the protocols of collective discourse and inquiry was understood to carry with it a risk of class domination. Newly emancipated from their old regime masters, the clergy and the nobility, the people felt themselves being drawn into the service of a new elite: the intellectual theoreticians and social managers who demanded allegiance to abstract values and complex systems of thought as the price of political and moral enfranchisement.

In a sense, the strategy of systematic analysis which the early modern period had devised as a means of reclaiming some measure of self-determination from the grip of social practice had been too successful. It had funded the emergence of a class of intellectual leaders powerful enough to overthrow the monarchy, but precisely because that class had identified their power with the truth of rational critique, rational critique no longer seemed class-neutral. In a world ruled by competing systems of analysis, the idea of system no longer carried in itself an aura of detachment from practice, much less of resistance to authority.

However, the specific anxiety on the part of "those who

believe" with respect to the growing power of "those who reason" should not blind us to their fundamental consensus with respect to the operations performed by Culture. If various parties alternately voiced their fear of domination by one class or the other, they did not significantly disagree about how a generalized regime of self-realization would work or what it should do. And what it should do was allocate functions and identity within society.

What was at issue in the Revolutionary debates on education was not, finally, whether an educational system would sort people into classes and functions, but whether that process was completely accessible and self-regulating, such that all people could participate equally in it, developing their inclinations and finding their place in society on their own, or whether on the contrary it was subject to manipulation or structured in such a way as to favor one constituency over another. As newspapers such as the *Feuille Villageoise* or research institutions such as the *Ecole normale* demonstrate, while the general deployment of analytic critique was intended to create a cohesive and coherent society, it was not expected to create a homogeneous one. On the contrary, it was assumed that the process of self-realization would be literal: people would realize their inclinations and abilities, and seek their place in society on their own.

This notion of self-selection is central to the ideology of Culture that develops in the modern era (it is in fact theorized at some length by Fichte in his 1794 *Gespräche über die Bestimmung des Gelehrters* (*Vocation of the Scholar*) at exactly the moment the Revolutionary discussions are taking place). Reassessing identity in its social and economic dimension, it posits that we can only realize our unique potential to the extent we can express it within the structures of possibility of our community. While we can always strive to modify those structures, we need some place from which to start. As Fichte notes, the ideal society would be concerned with the satisfaction of all the needs of its citizens and would be equally concerned with each. However, before one could construct such a society, one would need to have "an exhaustive inventory of all of the natural dispositions and requirements of mankind."[79]

The ethic of Culture offers a more efficient mechanism: it enlists every citizen in the disclosure and definition of his or her own inclinations and capabilities. One assumes one's place in society with a sense of self-determination, since it comes as a result of pursuing one's own interests.

Culture in this sense is not the accumulation of aesthetic capital, but the universal imperative to "make something of oneself," as well as the institutions and processes that disseminate that law and enable its enactment. This imperative places the responsibility for social hierarchy on the individual. By insisting that the first step in taking control of one's determination by social law is stepping back from the practices that enclose one and appropriating their force through systematic understanding, it downplays the constraints which material conditions of access to the resources for self-fashioning might have on this process.

Because it was difficult to overlook the substantial material mediations of a national educational system, the Committee's debates frequently bogged down in accusations of class privilege. Like the press, the school was flawed in one respect: behind its purportedly neutral structure, one could still see figures of authority and systems of discrimination in the persons of the administrator, teacher, priest, or orator, and in the location and accessibility of the schools. What was needed were forms of self-inscription explicitly dissociated from the spheres of the political or economic. Remarkably, these would come from the Commission itself, in the form of the ancillary cultural institutions it devised in the margins of its debates. While it failed to enact the great majority of the ambitious proposals brought before it, it left a substantial legacy in the less formal institutions of citizen building which it invented and funded. These also sought to fashion the citizenry (hence their administrative location under the purview of the Committee) but they did so by fostering precisely the unpredictable dialectic between critical autonomy and social conformity that the proposals for universal instruction had difficulty accommodating.

Today we take many of these institutions for granted: museums, theaters, natural history and botanical collections, learned societies and journals, national achievement awards, libraries, public gardens, agricultural and technological institutes, governmental culture ministries, zoos, a *Conservatoire des Arts et Métiers*, public speaking programs, national holidays and elaborate commemorative festivals. Some, like the official press and media, were explicitly motivated by and historically linked to political objectives. Others, like the museum or the literary contest, were designed both to facilitate individual aesthetic formation and to establish a national literary and artistic heritage as a symbol of social coherence.

But all had one thing in common: they deploy at one level or another the distinctive double rhetoric which simultaneously fosters conformity *and* individuation, and in fact extracts each from the other in a complex transaction that accommodates all members of the public. And all to one degree or another subvention the process of self-selection, inducing the public to distribute itself into ranks. What distinguishes these institutions from the school is their ability to perform this social triage relatively painlessly, guiding each citizen to his or her most appropriate social function and arena of self-realization without appearing to reintroduce class distinctions. This will become the hallmark of the modern Cultural enterprise of identity formation and the institutions that deploy it.

3

Instituting Culture

In the previous chapter we saw that the universal acknowledgment of the power of social practice in the eighteenth century was matched by a move to incorporate a broader spectrum of the population in the economies of public discourse that could counter that authority and rationalize society. In order that this deployment of rule-bound discourse might actually secure a more just, cohesive polity, the Enlightenment sought to universalize the ethic of self-conscious inquiry as self-realization. However, as the examples of the press and the debates on education showed, the initial mechanisms deployed to this end, whether unofficial or official, stumbled repeatedly on the potential contradictions embedded in both their ends and their means.

The political instrumentality of the periodical press, for instance, transgressed against one of the tacit conventions of Enlightenment critique with which it affiliated itself, namely the disclaimer of self-interested political intervention. This did not make it an ineffective political instrument, but it limited its capacities to unite the social body. Similarly, the Jacobin educational theoreticians' ambition to imbue the mind of the citizen with approved habits went against their commitment to autonomous judgment and a truth transcendent of local interests.

The more impartial endeavor that was needed found its most fundamental expression in social critique. Answerable to reason alone, and not political alliance or local interest; permanently striving to overcome the distortions of habit and custom in the name of a universal truth, Enlightenment critique grounded its moral claim in its transcendence of particular or national interest. It made the case for humanity and universal reason, and its court of appeal was individual conscience and experience.

The press and school had limited access to the more private

dimensions of experience. The former's overt instrumentality, its blatant self-interest, its impersonal mode of production, dissemination, and consumption, and the public nature of the issues it addressed all limited the extent to which it could incorporate personal experience or engage the felt moral sentiments of the individual. A significant part of what makes up identity in its particularity fell outside of the grasp of politics, and hence of political journalism: private memories and feelings, sense impressions, personal fears, local fantasies and histories, corporeal habits, etc. If the newspaper had difficulty addressing these private dimensions of experience, the school was conceived of as a means to repress them in order to foster a stronger identification with the nation. Its normative regimes provided even less access to particular experience. However, another powerful institution had arisen alongside the press and the public sphere which proved highly effective in organizing this side of subjectivity and bringing it into the public sphere. This was the new literary genre of the novel.

Mobilizing Subjectivity: the Novel

The origins of the novel and the reasons for its relatively sudden appearance as a dominant literary genre in the eighteenth century have been a topic of debate from the moment of its emergence to the present, and it is not within the scope of this study even to summarize the countless theories which have been proposed to account for it.[1] For our purposes it suffices to recall the key features of the genre – several of which are characteristic of modern fictional narrative in general, including the cinematic variety.

The novel differed in form and content from previous literary genres. It took as its content the sentiments, passions, and psychological dramas of individuals in contemporary social settings, which it typically presented as historical events, framed and authenticated by a first-person narrative or delivered by a pseudo-historical editor. In its attention to character, motivation, setting, and the temporal development of its plots, it exhibited a "realism" that set it apart from the precedent prose genre of the romance, despite their similar concerns with the depiction of love. In its choice of characters from all ranks of life, portrayed in everyday situations and coping with the demands of contemporary society, it distinguished itself from epic precedents and literature of the nobler sort more generally.

A second important feature of the new genre concerns its self-proclaimed didactic function. Although it frequently depicted conduct that could hardly be called exemplary or virtuous, it claimed for its tales a moralizing influence, on the theory that they provided readers with a necessary complement to their own limited experience, dramatizing vices to be avoided as well as the rewards of virtue. The exemplary function of literature was hardly a new idea, but the lessons of realistic fiction differed in their concreteness and specificity from the abstract morals of fables, sermons, or maxims. Conveyed by realistic characters who were immersed in a familiar material setting and struggling with a concrete problem defined by contemporary mores, the novel's message relied on a mechanism of identification or sympathy, rather than abstract moral principles. Readers grasped the liabilities or rewards of different behaviors by living through them with the characters. There was of course a pleasure associated with this vicarious experience, and this accounted for the negative evaluation the new genre received from conservative forces. While the genre's proponents justified it by appeal to its moralizing potential, reactionaries singled it out as an incitement to vice and sloth, and an irritant to the passions.

These criticisms often focused on a third feature of the new genre, namely its identification with an intimate, voyeuristic mode of reading and pleasure. Unlike traditional inspirational works, which were generally read aloud in a collective setting such as the family and were reread programmatically for their exemplary value, the novel was devoured silently and in solitude, and generally only once or twice. Rather than an incitement to reflection, novels seemed to tempt readers with a world of passion into which they could lose themselves in their leisure hours, giving reign to their most repressed fantasies and private urges. Novel reading was asocial, private, and empathetic, and it involved the consumption of multiple texts, the immersion of the individual consciousness in the narcotic of multiple worlds and consciousnesses.

There are other ways one could characterize the new genre –

for instance its mode of production, dissemination, and marketing; however, the formal traits summarized above are the most pertinent to our discussion. For they made the novel a natural medium for expressing and overcoming the divergent imperatives of modern social identity, melding the realization of individuality with the assimilation of norm and law.

In its content and form, the novel gave literal expression to the fusion of society and individual. Delivering its generalizable vision of contemporary sentimental and social life through the experiences of a particular character, it depicted the coming into being of morals and the law as a function of individual self-awareness. The use of the first-person narrative voice (nearly ubiquitous in the eighteenth century) further reinforced this message: general patterns of social behavior emerge and take on meaning only within the consciousness of an individual mentation that narrates "my" experience. The laws that give the social order its coherence do not emanate from official channels in the form of general rules; they are concocted by individuals on the basis of personal experience, and they take the form of empirical conclusions. As if to acknowledge this principle and its centrality to the genre, several of the most influential works of the century, such as those of Richardson and Rousseau, take as their explicit theme the genesis of social order on the basis of individual conscience.

Further, these fictional dramas of self-realization and social ordering were presented as such: most eighteenth-century novels expressly thematized the endeavors of individuals to understand, navigate through, or triumph over society's tacit codes and protocols. To that extent readers of the novel could be said to encounter themselves as social agents in a particularly graphic and straightforward way. Confronted by the drama of their own efforts at social advancement, readers could not help but become self-aware. The novel in this sense succeeded both in articulating and fostering a process of self-confrontation which subsequent aesthetic theory would seize on as the key to self-realization.

The new way in which novels were read also made the genre singularly well placed to mobilize the private dimensions of experience and reconcile them with shared categories. Long before theoreticians like Baumgarten or Schiller isolated the fusion of the sensory and the intellectual as the key feature of aesthetic experience, fiction was already operating such a fusion. This occurred in the way it stimulated the creation of an imaginary world. As those who feared its influence sensed, fiction unleashed a particularly powerful form of imaginary activity. The scenes which individual readers concretized in their minds enjoyed both the authority of universality or ideality and the vividness and persuasiveness of remembered experience.

This is because when we flesh out a scene from a fictional narrative in our mind's eye, we imagine it on the basis of our past experience, or more precisely we cobble it together out of various fragments or aspects of our experience, which we reconfigure according to the stipulations of the narrative: readers of French literature who are familiar with Paris will image passing references to "La Coupole" quite differently from those who have never been there. The images, however ephemeral, that fill our minds when reading novels are at all times both familiar and new, reassuring and seductive, general (because based on conventional categories and qualifiers expressed in the text) and particular (because built up in their givenness out of fragments of our past experience).

It is in part because of this powerful mode of representation that the eighteenth-century novel could engage the reader's moral conscience so effectively: fabricated out of the passions and experience of their readers, the social and psychological dramas of fiction objectified those passions and forced the readers to confront them and understand their power. At the same time, by idealizing the virtues, novels provided models for emulation and admiration that not only inspired individual readers but convoked society under a single ideal.

In a very general sense then, the novel derived its identity as a new and controversial genre from the mechanisms of self-confrontation, social fusion, and moral emendation it deployed and refined as part of its distinctive form. One might complete this picture by noting that the genre's thematization of the interplay between individual and collective, freedom and law, had the predictable outcome of fomenting intense discussion in the public sphere. One of the primary "pretexts" to the questioning of customary practices and accepted values, novels came under intense criticism early on as agents of social destabilization, particularly as regarded women. Ironically, this claim generally focused on the novel's seductive capacities. Its ability to captivate the minds of women with its immoral tales of love (a thematic *sine qua non*) was a recurrent concern, notwithstanding the ample evidence that fiction caused people to reflect, judge and question, at least as often as it entranced them.

In fact, the most important feature of the new genre was the one it concealed the most completely: it elicited and authorized multiple and incommensurate cognitive and affective responses. As a point of entry into this subtle structural characteristic, let us consider the model of reading most often associated with the genre.

Absorption and Reflection

Although most of fiction's detractors stressed its narcotic capacities – and some contemporary evidence indeed suggests that the new genre had the ability to excite some readers to the limits of self-control – there is also built into it an explicit incitement to critical distance. One can discern this most clearly in the "editor's" statements that preface most of the works of the period. Drawing on the Aristotelian mandate that literature amuse and instruct, these typically argue for the moral usefulness of the narrative by insisting on its capacity not just to amuse, but to stimulate *reflection* on the part of the reader. In other words, fiction presents its examples *as examples*, as tokens of a type, even as it acknowledges the inevitability of sympathetic identification which will relate to them as particulars.

Fielding's novels present perhaps the most graphic illustration of this move. Although they are rife with realistic detail, the characters they depict function more as social types or embodiments of human nature than actual individuals. Fielding admits to depicting "not men, but manners; not an individual, but a species."[2] However, he insists, this does not make his characters any less real; on the contrary, the fact that people behaving in such ways have always existed and still can be found confirms their "reality." Thus, à propos of the lawyer in *Joseph Andrews*, he notes:

> The lawyer is not only alive, but hath been so these 4000 years, and I hope G_____ will indulge his life as many yet to come.

He hath not indeed confined himself to one profession, one religion, or one country; but when the first mean selfish creature appeared on the human stage, who made self the centre of the whole creation; would give himself no pain, incur no danger, advance no money to assist, or preserve his fellow-creatures; then was our lawyer born; and whilst such a person as I have described, exists on earth, so long shall he remain upon it.[3]

Remarks like this may reassure the reader of the novel's value as a portrait of human society, but they also require for their appreciation the dispassionate detachment of the literary critic. We cannot simultaneously assess the characters' value as tokens of a type and identify with them as if they were individuals. In foregrounding the "typical" value of its characters, fiction opens itself to a double assessment, inviting the reader to identify and sympathize with them, thereby internalizing their example, but also to assess the typicality of that example – the degree to which the character corresponds to an actual social type.

Fielding's works represent an extreme dramatization of how fiction alternately invites its readers to engage in dispassionate reflective judgment and seduces them with its concrete detail. However, a similar ambivalence between reading as identification or sympathy and reading as analysis animates all fiction. In the eighteenth century it is ubiquitous in the prefatory apologies and editorial explanations that frame each work, but in later realist fiction it persists in more subtle forms in the evolving conventions of narrative. To give just three accessible examples: one can perceive such a tension in nineteenth-century realist fiction in the clash between the omniscient narrative voice, the dialogues, and the inner voices of the characters; in the preponderance of material description that implicitly enlists the analytic, taxonomic capacities of the reader even as it creates a denser material world in which to become entranced; and in the ironization of the characters and the destabilization of the narrative voice that calls into question the intention of the author even as it expresses it.

It is important to note that the novel's contradictory solicitations are not imperatives; to evaluate the type *as type* requires a bit of extra effort which the average reader might well forego. This is a crucial feature of fiction: the activities it educes are not all of a uniform nature; many are only implied, while others are urged on the reader. This variability is inherent in the genre's social instrumentality, for the choices offered the reader and the subtlety of the responses they allow are what enable fiction to perform its multiple functions of social consolidation and social triage.

The novel is a particularly effective instrument of social cohesion precisely because of its ability to mobilize a broad spectrum of responses and thus to address a public of varying capacities and interests. Conversely, to the extent that it makes such varying capacities and responses visible, it provides a subtle but precise means of classifying people (which it shares with many other Cultural institutions). The reactions it accommodates might range from the simplest emotional identification to the most sophisticated abstract judgment, but it authorizes each of these discreetly, such that whichever way one chooses to read, one will feel legitimated by the narrative itself and remain to a large extent unaware of the alternatives. This is a difficult concept to grasp abstractly, but easy enough to illustrate with an example.

Rousseau's *Julie, ou la nouvelle Héloïse* is arguably the most influential novel of the century – and one of the most complex and difficult to read. Thus it is not surprising that Rousseau composed a lengthy dialogued preface, the *Entretien sur les romans* [A Conversation about Novels] intended to provide both guidance to the readers and an insight into the author's ambition for his text (although for material reasons it was actually published separately a few weeks later).

Julie is a novel that might be said to thematize the conflicted imperatives of Culture. It allegorizes the formation of the ideal state and explicitly associates it with the transformation of the individual consciences of its subjects. For the peasants and simple folk this occurs through the adoption of habits and routines determined by an enlightened lawgiver. The protagonists, however, internalize certain principles by systematically – and at great length – discussing and analyzing them until they become imbued with their logic. By their example, these two types of subjects situate virtue in the merger of individual identity and shared law.

Acknowledging from the outset that his novel is a kind of social allegory, Rousseau presents it in the *Entretien* as an instrument of social coalescence: a model for rural people of virtue to follow in order to achieve happiness and find satisfaction in their simple state. In the course of his discussion with an unnamed interlocutor, he envisions his ideal readers as a chaste rural couple who will be transformed by the charming spectacle of the novel's central figures, inoculated against the lure of urban vice and worldliness, and imbued by the example of the rural utopia with a newfound respect for their own humble state:

> I like to imagine a married couple reading this collection of letters together, drawing from it new courage to tolerate their common tasks, and perhaps new ideas for making them useful. How could they contemplate the happy household scene in it without wanting to imitate such a sweet model? How could they grow warmhearted at the charm of a marriage, even one deprived of the charm of love, without their own becoming stronger and tighter[4]

Even this brief citation reveals that for Rousseau *Julie, ou la nouvelle Héloïse* was meant to effect the fusion of individual with social order, and that in two distinct ways: by stimulating ideas and providing a model. For Rousseau, the latter is much the more important mechanism. The sublime vision the novel offered its "viewers" not only would *represent* the harmonization of individual happiness with social prosperity but would actually *effect* it by infusing the readers with an internal certainty of "new courage." Transfigured by the vision of domestic bliss and social harmony they would absorb, the ideal readers would return to the real world with a new appreciation for the value of collective endeavor and self-restraint: "upon putting down their reading they will be neither saddened by their condition nor repulsed by their chores. On the contrary, everything around them will seem to take on a cheerful aspect; their duties will appear noble in their eyes; they will rediscover the natural pleasures"[5] Having quite literally seen themselves in the book, the ideal readers internalize the law of virtue and accept their lot in society with joy and a sense of self-satisfaction.

This is sympathetic reading at its most paradigmatic and it is not surprising that Rousseau evokes it, for it was widely accepted as the kind of reaction that fiction characteristically induced. Indeed, if we are to believe the voluminous correspondence that Rousseau received after publication, many readers indeed reacted in just this way. Charles-Joseph Panckoucke, for example, describes his experience in these terms: "your divine writings, sir, are fires that consume me, they have saturated my soul, fortified my heart, enlightened my mind . . . What tears I shed, what sighs, what pains! Since the happy day of this reading I burn with the love of virtue."[6]

But if we take Rousseau's tableau of entranced reading at face value, we are missing the complexity of his gesture. By *announcing* his intention to enthrall the reader with the reflection of that reader's own situation, and by associating the reader with simple country rustics, he imposes on the actual reader of his theory a critical distance that makes such absorption all but impossible. For as an abstract argument about reading – which it is – the *Entretien*'s lesson cannot be extracted by means of the operations it prescribes; the engagement it requires of *its* reader (who is also the presumed reader of *Julie*) is totally incommensurate with the mute absorption of the country couple. The only characters the preface gives us to identify with are Rousseau and his sophisticated Parisian interlocutor, who philosophize about – and thus objectify and distance themselves from – the purely theoretical construct of the provincial reader. While never relinquishing its ostensible preference for reading as imitation, the dialogue entangles its presumed novel reader in a series of abstract propositions more properly the concern of the critic, touching on literature, culture, authorship, fictionality, and the relationship of the city to the country. Untangling these various issues – indeed, even keeping track of who is speaking at any given moment in the dialogue – requires a level of intellectual effort completely at odds with the affective absorption of the ideal readers.

The image of the enthralled country folk veils this more actively analytic form of subjectivity even as it elicits it, by constructing an ideal with whom the real readers are all the more incapable of identifying in that it has been reduced to an object of dispassionate analysis and no small measure of condescension. Thus, in a move strangely premonitory of *Madame Bovary*, Rousseau's dialogue proposes a lesson about novel reading that cannot be taken at face value, since it is invalidated by its own mode of presentation. Even if we somehow desired to assimilate unreflectively the preface's theory, we would be unable to do so, since Rousseau and the unnamed *homme de lettres* support opposing views through most of the dialogue, neither of which emerges as conclusive.

In a sense, though, while the *Entretien* discourages its actual readers from identifying with its supposed "ideal" readers, it also rewards them with the satisfaction of knowing more than the rural couple. To the extent they notice that they cannot read sympathetically, they become aware of their difference from those readers and of their greater sensitivity to the mechanics and rules of reading. *Understanding* the way texts affect them, they feel more in command of themselves than those who do not. The plot of *Julie* will argue at great length that this self awareness is a first step toward virtue and an indispensable prerequisite to exercising moral and political authority.

This does not mean that other kinds of readers do not exist or that their responses are not valid. The novel in fact sustains and exploits the tension between different kinds of subjectivity, eventually linking it to a difference in political enfranchisement as well as a gender distinction.[7] The range of subject responses it portrays in its characters and authorizes in its readers corresponds to the range of social functions individuals can assume under the paradigms of self-realization it deploys. This is the foundation of the mechanism of self-selection or autotriage that Cultural enterprises systematically enable.

Reading as Autotriage

In its plot as in its preface, Rousseau's novel advises us that it is not simply addressed to a single kind of reader or reading, but many, and it implies that the difference between these is a useful index of one's social and political role. In its plot, as in most eighteenth-century plots, this principle is enacted in terms of the social and moral authority that accrues to analytic sophistication and those who deploy it. Just as the utopian society depicted in *Julie, ou la nouvelle Héloïse* is composed of different classes of individuals, from the simple farm laborers whose virtue is constructed through carefully engineered work habits, social rules and rituals, to the managerial class of the lords of the estate who prescribe and oversee the application of those routines and rules, so too the narrative form of the novel posits a broad spectrum of readers and types of reading, from simple absorption and emulation to abstract theoretical critique. Readers who doubt the plausibility of such a broad response – or Rousseau's intentions to elicit it – have only to consult the massive correspondence his novel elicited, which testifies amply to the success of his strategy.

One thing all these reactions have in common is self-conviction: each feels legitimated by the narrative, even to the exclusion of other responses. It is understandable that the most naive readers are convinced their response is the correct one – the one that was encoded in the narrative. The way they read makes it literally impossible for them to perceive alternate interpretations. Conversely, readers who recognize the possibility of alternate readings take the fact of this recognition as proof of their own sophistication – and that of the author.

As intimated above, we can see how this works in the *Entretien*. A lax reading of the dialogue could easily stumble on the complexities of the theoretical debate, but it would not miss its own celebration in the foregrounding of the ideal couple: someone who had effectively identified with the characters of the novel and reassessed his or her humble existence accordingly would see in Rousseau's argument a validation of that response. On the other hand, readers who saw in the novel's plot an allegory and understood the characters as mere components in a pedagogical mechanism would find confirmation of their hypothesis in the naive response of the "ideal" readers, who are invoked in the preface to substantiate Rousseau's theory of didactic fiction. In other words, the ideal couple with whom the naive reader identifies will appear to the dispassionate sophisticated reader as a predictable rhetorical device designed to illustrate how novels might work (for the masses) and not as a model to be emulated. Again, to the extent they are truly naive, unsophisticated readers simply will not perceive alternative paradigms of reading, while sophisticated readers will take their perception of other possible ways of reading as confirmations of their own perspicacity and literary sophistication. Needless to say, between these two extremes, and subject to further differential mechanisms deployed by the text, one can imagine a host of intermediate positions.

What is interesting about this process – and paradigmatic of high Cultural practices in general – is that it implicates subjects in the determination of their own social status, by correlating their decision to apprehend a discursive representation in a certain way with their capabilities, class affiliations, and educational formation. This is the mechanism of autotriage: by the way they choose to read, readers *sort themselves* into groups.

Rousseau's *Entretien sur les romans* illustrates in particularly graphic terms how a narrative can underwrite such social triage even as it encourages the formation of individual identity. However, his short essay is paradigmatic of the genre of the novel in general, which always underwrites at least two different registers of response by conventional definition and rhetoric. Novels by definition announce themselves as fiction – as narratives that have no direct link to reality and are consequently immune to disproof. But at the same time they present themselves as accurate representations of social reality (this is particularly the case in the eighteenth and nineteenth centuries) that merit considered reflection.

"Realistic fiction" thus by definition at all moments invites and authorizes two diametrically opposed responses: the sympathetic and the critical or evaluative. The former envisions readers to be literally enthralled by an ideal spectacle of their own imagining (since they necessarily flesh out or concretize the fictional world on the basis of their personal knowledge and experience). In this mode they simply gaze upon and absorb the example of the drama that unfolds before their eyes – like Rousseau's rural couple. At the other extreme lies what one might term analytic reading or abstract interpretation. This involves grasping the characters as types and the plot as an allegory or paradigm, and, once again drawing on the reader's own past experience, formulating an abstract proposition about the meaning, effect, or value of the novel. In addition to these extremes one can imagine various other subjective stances, among which the reading conscience might shuttle.

It is important to understand that while different kinds of cognition may be associated more strongly with one kind of writing than another, many can be available concurrently at any moment in any novel. For instance, a particularly rich descriptive passage such as the evocation of fog that opens Dickens's *Bleak House* might simply absorb a reader in wonderment, but it could also trigger recollections of London (or of other foggy places), arouse a smile by its jaundiced tone, jar the reader into an abstract analysis of its remarkable narrative style, or simply bore – to mention only a few possibilities. It is this constant availability to multiple kinds and intensities of cognition which underlies the novel's value in bringing the reader's experience to the level of self-awareness and making it potentially available for comparison with other possible kinds of response. For by electing one kind of reading over another readers discover and display their sense of identity, as well as their level of formal preparation, familiarity with the genre, and even, as in the case of Rousseau's ideal couple, or a description of fog in London's legal district, their regional or class affiliations. It is not even necessary that other individuals be aware of the reader's response for this to occur. The reader, for instance, who is baffled or disconcerted by his or her inability to parse Dickens's prose or situate the scene in London (having never been there) will be made aware of that fact on some level by the description. Self-situation and self-definition occur even in solitude.

The process in question is powerful (1) because it is subtle, private, and ubiquitous, and (2) because it is grounded in the free will of the reader. The cognitive responses that make apparent the capacities and desires of a reader occur as the result of that individual's free initiative, as conditioned by the conventions he or she perceives in the text and acts upon. The novel cannot make us read it; nor can it force a particular kind of reading – although it can lend itself to one kind or another. The pleasure of novel reading lies precisely in the options it leaves to the reader, in the latitude it affords us in deciding how fast or carefully to read; how much attention to pay to descriptions; what parts to skip over or whether to read the end first; which characters to like and dislike, identify with or forget; whether to pause and reflect or chat with a friend about it; and so forth. It is because of this freedom that the particular meaning or understanding we take from a book so perfectly expresses our opinion, so securely affixes our conviction. Because we freely select our ways of reading and freely elaborate the "readings" they generate, we become through the novel the agents of our own articulation as individuals, the authorities behind our social calibration.

The other important feature to this process pertains to its built-in self-limitation or self-blinkering. To the extent that both our understanding of the text *and* of our way of reading find articulation within that way of reading and the limitations it implies, we necessarily remain more or less blind to alternatives: either to alternative ways of reading altogether or to the viability or equivalence of the alternatives that we recognize. Within any given work our interpretation and our grasp of *how* we read are constructed by *the way* we read; consequently we cannot be convinced that a different way of reading is possible or better: should we become so convinced, we have by definition adopted *that* reading and become as convinced of its superiority as we were of our former reading's. One might object that sophisticated literary types regularly acknowledge the plurality of the text and the validity of competing readings. However, this gesture of generosity is merely itself a further and very self-conscious kind of reading: one which includes as part of its claim to superiority the awareness of competing models and incorporates their conclusions into its own as a means of going beyond them.

I insist on these two features of self-administration and self-limiting awareness because they are key to the effectiveness of the novel as a Cultural institution – and to Cultural enterprises in general. By which I mean an institution or practice that addresses the conflict between social uniformity and self-individuation, general law and personal autonomy, equality and hierarchy, by enabling a form of self-realization that expresses itself as the mastery of social law and collective norms, that finds individual identity within the terms of the community, freedom within its ability to articulate the law, uniqueness in its particular expression of the normative.

Novels trigger just such a fusion by inducing the expression of individuality and autonomy, absorption and reflective judgment within shared social structures, values, and terms. Fiction compels us to apprehend the world – and ourselves in that world – through social values and categories. One might express the transaction serially: novels stimulate us to image forth a social world on the basis of our personal experience; to intuit ourselves within that objectified world; to reflect upon it and having reflected, to formulate an assessment of its meaning; and to defend that assessment and its means of production as our own, as underwritten by the book. It is in this last moment that the fusion of particular and general, freedom and law occurs most explicitly; for in appealing to the text as the guarantor of our reading, we tacitly acknowledge our embeddedness in and dependence on its conventions, rules, shared protocols: we can only express ourselves (or defend our reading) by appeal to scripts, categories, and procedures that are by their very nature and that of the institution that disseminates them collectively determined. To appeal to the text is to acknowledge its law.

The novel's integration of freedom and law, individual and collective identity, is similar to, but more powerful than that occasioned by the newspaper: it involves the individual at the level of particular, private experience; it mobilizes both the reflective and the sensory faculties (by drawing on past sensory experience in its concretization by a particular reader); it engages more of the subject's personal energy and thus a deeper commitment; it carries no ostensible political consequences. This more powerful paradigm for articulating and reconciling the two imperatives of social identity emerges at the level of practice in novels, but also in other activities that involve the concretization and apprehension of virtual worlds on the basis of conventional representational artifacts: the theatre, most notably, but also music, poetry, and certain kinds of collecting. By the latter half of the eighteenth century, the effectiveness of this process as a form of social glue is indisputable, its mechanisms increasingly apparent. It finds its theoretical elaboration in the new category that emerges concomitantly – but not coincidentally – with both the rise of the novel and the emergence of "culture" as a concept: namely, the aesthetic.

The Concept of the Aesthetic

The concept of the aesthetic was first proposed in the middle of the eighteenth century by the German philosopher Alexander Gottlieb Baumgarten in his 1750 treatise *Aesthetica* as a means of bringing the sensory and affective experience of beauty within the realm of systematic understanding. Within the account I am elaborating the sensory represents a last threshold of sorts. Having extended the claim of systematic knowledge and discursive authority to not only the natural world, but the social and the political as well, the Enlightenment needed to demonstrate that even the body and the emotions could be brought under control

by reason.[8] The notion of the aesthetic does just that by rationalizing sensory affective experience and associating the awareness
of its mechanisms with a heightened moral sensibility. It thus
extends the logic of systematic analysis we have followed from
the Renaissance beyond the limits of the material and social,
inscribing even the most private ineffable kinds of experience
within the laws of discipline. Henceforth all particular experience
can be thought of in terms of the assimilation and mastery of
systems, norms, and shared protocols. Aesthetic theory refines
and clarifies what I have called cultural logic and makes it
available for further conceptual elaboration and implementation
at the institutional level.

That even the particular experience of beauty leads to reflection
and the articulation of judgments in conventional analytic terms
will have become a given by the nineteenth century: in his lectures
on aesthetics Hegel will insist that for the contemporary mind the
work of art is no longer a self-sufficient embodiment of the
transcendent as it was in antiquity, but rather a stimulus to
judgment and reflective examination. By formulating how such a
conversion of the (sensory) particular into the universal (rational)
might occur, aesthetic theory both confirmed and facilitated the
colonization for social needs of that part of individual experience
which other kinds of knowledge could only clumsily address.

The second consequence of aesthetic theory was to extend the
compass of discursive authority. Because systematic rational analysis by definition culminates in discursive propositions, the effect
of rationalizing sensory experience was to draw private experience
into the realm of abstract discourse, or, put more strongly, to
disqualify as morally illegitimate any form of experience that did
not find expression in the shared categories of public discourse.
Theorizing the translation of private experience into shared category as a universal imperative, the aesthetic brought the totality
of legitimate human experience under the jurisdiction of shared
discourse and its collectively negotiated categories. This is turn
opened that experience to regulation and normalization by society
and the state.

Whatever their putative function, the institutions developed to
promote aesthetic Culture and the aesthetic development of the
individual and nation all entail the colonization of particular
experience by shared practice – or, which is the same, the

expression of private experience within shared categories. Some of these, like the national art museum, were explicitly sponsored by the state as a means of furthering and regulating the intellectual and moral development of its citizens. Others, like literature and the fine arts, developed less systematically. However, all shared one central feature: they invited individuals to "cultivate" themselves, and defined such Culture as the reformulation of one's most intimate and inarticulate experiences in categories of social practice.

This leads to a third feature of aesthetic theory that underwrites and legitimates the logic of Culture: its emphasis on educational programs designed to construct the ideal aesthetic person. Aesthetic sensibility is inseparable from the processes of its acquisition, since, like Herder's reason, it is formed dialectically in experience. Under the rubric of "Bildung" or "cultivation," this process forms an essential component of our modern notion of education. And it carries with it a barely concealed strategy for identifying the individual's proper station in the social, political, and economic hierarchy.

More forthrightly than its antecedent forms of discursive engagement, aesthetic Bildung correlates the acquisition of aesthetic refinement to social rank and economic function. And it specifies the quest for one's place in society to be a moral imperative, since society can only attain its harmonious expression if each person has located his or her proper station and function. Bildung is a mechanism of status allocation that is superior to previous principles of social rank (such as birthright or fortune) precisely in that it is largely self-administered: one undertakes one's formation with the expectation that it will help one realize one's particular aptitudes and find one's place in society.

The ideological ramifications of the aesthetic are of course far more complex than this, as Terry Eagleton and others have demonstrated.[9] It is more or less taken for granted now that the aesthetic is one of an array of ideologies and institutions deployed in the modern era for constructing, classifying, and regulating subjects. However, the preceding discussions should make clear that the aesthetic is not so much the innovation of a particular political or economic system, or class, or era, as the inevitable extension of ways of thinking about authority, identity and system that had been developing for centuries. Aesthetic theory gives coherence and legitimacy to assumptions about individual identity that were already in circulation; it makes sense of processes of social formation that were already underway. And in so doing it makes them available for further refinement and institutionalization.

In other words, the aesthetic represents a final component in the Enlightenment universalization of discursive authority. One might well ask why a new category was necessary to recruit the experience of the senses for rational discourse when substantial discussions of art and beauty, not to mention the sublime and taste, already existed. The answer lies in the universality of the mechanisms postulated by aesthetic theory. Unlike histories of artistic production which focused on the genius of the creative artist, or art criticism, which relied on traditions of connoisseurship and specialized terms of analysis to rank specific works, aesthetic theory posits faculties and experiences that are common to *all* people. The dialectic of spirit and senses that it describes is fundamental to human consciousness itself, its ethic of self-formation pertains to everyone.

That this is the case is apparent already in the early theories. Perhaps the most influential was that of Friedrich Schiller. In 1793, even as the Committee on Public Instruction was struggling with the issue of forming the perfect citizen, Schiller was formulating a different model for attaining the same ends in his now classic *On the Aesthetic Education of Man in a Series of Letters.*[10] Schiller's decisive contribution to the development we are tracing can be located in two areas. First, he explicitly formulates human life as a dialectic between form and sense, and specifies that the antagonism between these two drives is not a dilemma to be overcome, but a constitutive dynamic of human identity whose energy can be sublated into the highest form of being. Second, he correlates this sublation of our competing drives to the overcoming of the tension between autonomy and law. The aesthetic becomes explicitly in his work an ideology of state formation.

The Dialectic of Subjectivity

The aesthetic as Schiller formulates it encompasses far more than the political or civic dimension of life; it addresses the very consciousness of being human that all people share. As he sees it, humanity is torn between two impulses: one caught up in feelings, nature, sensuous reality, the present, phenomena, historical time, and contingency; the other characterized by consciousness, reason, form, the spirit, necessity, the ahistorical order of the eternal, and morality. Our moral, rational side Schiller associates with the imperatives of political and social unity, our natural sensual side with the drive to self-expression and individuation.

On the one hand, we experience ourselves in historical, material reality as pure actuality and particularity. In this realm of Nature, we answer to the *exigency* of *phenomena*, whose demands we *feel* through our *senses*. This, Schiller calls the "sense impulse" or sense-drive [sinnliche Trieb]. At the same time, though, we answer to a "formal drive" [Formtrieb] which proceeds from our *rational* nature and imposes *unity* on our diverse manifestations and our personality by affirming their *necessity*, using *reason* to configure phenomena according to *laws* of *morality*.

These antitheses can be conceptualized in terms of identity and change over time: we *exist* only to the extent that we change over time, yet we exist as *ourselves* only to the extent that we remain the same over time: "only as he changes does [Man] *exist*; only as he remains unchangeable does *he* exist."[11] The same paradoxical tension structures our sense of agency: "the sense impulse wants to *be* determined, to receive its object; the form impulse wants to determine for itself, to produce its object."[12]

One might summarize Schiller's oppositions schematically:

reality	form
sensuous	spiritual
actuality	necessity
material	rational
historical	ahistorical
inclination	duty
exigency	law
Nature	Reason

Subjective	Objective
multiplicity	unity
phenomena	morality
demand of Feeling	demand of Reason
contingent	autonomous
the sense impulse: time	the formal impulse: gives
merely occupied by	harmony to the diversity
content; physical existence	of man's manifestations,
	and maintains his identity
	through time

Schiller's model, like the proposals of the Committee on Public Instruction, recognizes the conflicting imperatives of critical analysis and reflexive habit, freedom and law, particularity and universality. However, Schiller not only considerably enriches this menu of antithetical drives under the general framework of the sense/reason opposition, he also makes the tension between these drives *structurally constitutive of subjectivity*:

> [Man] can never learn really . . . to be in the full sense of the word a man, so long as he satisfies only one of these two drives exclusively; or both alternately; for so long as he only feels, his personality or his absolute existence remains a mystery to him, and so long as he only thinks, his existence in time or his condition does the same.[13]

We cannot realize "all" of ourselves and become individuals operating within the world unless we somehow answer both of these conflicting demands simultaneously. If we give ourselves over entirely to our senses, we lose the enduring content of our identity – our subjectivity – which allows us to sense the outside world in the first place. Conversely, if our rational drive substitutes thought for sensation and obliterates the world with our form, we lose the objective reality off of which subjective certainty defines itself. Thus the paradox that "only insofar as [Man] is autonomous is there reality outside him, is he receptive to it; only insofar as he is receptive is there reality within him, is he a thinking power."[14] The same paradox can be expressed in terms of the conflict between two systems of determination and their effect on human freedom:

> The sense drive excludes from its subject all autonomy and free-
> dom; the form-drive excludes from its subject all dependence, all
> passivity. Exclusion of freedom, however, implies physical necess-
> ity, exclusion of passivity moral necessity. Both drives, therefore,
> exert constraint upon the psyche; the former through the laws of
> nature, the latter through the laws of reason.[15]

This formulation makes social identity as well as the individual's sense of self a function of antithesis and tension. The opposition between autonomous rational critique and unconscious prejudice which obsessed the Enlightenment with respect to the collective behavior of the community is refined by aesthetic theory into a tension we feel at every moment of our being, and which is in fact constitutive of our being: between thinking and feeling, moral law and natural law.

The same opposition can be expressed in terms of the state, which, as Hegel points out in his assessment of Schiller, represents in objective form the attempted unification of the ideal, general-ized subject with the diversity of actual individuals. Schiller underscores this in his stipulation that

> a political constitution will still be very imperfect if it is able to
> produce unity only by suppressing variety. The State should not
> only respect the objective and generic character in its individual
> subjects, but also their subjective and specific character, and in
> extending the invisible realm of morals it must not depopulate the
> realm of phenomena.[16]

The task of the moral state is precisely to meld the conflicting impulses of universality and particularity, such that each finds its logical ground in the other, the idea of freedom being expressed in the law itself. On the one hand, the State sublates (to use Hegel's language) the individuality of its subjects into law, rights, and customs; on the other, the individuals making up the state must "raise themselves to the level of the generic" overcoming the antithesis of feeling and reason, necessity and freedom, particular-ity and unity.[17] Aesthetic education is what makes this possible, by channeling the individual's inclinations, desires, feelings, and impulses into the realm of reason, with its universalizing benefit. In the process, reason itself and the spirit are reunited with the natural world of the senses and shed their disembodied abstract quality.

The success of this transaction depends on a dialectic between our two drives, neither of which can overwhelm the other without undermining its own claim. To meet both of their demands Schiller proposes an intermediate category or state in which both drives find full realization: "the play impulse" [Spieltrieb]. It is here that the aesthetic properly speaking is produced. While the sense impulse "demands that there be change, that time have a content" and "the form impulse demands that time be annulled, that no change occur," the play impulse has as its object "the annulment of time *in time* and the reconciliation of becoming with absolute being, of change with identity."[18] But what is the object of play? what brings the play impulse into play? If the object of our form impulse is *form*, that of our sense impulse, material *life*, the object of play can only be living form – or what we normally call beauty: "Only as the *form* of something *lives* in our sensation, and its *life* takes *form* in our *understanding*, is it living form, and this will always be the case whenever we judge it to be beautiful."[19]

The experience of beauty simultaneously energizes and harmonizes our two impulses: "Our psyche finds itself, in the contemplation of the Beautiful, in a happy midway point between law and exigency . . . the material drive and the formal."[20] As the *embodi ment* of pure *form*, beauty sublates the opposing impulses of Man, intensifying each, yet preserving the irremediable alterity of each with respect to the other, such that "we find ourselves at the same time in the condition of utter repose and supreme agitation."[21]

What is involved here is no simple compromise. Schiller takes pains to point out that "the distance between matter and form, between passivity and activity, between sensation and thought, is infinite, and cannot conceivably be mediated."[22] Rather, Beauty transports us to an entirely new level of being; in a dialectical *Aufhebung*, "both conditions entirely disappear in a third, leaving no trace of division behind in the whole."[23] It is in this moment of dialectical sublation that we achieve the impossible harmonization of our divergent impulses towards reality and ideality, change and form, phenomenon and truth. Both pure feeling *and* pure thought, absolute beauty consists not of "lawlessness but harmony of laws," "not in the *exclusion of certain realities* but in the *absolute inclusion of them all*, so that it is therefore not limitation but infinity."[24]

There are several ways to figure this optimistic scenario. By promising the "absolute inclusion" of all "certain realities," the aesthetic moment provides a way of conceptualizing the imposs-ible identity of particular existence and social norm, individual will and collective law. As Schiller confidently predicts: "if the inner man is at one with himself, he will be able to preserve his individuality [Eigentümlichkeit] however much he may universal-ize his conduct." He can do this because he assumes that just as the object of beauty becomes in the aesthetic experience the timeless expression of personal truth – merging individual (exist-ence) with the law (of form) – so too in citizenship "the State will simply be the interpreter of his fine instinct, the clearer expression of his inner legislation."[25]

In the simplest political terms, the aesthetic operates the merger of freedom and obligation. Freedom, Schiller says, "first arises only when Man is *complete*, and *both* his fundamental drives are developed."[26] For as long as he is subject to the "one-sided constraint of Nature in his perception and . . . the preclusive legislation of Reason in his thinking" he is doubly hamstrung.[27] Conversely, in the contemplation of beauty

> The mind . . . passes from sensation to thought through a middle disposition in which sensuousness and reason are active *at the same time* . . . This middle disposition, in which our nature is constrained neither physically nor morally and yet is active in both ways, preeminently deserves to be called a free disposition; and if we call the condition of sensuous determination the physical, and that of rational determination the logical and moral, we must call this condition of real and active determinacy the *aesthetic*.[28]

Of course *absolute* beauty – "the most perfect possible union and equilibrium of reality and form" – is never attained: "in actuality there will always be a preponderance of one element or the other, and the utmost that experience can achieve will consist of an oscillation between the two principles, so that at one moment it is reality and at another form, that is predominant."[29]

This unattainability is a key feature of the ideal of behavior that the aesthetic implicitly specifies. For Schiller's concept of aesthetic fulfillment does not merely function as a theoretical description; it inscribes the subject in an ethic of permanent deferral.

The Deferral and Division of Identity

As recent commentators have argued, aesthetics comprises an ethical program that associates moral superiority with the continual problematization of one's experience.[30] Enrolling the subject in a dialectic of selfhood that by definition can never be fully achieved, but is continually repeated and refined, the aesthetic substitutes the symbolic pursuit of fulfillment for effective action on material reality.

The value for the state of this permanent deferral is apparent at first glance: permanently aspiring towards a more perfect dialectical sublation of individualism and social conformity, free will and obedience, the aesthetic subject engages a process of self-realization that expects no end, demands no reconciliation of the conflicting demands which liberal democracy places upon its citizens. In concrete terms aesthetics teaches us to strive for and believe in, but not to expect in any immediate future, the perfect harmonization of our wills and desires with the laws and requirements of the state. To which one might add that by envisioning life as a continual striving after a better state, aesthetic theory neatly synchronizes the subject with the dynamics of desire and the market.

But what does the deferral of identity mean in practical terms? In our brief analyses of the newspaper and the novel, we have seen how their particular modes of apprehension might serve social coherence. How might the aesthetic transaction with its deferral of closure reconfigure the subject? The answer lies in the specialized cognitive transaction which aesthetic experience entails: aesthetic judgment or interpretation.

For Schiller, humans, like any animals, are constrained by the condition into which they are born. In society, these constraints are imposed by the state.[31] However, unlike animals, we have the ability to change the status of our situation by reconceptualizing its blind need into a logical imperative, freely conceived: "[Man] possesses the capacity of retracing again, with his reason, the steps which [Nature] anticipated with him, of remodeling the work of need into a work of his free choice, and of elevating physical into moral necessity."[32]

Fundamental to this operation is the structure of self-confrontation through which aesthetic experience reinforces the subject's self-awareness. While aesthetic judgment takes the outward shape of a reaction to a work of art, it actually represents the mind formulating it and is thus an instance of self-expression and self-awareness more than of critique. As Hegel explains in his aesthetic theory, since the human spirit has the capacity to consider itself in all of its products, and art is a product of the human spirit, it follows that when we confront art we apprehend our own spirit:

> Just as works of art, rather than thoughts and concepts, represent the development of the concept from itself outward, an alienation towards the exterior, so the power of the mind lies in not just apprehending itself under its proper form of thought, but also in recognizing itself as such in the exteriorized form of feeling and sensitivity, in short apprehending itself in its other self, while transforming this alienated form into thought and thus bringing it back to itself.[33]

Confronting the feelings and sensations triggered by the work of art and converting them back into reflective thought, we rediscover ourselves in our aesthetic assessment.

The aesthetic work induces self-confrontation in two senses. First, it objectifies the human passions, making them available to contemplation and critical reflection. For Hegel, this is how art softens and refines human mores: our passions lose their power over us simply by virtue of becoming objects of representation, separate from us, and hence open to our free reflection and judgment.[34] Understanding ourselves, we can moderate ourselves. Schiller specifies this moment of separation — which refigures the stance of critique — as the constitutive moment of our identity and knowledge of the world:

> So long as Man . . . accepts the world of sense merely passively, merely perceives, he is still completely identified with it, and just because he himself is simply world, there is no world yet for him.

Not until he sets it outside himself or *contemplates* it, in his aesthetic status, does his personality become distinct from it, and a world appears to him because he has ceased to identify himself with it.[35]

At a second level, however, this self-conscious contemplation seems to lead to a secondary reflection or abstract judgment. That this is the case is not immediately apparent. The visual or musical art work generally associated with aesthetic apprehension does not deliver abstract lessons per se. And superficially at least, it seems to differ from the novel as pioneered by authors like Fielding and Rousseau in that it does not seem to stimulate conceptual discourse: one can presumably gaze at a beautiful sculpture and judge it beautiful without articulating that feeling.

In fact, however, the aesthetic experience always involves an act of critical judgment. Even if that act only expresses the subject's experience by declaring the work to be beautiful, it implicitly demands assent, and does so in the abstract conventional terms of shared standards, rules, and norms. Hegel expresses this in the contrast he draws between the way ancients viewed art and the way it is viewed in the modern era, when all particular phenomena are grasped from the viewpoint of the general and abstract. For his contemporaries, he maintains, art is quite different from what it was for the Greeks. It no longer inspires the awe which former ages accorded it, because it no longer embodies the divine or elicits belief. Rather, it triggers reflective judgment on the part of the viewer: "what works of art induce in us today, besides immediate enjoyment, is simultaneously our judgment . . . art invites us to reflective thought."[36]

This culmination of the aesthetic experience in an assessment or interpretation of the work of art is especially visible in the institutions of high Culture, which extend the discursive imperative of the newspaper and the novel to the experience of beauty. Literature, the art museum, the historical society, the symphony or the opera encourage us not just to gaze and listen, but to think about what we see and hear, and to recount our experience to others. They also define public cultural spaces where such accounts can be produced and circulated, providing not only an expression of our individuality but an index of our standing.

It is clear that aesthetic judgment integrates the subject's will with the rule(s) of the community, by channeling the expression of personal feeling and individual experience through the normative parameters of analytic critique. Less clear are the reasons for our willingness to articulate such judgments. Why is it we so gladly express our aesthetic judgments, whereas few of us feel inclined to write letters to the editor or engage in serious political debate? The answer lies in the aesthetic's refusal of closure.

Aesthetic judgment can formulate itself with self-assurance because it knows itself at some level to be immune to repudiation. The immunity is built into all aesthetic practices by virtue of their dialectic of permanent deferral. Indeed, the consolation of symbolic self-fulfillment which the aesthetic offers us would have little value, were it susceptible to discrediting. After all, if aesthetic judgment is at heart the expression of our own self-awareness, our identity is at stake, albeit it in the form of a symbolic representation. To lay ourselves bare, we require advance assurance of our validity.

It is this assurance that the open-endedness of the aesthetic transaction provides. Although it is fully determinate the aesthetic cannot be limited to any single determination. "Beauty produces no individual result whatsoever," Schiller declares, "it discovers no individual truth," by which he means not that it does not impel *us* to generate such truths, but that in and of itself, it authorizes no particular determination (but rather *all*). The aesthetic positively un-determines Man in order that he might "make of himself what he chooses"; it restores to him "the freedom to be what he ought to be":[37]

> By means of aesthetic culture . . . the personal worth of a man, or his dignity, inasmuch as this can depend solely upon himself, remains completely indeterminate; and nothing more is achieved than that he is henceforth enabled by the grace of Nature to make of himself what he will.[38]

This axiomatic exclusion of any particular determination is a crucial feature of our modern Cultural institutions, all of which are constructed on the logic of the aesthetic. It legitimates multiple interpretations and locates the value of the aesthetic object and the individual acts of judgment that define it in the non-propositional realm of virtual truth and subjective self-expression. Aesthetic judgments are open to negotiation, revision, even repudiation in terms of reigning styles or norms, but they can never be invalidated as expressions of subjective taste and of the individuals that produce them. As Kant succinctly put it, "taste claims autonomy."[39]

Even at the level of abstract interpretation, a bad painting or work of fiction cannot be "wrong," if only because it doesn't say any particular thing. It is rather the occasion for some person to say some particular thing. And because whatever that subject says is grounded in a dialectic of living form to which no one else has access, it can never be definitively invalidated as an expression of the person that produced it. Whatever I say a painting means for me it *does* mean for me. Our aesthetic judgments necessarily reflect our experience (in all senses of that word). It is this feature that allows us to be so certain of our pronouncements: to the extent they express us as well as the aesthetic object (as we experience it), they are necessarily accurate and valid.

This does not mean that aesthetic judgments cannot and are not used to rank, discredit, or glorify the persons to whom they are attributed. However, such allocations of status occur as secondary assessments of the critical capacities of the subject or of his or her critical discourse considered relative to that of others or to certain traditions of expertise and their methodologies. Blatantly normative, these secondary assessments cannot impinge on the value the underlying aesthetic experience has for the individual. If people pursue Culture and express their tastes, knowing full well that it will classify them socially, it is because the aesthetic carries its own compensation in the form of an augmented sense of self. As Hegel put it, "the spirit finds only itself in the products of art."[40]

From this perspective, the secondary judgments which others might level at one's reactions are to a large extent a matter of indifference: they articulate social boundaries but no more so than do the expressions of personal reaction off of which they play. The father who roundly declares "My six-year old could paint that" when confronted with a Jackson Pollock is not just exposing himself to disdainful glances and imputations of philistinism, he is also by his gesture consolidating his sense of self, displaying his social affiliations, and strengthening the identity and community of like-minded persons to whom the remark is tacitly or actually addressed.

Aesthetic Practice and Social Stratification

At the level of self-realization, the discursive judgment which modern Culture associates with and demands of the aesthetic experience is immune to evaluation. It is this feature of Culture that reassures the broader public that their increased participation in Cultural events will always pay a dividend in a stronger sense of self – even if that sense of self comes with an implicit status affiliation. That is what allows the Culture to draw private experience into public discourse, where it can be regulated: with its promise of self-validation, the experience of the aesthetic induces people to translate their affective reactions into conventional units of meaning and publicly sanctioned categories.

Of course, at a higher level of analysis within the rituals of high Culture, expressions of aesthetic experience are explicitly made the object of collective discussion. The institutions that facilitate and encourage our apprehension of beauty also classify us on the basis of our ability and willingness to conceive and express our personal reactions in ways sanctioned by the larger community. As in the case of the novel, what is involved here is a form of social triage that is relatively inoffensive to the extent that it is voluntarily assumed by the subject being classified. However, in its institutional forms, aesthetic triage is far more powerful than that exercised by print instruments that are consumed in private. For one thing, it *requires* that one articulate one's reaction, thus engaging to some degree at least the authority of the public sphere. For another, the distinctions it imposes are perceived differently and carry different meanings for different constituencies (as the example of the proud philistine suggests).

Institutional Culture's mechanisms of social hierarchization go well beyond the explicit subordination of student to teacher, amateur to expert, beginner to connoisseur that structures its procedures of indoctrination. Beneath its ostensible concern with the apprehension and comprehension of timeless beauty, aesthetic practice conceals a powerful mechanism for recruiting individuals into assuming responsibility for their own positioning. Its ethic of self-realization draws the individual desirous of being "culti-vated" into a new system of social differentiation and political qualification based not just on familiarity with the traditions, idioms, and artifacts of one's "culture" and on facility in inter-preting them, but also on the familiarity with and acknowledg-ment of one's own inclinations and dispositions.

The need to classify and rank the members of society is hardly an explicit priority of aesthetic theory, but the value of aesthetics for just such a process does find acknowledgment there. The roots of the principle are already visible in the early theories of Baum-garten, who asserts, in his 1750 *Aesthetica* (§27), that "the beauty of aesthetic insights considered as an accomplishment of the beautifully thinking person can be neither greater nor of a nobler kind than the living powers of that person." Accordingly Baum-garten includes in his outline of aesthetic knowledge all of the qualities which "beautifully thinking" people must have. Nat-urally, if superior people produce aesthetic insight, it follows that people who do not achieve such insights are inferior.

Baumgarten does not follow his thinking to its logical con-clusion – that relative aesthetic reactions can be used to index people – but Schiller does. Some people, the latter maintains, are unable to tolerate the indeterminacy of the aesthetic temper for long; these "press impatiently for a result which they do not find in the condition of aesthetic boundlessness," and their sojourn in the aesthetic is barely perceptible. Quite different is the behavior of others who "find their enjoyment more in the feeling of *total capacity* rather than any *individual* application of it." These latter can no more ". . . bear limitation" than can the former tolerate "vacuity."[41] There is more at stake here than a further classifica-tion on the part of a man who loves binary distinctions. Schiller immediately assigns these two types of people two very different ranks and functions in society: "I need hardly mention that the former are born for detail and for subordinate occupations, the latter – supposing that they also combine this capacity with a sense of reality – for the whole and for distinguished roles in life."[42]

Schiller's is a particularly bald statement of an assumption that circulates more tactfully in later theories of culture in the nine-teenth century. Like Matthew Arnold, he associates self-cultiva-tion with the health of the society, but he also directly links it to the exercise of power, the individual's career, and the social exclusions it will operate. It is not just that aesthetic activity will promote a higher level of civilization or a healthy state by helping people realize their potential and express their individuality; it will also in the process furnish a concrete means of discriminating between those who are fit to govern and those who are not.

Schiller's aside may reflect an unspoken assumption on the part of those promoting Culture and the aesthetic as a means of "improving society," but it is an assumption which risks undermining the whole enterprise when articulated so ingenuously. Post-Enlightenment Europeans were only too aware of Culture's potential as an instrument of social stratification. As the famous chemist Lavoisier remarked, an educational system based on different tracks according to inclination and ability could not help but produce a two-tiered society: one class, those who devote themselves to "the study of languages and literary objects," would be "destined for public service," while "the others are destined for mechanical arts."[43] Another writer on education rightly noted that were such a system adopted, it would have the effect of reinstating a privileged class little different from the clergy.[44]

In fact, the turn to aesthetics was intended to sidestep just such issues. If Schiller prefaces his indiscretion (which occurs in a footnote) with the telltale "I need hardly mention . . .," it is because at this early stage in the formulation of high Cultural ideology, he feels he *does* need to mention it: he cannot be sure that the political utility of his method will be obvious, steeped as it is in abstractions and references to inner, felt realities. By the end of the nineteenth century no such elaboration will be necessary: that cultured people are "naturally" the best qualified to run the country and the economy will quite literally go without saying.

The Politics of Disinvolvement

The political implications of the aesthetic go beyond its obvious value as a subtle program of autotriage. For it also appropriates and clarifies the claim of political disinterest we have associated with critique, and develops it into a particularly ambiguous strategy of (dis)engagement, the exact political effects of which are a matter of perennial dispute.

From one point of view the emergence of the aesthetic seems merely a useful moment in intellectual history: a successful job of crystallization and conceptualization that provided a framework for understanding institutions and practices that were already well established. Indeed, as the previous chapters suggest, many of the diverse practices and assumptions which it weaves into a coherent pattern had been working themselves out for centuries. However, by theorizing a domain of value and a form of practice structurally analogous to the dialectic of individual and law being acted out in the political sphere, yet *a priori* free of political interest by virtue of its concern with the ideal value of beauty, aesthetic theory makes possible high Culture's "a-political" rehearsals of political subjectivity.

The key move here can be found in Schiller's theory, where the capacity of aesthetic experience to integrate the individual into the state is grounded precisely in its freedom from the partial interests which might alienate any given person. Aesthetic experience constructs identity and selfhood safely outside the zone of political interest, within a domain of absolute value that by definition exceeds governance: "Art, like Science, is free from everything that is positive or established by human conventions, and both of them rejoice in an absolute immunity from human lawlessness. The political legislator can enclose their territory, but he cannot rule within it."[45]

Answering to the absolute value of beauty alone, neither the work of art nor the subjectivity it entails can be subordinated to political expediency. This is what guarantees the aesthetic's unifying force for the nation and humanity at large: whatever our political affiliations or immediate interests, the aesthetic will accommodate us – provided we put them aside in deference to the universal appeal of beauty. Nor by the same token can artistic value be assessed in terms of the work's exchange value. This doctrine of art as an autonomous sphere is central to its institutionalization in the nineteenth century as a form of moral instruction and a refuge from the vulgarities of the marketplace and the strife of politics.[46] As Marxist commentators will subsequently point out, by the same token it disqualifies immediate action in the real world in favor of a mediated symbolic representation of the autonomy and equality which the state promised but could not deliver.[47]

Aesthetics trains the subject for life in an orderly society of free individuals by severing self-realization from the unconditional pursuit of material equality. This strategy reflects the doctrines of egalitarianism in vogue at the close of the Enlightenment, which held that while all people were equal in terms of their political rights, they were not equal in capacity or professional inclination. For an egalitarian society to function smoothly, individuals needed to recognize the practical limitations to their freedom and learn to renounce the dogged pursuit of self-interest in the interest of administrative and economic efficiency.[48]

Schiller expresses the sequestration of aesthetic activity from the sphere of the political as if it were of benefit to those involved with art, whose freedom of expression comes with freedom from the bothers of political involvement. However, cordoning off the aesthetic from the political and economic serves the state's interests as well. By defining an arena of activity that is by convention apolitical and virtual, rather than actual or material, aesthetics makes it possible to apprentice subjects to habits of self-assertion and autonomy that carry no risk to the state, although they inculcate the subject with the values of the state. Like Kant's disinterested "public use of reason," aesthetic formation occurs within a space unsullied by political or economic struggle and accustoms us to accept that space as the compass of our self-assertion. Yet this space is saturated with the idioms of expression, strategies of analysis, rituals of evaluation, and traditions of hierarchy that undergird prevailing structures of power, and expressing ourselves within Culture, we absorb those values. It is no doubt for this reason that the French Revolutionary Boissy d'Anglas called the cultivation of the arts "a sweeter surveillance" than direct political oversight: it both energizes and channels the indolent and defines a harmless outlet for the enthusiasm and exaltation of the politically agitated.[49]

From one perspective of analysis then, aesthetic Bildung is a quintessential form of Althusserian interpellation: it divests us of idiosyncrasy and calls us into the rules of our society. Motivated by the promise of autonomy, inspired by the ideology of self-construction, we assimilate our community's dominant lexicons and ways of thinking at our own initiative. Even as we exercise our aesthetic judgment, we learn to think about ourselves in certain ways, in certain terms; we construct our identity out of the experience of collectively sanctioned artifacts, texts, sounds, and ceremonial spaces. And we do so with enthusiasm because we believe our actions to be invulnerable to disqualification and free of immediate political consequence. We can express our aesthetic judgments with as much stridency as we wish; we can like, dislike, or produce any kind of art we wish, secure in the belief that our taste has no immediate concrete linkage to our political status or the stability of the state.

The aesthetic's separation from other forms of endeavor is important not because it shelters the state from our powerful acts of individuation or vice versa, but because it reassures us in our aesthetic initiative and draws us more deeply into the normalizing mechanisms of institutionalized practice. The promise of aesthetic-cognitive autonomy is one of the things that makes us so willing to devote ourselves to the pursuit of Culture and work so hard to assimilate the traditions and norms it conveys. Learning to think for one's self is at the very heart of the high Cultural machine.

But does the sequestration of art necessarily foreclose on its political instrumentality? Schiller clearly thinks so: his artist must "resign the sphere of the actual to the intellect, whose home it is," and he advises the young artist intent on effecting social change not to intervene directly in the political or social order, but merely to "give the world you would influence a *direction* towards the good, and the quiet rhythm of time will bring about its development."[50] Presumably the same advice would apply to the consumers of art tempted to engage in political critique. Like Kant's good taxpayer, they should circulate an abstract argument about the injustice of the system, rather than taking concrete action. Were this the extent of the aesthetic's political value, we could understand it as an instrument of displacement, a neutralizing maneuver designed to channel potentially dissident intellectual energies into politically inconsequential activity.

However, remembering Koselleck's argument that the Enlightenment critique of absolutism could foment the French Revolution not in spite of but *because* of the strict boundary between politics and private morality, one might surmise that the apolitical status of the aesthetic might likewise secure for it a covert form of political agency. Like Enlightenment calls for reform which were made in the name of universal truth and morality, the aesthetic might be all the more powerful in that it claims to transcend political interest: "by the yardstick of the laws of the moral world, social and political reality is not only incomplete, limited, or unstable but also immoral, unnatural and foolish. The abstract and unpolitical starting point allows a forceful, total attack on a reality in need of reform."[51] Discourse that claims only to disclose universal value is politically valuable precisely because it is more difficult to attribute to personal interest.

Along similar lines, it has been argued that the aesthetic withdrawal from mundane reality is a form of "ethical preparation" that functions as "the condition of access to a level of ethical being from where the whole of society can be judged and found wanting."[52] Kant argued that aesthetic judgment lays claim to universality, if only because to pronounce an object beautiful is to assert that it is so for all people. Thus, even if aesthetic judgment leads to a critique of social, political, religious, or economic institutions, it can claim immunity to regulation on the grounds that it is not concerned with local phenomena so much as universals. In this way, aesthetic theory enables critique and puts it beyond the grasp of the state. Occasioned by beauty, concerned with timeless universal values, how could it threaten the state? Its operations, however much they may involve or culminate in critical judgments, will always protest their innocence.

This strategy of disingenuous critique has often been associated with the novel – suggesting once again that it is a prototype for many of the operations of institutionalized Culture. One of the things that makes the new genre so controversial is that even as it acquires moral authority from the eighteenth to the nineteenth century, individual works begin to broadcast their lack of commitment to reality by admitting the label of "fiction" into their self-definition. The traditional eighteenth-century conceit of the genre was of course that it *was* involved with social reality – that it was based in history or the real experiences of actual people and could therefore hardly be criticized if the tales it related were morally reprehensible. So for a narrative to call itself a "novel" or a "fiction" is to repudiate its original claim to utility. However, this bad faith gesture marks the genre's political commitment, rather than its withdrawal from politics. For by establishing a domain of virtual reality distinct from that of actual politics, fiction could attack political and social structures from the outside: its critique could implicate real people and events, even as it claimed to affect only imaginary ones, or at best representations of historical people and events. This cloak of disinvolvment is deployed equally efficiently by dissident fiction and fiction in the service of the dominant political faction: the mantle of aesthetic disinterestedness allows the latter to infuse the readership with its values and paradigms of subjectivity all the more effectively.

Grounded in the logic of the aesthetic, modern institutions of high Culture are politically ambiguous, alternately decried and espoused by Left and Right alike. Indeed, their primary attraction to their earliest theoreticians was precisely that they could do political work without appearing to do so. Art itself had long been associated with the political domain, where it had been perfected as a means of political regulation by Louis XIV and those who emulated him. And of course public art continued to function as an explicit tool of social control in the work of artists like Jacques-Louis David, even after the politically disinterested discourse of aesthetic "appreciation" had been put into place. However, aesthetic theory made art an instrument for regulating *all* the people and doing so from the inside, not by dazzling them with symbols of majesty, but by shaping their sense of themselves and giving them responsibility for articulating the history and legacy of values to which they answered. Aesthetic theory brought the law inside the subject and installed the subject inside the law; and when it did so, it changed the meaning and use of art.

The Cultural Institution and the Work of Art

The new Cultural institutions that appear in the wake of the French Revolution find a flexible and subtle instrument of social regulation in aesthetic theory, one that can incorporate the conflicting imperatives of the modern state: individualism and social homogeneity, law and order grounded in freedom. Ostensibly devoted to encouraging individual self-perfection, Cultural institutions arise from the need for coherence in the state: most of those we are familiar with today were explicitly proposed to that end by the Revolutionaries. If they mark off a domain where freedom can be exercised, it is to ensure that no one evade the law. They govern not by appeal to political doctrine, but by folding the particularities of experience into universal law, building individuals out of codified practice.

The aesthetic enters the state through the institutions of high Culture that were conceived at the end of the eighteenth century as a means of forming a coherent, obedient citizenry out of a diverse population of conflicting interests. These institutions were designed specifically to recruit the critical initiative of the individual into assimilating positive values even as they disassociated such initiative from political action. They bred autonomy, but it was autonomy of aesthetic judgment, normative in that it assimilated the individual to state-sanctioned modes of self-assertion, but politically inconsequential in that it redirected the citizen's critical energies away from questions of government or class interest and towards the determination of beauty and taste. In compensation for their enthusiastic espousal of this task, the citizens gained a sense of augmented virtue, and perhaps also the elusive promise of eventual political and social effectiveness, the lack of immediacy of which was supposedly offset by its resistance to direct state regulation.

These institutions of Culture are familiar to all of us, because we have all been formed by them. Some of them I mentioned at the conclusion of the previous chapter. They include first and foremost the schools, but also public libraries, historical societies, natural history museums, art collections, operas, orchestras and chamber music societies, observatories, sculpture gardens, dance companies, literary clubs, public monuments, and poetry readings, to mention just a few. Most of these have clear antecedents in the early modern period as elite practices, but were funded as *public* resources only subsequent to the Enlightenment, as part of the continuing generalization of the logic of culture to the people.

Cultural institutions differ from other socio-political forms in the operations, types of subjectivity, and kinds of objects they presume. Their operations meld into a single ongoing dialectic the two strategies of normalization we have noted in discursive institutions such as the novel, the press, and education: indoctrination through example and internalization through analysis. They provide exemplary material to be absorbed, emulated or assimilated as a frame of reference: the ideals, values, facts, and artifacts that set the parameters of our self-realization. But they also provoke and fund a process of rational critique and aesthetic judgment which takes place within that framework and appropriates its categories to construct self-awareness and a sense of individuality. This process occurs under the aegis of autonomous self-expression but it integrates the subject into social norms through the discursive protocols it prescribes: we learn to express our opinions and defend our judgments using methods and categories specific to our culture.

These two different modalities of indoctrination correspond to the two modes of apprehension we recall from Rousseau – the absorptive or emulative and the analytic or reflective – and two visions of subjectivity, as determined or autonomous, habitual or disciplined. They correspond as well to two different conceptions of the object that is actualized in the aesthetic experience: as reservoir of value and embodiment of a legacy, and as the occasion and product of interpretive initiative.

These different understandings of the art work are most obvious in the contrasting conceptions of art that were in circulation at the close of the Enlightenment. We recall Hegel's observation that art no longer had for his contemporaries the self-sufficient vital plenitude it enjoyed in classical culture but had become rather the pretext to discourse and abstraction. This lament was reiterated by the French art historian, Quatremère de Quincy. For him true art was a product of sentiment and took its meaning from its embeddedness in religious, political, and social reality; what distinguished the classical period was that people actually believed in the existence of the beings represented in their art.[53]

The two attitudes to which Hegel and Quatremère de Quincy refer index two conceptions of the art work: as an embodiment of ideality which infuses the subject with moral value, and as a vessel which acquires its meaning and value from the uses to which the subject puts it.

As the embodiment of an ideality, art fulfills an *exemplary* function. It provides ideals and forms which different groups and generations can emulate (or shun, in the case of negative models) or unconsciously assimilate through habit. Art in this sense defines the values of the subject. However, to the extent that the experience of art culminates in reflection and aesthetic judgment, it functions as a *discursive locus*. In this sense it is the subject who determines the value of the work of art. This process also regularizes the citizens, but it does so under the guise of individuation, by engaging each subject in a process of self-expression that occurs within consistent forms of inquiry and ways of thinking, even when it does not impose a single content or model on them.

The institutions of Culture partake of both of these strategies at all times. On the one hand they define a set of artifacts and rituals purported to embody the foundational beliefs and traditions of the community, and they demand that the individual acknowledge and assimilate them. On the other hand, they demand that the individual invest these artifacts with value and meaning, in a critical response that expresses his or her personal experience and testifies to the mastery of the society's accredited forms of analysis and comprehension. Both of these processes occur simultaneously in the high Cultural dialectic: in asserting their autonomy and expressing their individuality, the members of the community assimilate, reiterate, and revise their culture's structures of thought and frameworks of judgment.

This double process is inaugurated by forms such as the novel and the theater, but the new institutions explicitly concerned with the aesthetic, such as the museum, went well beyond merely provoking the dialectic. They specified that one not only assimilate shared values through one's acts of individuation, but that one *be aware* that one was doing so and confirm that awareness in a special account of one's experience. This demand constitutes a crucial innovation of high Cultural institutions, all of which urge us not just to master certain traditions and values, but to conceptualize our embeddedness in them.

This imperative is Culture's legacy from critique. It draws us into the values, concepts, artifacts and traditions of the community, but it also encourages us to take our distance from – and to change – those values and traditions by talking about our experience. Indeed, the highest form of Cultural refinement confirms its mastery of shared values and practices *by* expressing and critiquing its own entanglement in them. Just as Enlightenment critique engendered new values and practices in its wake, high

Culture demands that its practitioners take an active role in the articulation of their society's legacy.

Culture in this sense is not just a symbolic distillation of practice, but a process for enlisting us in the production of such symbolic distillations, if only at the level of shared conversations and expressions of taste. Culture compels us to acknowledge our judgment as our own. It is a set of practices and artifacts, but also a process of induction. When we apprehend and critique a Cultural object – indeed, when we apprehend *any* object *as* a cultural object – we acknowledge that it is the product of human intentionality and hence the result of initiatives like our own. Assuming responsibility for its production, we submit to its laws.

What is involved is a dialectic of reciprocal production, in which subjectivity is shaped by the object it shapes, and vice versa. This reciprocal action is manifested most clearly in the metaphor we use to convey it: that of the Cultural *work*. Cultural work is constantly underway. It is constantly expended and reproduced by the public in transactions of regulated disclosure: displays or performances in which the value and identity of the work are reasserted and redefined by the public in a dialectic of present and past, institutional value and individual assessment.

We acknowledge this dialectic in our assumption that the identity and meaning of a work of art – say *Hamlet* – does not fully reside in any single performance, transcription or material support (such as a manuscript) but in the constantly changing value, meaning, and use that work has for the community that so identifies it. Cultural value continually circulates and is renegotiated through individual events of aesthetic apprehension, which approximate in their structure Schiller's paradigm of aesthetic experience. The objects they involve are heterogeneous, knitting together the perceptual and the discursive, the private and the public, the past and the present, the idiosyncratic particular experience and the shared general account.

It hardly needs reiteration at this point that if participation in the negotiation of cultural value fosters a sense of interpretive autonomy in the subject – a feeling of freedom and individuality – it also makes manifest the rules and values of the culture and to that extent reinforces the individual's sense of being determined by received traditions and collective habit. The genius of Culture is that it resolves the tension between these two feelings by manifesting the rules of the culture as products of the subject's free assessment. This feeling of simultaneous freedom and constraint is reflected in the mix of reverence and repudiation which "cultured" people display towards their culture, celebrating and reasserting the traditions that bind and define them, even as they contest, transgress, and rewrite those traditions.

It also goes without saying that Cultural institutions, like all systems of rule-bound discourse, apportion status and distinction. Like the novel, Culture addresses multiple publics and underwrites multiple cognitive enterprises and conflicting meanings *simultaneously*. This multivalence is what guarantees the process of autotriage by which individuals apportion themselves into classes. The genius of the Cultural institution is that it makes individuals see this apportionment as the result of their own decisions or initiatives. Accordingly, they feel themselves in control of their social status in ways which other mechanisms of stratification – such as fortune or rank – do not afford. Perhaps nowhere are these processes embodied more vividly than in the art museum, which in many senses defines the archetypal high Cultural institution of the modern era.

Constructing the Subject: the Art Museum

The museum is in many respects the quintessential Cultural institution. If it is the place *par excellence* that one visits to "get Culture" and to study or learn about other "cultures," that is because its development and structure are inextricably bound up with both the Cultural ethic of self-improvement and the objectification of social values and traditions as "culture."

Much has been written about museums in the past two decades, concerning not only their origins in the royal and aristocratic collections and *Kunstkammer* of the Renaissance and their development in conjunction with the ideology of enlightenment, but also and especially their complicity in the formation of the modern state and its ideologies.[54] As with the novel, it is beyond the scope of this study to account for all of the ideas and models that have been formulated on this subject. However, to understand how the museum functions today, it is necessary to keep in mind the general framework of its emergence.

Museums have their origins, both materially and conceptually, in the collections of the wealthy and the privileged. Historically, they displayed the wealth of the collector, but also his cognitive power. The acquisition and display of beautiful, curious, or rare objects in the Renaissance confirmed the collector's access to the secrets of the universe contained in those objects, which mediated between the visible and the invisible, the material world and the order that subtended it.[55] The collection indexed its proprietor's access to this realm of hidden meaning and placed outsiders who were granted access to the collections in a subordinate position. Paying their respects to the collection, they acknowledged the status of the collector. Although the evolution of the collection into the museum during the early modern period occurs in tandem with a series of epistemic shifts in the structure of knowledge, museums remain fundamentally concerned with articulating the relationship of knowledge and ownership to identity, power, and status.[56]

The Enlightenment constitutes a capital moment in the history of the museum. As part of its progressive social agenda it sought to undo the linkage between wealth and knowledge, by converting the private collection into a public museum. Beginning in the eighteenth century and continuing to the present day, the practice of donating a private collection to the state both acknowledges and claims to remedy the unequal distribution of power by making the systematic understanding of the natural world, history, and art available to the public. The first such collections were of several sorts: botanical collections such as the Jardin des Plantes in Paris, founded in 1633; scientific collections and libraries, such as the British Museum, created out of the Sloane collection in 1759; mixtures of natural history and historical objects, such as the Ashmolean, inaugurated in 1683 at Oxford; or collections of paintings, sculptures, and art objects, such as the Muséum National des beaux-arts, which would become the Louvre and define the prototypical art museum for modernity.[57]

By the time the Louvre opened in 1793, the logic underlying all these collections was firmly entrenched: objects of scientific, historical, and artistic value belong to all the people. The knowledge they embody cannot be owned. Making the collection accessible to all of the people makes its knowledge available to them – and if they persevere in their aesthetic education, they can eventually also achieve some measure of the power and status that come with that knowledge. This redefinition effects the status of the collected objects as well, which can be understood henceforth to body forth the heritage and identity of the community rather than the power of an individual. Belonging to all members of the community (nation, state, city, ethnicity, etc.) for all time, they have become part of the patrimony – elements of a "culture."

Of course, when the museum makes the power of the collection available to the public, it is with the understanding that they will conform to certain rules of behavior, emulate certain modes of subjectivity and exercise self-discipline. From its earliest theorization as a public institution, the museum has been understood as an instrument for forming the citizenry. Indeed, Revolutionary plans for a French museum of natural history specified the formal courses of instruction that would be given. The public art museums that emerged in the late eighteenth and nineteenth centuries were intended to shape the public's taste through the aesthetic. As the Berlin Royal Museum's first director put it, "the first goal of a museum is to promote the spiritual growth of the nation by the contemplation of the beautiful."[58] But in addition to cultivating aesthetic judgment, museums infused the citizenry with a shared heritage and a framework for understanding it.

On the one hand, they were intended to inspire the public and provide exemplary instances. The artist Jacques-Louis David is no doubt thinking of this when he declares that the Muséum National – the future Louvre – "is not a trifling collection of frivolous luxury items, destined only to satisfy our curiosity. It must become an important school. Teachers will take their young pupils there; the father will take his son. At the sight of the productions of genius, the young man will feel welling up in him the type of art or science for which nature destined him."[59]

On the other hand, the museum would stimulate discourse and analysis. The formation of the nation required more than the passive contemplation of the works. "The mute eloquence of monuments and masterpieces elevates the soul and enlarges the scope of the mind and the imagination: but it does not suffice as instruction."[60] To function properly, the work of art needed to invigorate the public's analytic enthusiasm and thus find its way into their discourse and conscience. The museum ensured this would occur by mobilizing the public's attention around a set of objects specified to embody their heritage and providing a site and set of rules by means of which they could pay homage. The displayed collection gave tangible form to the nation's identity – its "culture" – but only to the extent the visitors acknowledged it as such. The museum made individual Culture and national (and ultimately universal) culture dialectically constitutive of each other: the development and theorization of collective identity was inseparable from the individual assessments that acknowledged and engendered it.

That museums stimulated the critical spirit of analysis was an assumption shared by their proponents and detractors alike. Indeed, for its most vocal critic of the period, Quatremère de Quincy, that is *all* the museum stimulated. Severed from their social setting and massed in collections and museums, works of art were no longer capable of animating the moral spirit of the people; they merely provoked an attitude of idle curiosity or, worse yet, the cool detachment of the critic. "Everything there . . . speaks to us of Art and its devices, of the secrets of its science, the means of studying it; everything there puts you on your guard against its seductions. Curiosity and the critical attitude are there to prevent emotions from getting to our soul or penetrating it."[61] Quatremère's observations open an issue fundamental to museum theory: what kind of ethical and cognitive postures do museums foster, and what are their political and social ramifications?

Modern commentators have speculated intensively on the museum's effect on the public, focusing generally on the epistemic shifts or ideological affiliations reflected by various display strategies.[62] There are indeed many ways the museum can affect our experience, not just in the grouping and hanging of the art, but through the rituals of viewing it enforces: the itinerary that is imposed on the visitor through the disposition of the spaces and the partitioning of the exhibit into stages or periods or schools; the labels, explanatory texts, and recorded commentaries that explain the "significance" of the works for the willing listener; the protocols of veneration, covering admission, dress and conduct; and even the logistics of access, such as the placement of the museum building, memberships and sponsorship, the reservations one must make for special shows, and the price one pays for them.

In addition to these tangible manifestations of regulation, the museum deploys subtler influences on our ways of thinking through the systems of classification it endorses, the unspoken historical filiations it appeals to, the inclusions and exclusions it operates, even the language it uses. And of course the museum reminds us constantly of the unequal distribution of knowledge and power by its administrative structure: directors and curators decide what to purchase, have access to all of the works in the collection, including those not on display, claim to know what is authentic or important and what is not, and decide on that basis what to let us see, and under what conditions.

The fact that museums can affect how we think by their way of displaying objects is something the founders of the first great national collection, the Louvre, were perfectly aware of. Indeed, what made the idea of the museum so attractive to the political engineers of the French Revolution was precisely its ability to structure the people's cognitive habits and intellectual reflexes. As Quatremère de Quincy noted at the beginning of the nineteenth century, just as the mode of presentation of the object in the museum affects the qualities we attribute to it and the way we use it, so too does it modify our faculties for dealing with it, augmenting or diminishing our capacity to be affected by it. The "theatrical" setting and the physical disposition of the works instigate not only new relationships and perspectives of analysis, but also a shift in the "point" or finality of art and the legitimation of a new form of judgment.[63] Rather than being moved by the art, we compare and contrast it, construct a history of its production, rank the accomplishment of its various practitioners. At one point in his polemic, Quatremère exclaims that to assemble the "debris" of displaced art works in a museum according to an artificial scheme of classification is to "kill art in order to make history out of it."[64] History implies discourse, and Quatremère's lament suggests that while in the durability of its collections the museum may seem a monument to the material reality of a society, in its strategies of exhibition and pedagogy, it actually compels the subject to transpose visual experience into the critical language of historical abstraction.

Looking at the evolution in museum pedagogy over the past

two centuries, it is abundantly clear that this is the trend. It had always been assumed that the final measure of aesthetic judgment was a discursive product: the knowledge of art necessarily implied the ability to *explain* why one artist was superior to another.[65] In fact, one of Quatremère's contemporaries, George-Marie Raymond, argued that rational assessment was the *primary* reaction that an art work elicited: "we cannot see a painting without starting to reason on the means of art."[66] The museum maximizes this tendency by inviting comparison of paintings and framing them in an historical account. By the early nineteenth century, both the heterogeneous jumble of the curiosity cabinet and the contrastive hanging that juxtaposed artistic techniques had begun to give way to display according to chronology and school.[67] Over time, the imperative to convert visual information into discourse becomes more pronounced, resulting in ever more intrusive technologies of commentary. Early museums – even those envisioned as institutions of public education – did not generally include labels for their displays; at best a list or catalog identified the works.[68] Subsequently, labels were added and itineraries defined; more recently, notices have been appended to the displays, and guided tours provided, firmly situating the meaning of the work within an authoritative historical context. Extensive catalogs, tape recordings, headsets and talking wands form the most recent addition to this technology, which is supplemented by a host of secondary documentation and paraphernalia that can be acquired by the visitor at the museum "shop" – occasionally located like a way station midway through the itinerary.

Of course, this incitement to discourse is not limited to the art museum. The museum of technology or the historical institute impel us to discourse even more forcefully. While the students visiting the historical diorama or natural history display may not articulate their responses in terms of beauty, they *are* expected not just to absorb the examples they have observed, but to *talk* about what they saw, what it meant, where it came from, why it is important, what it made them feel, and so forth.

These heavy-handed techniques for administering the museum visit and insuring that our visual experience is converted into verbal account are not recent innovations or secondary phenomena but manifestations of the museum's grounding logic, its enduring wager as a Cultural institution. All Cultural institutions instigate discourse. The originality of the museum lies in its reliance on *objects* to this end, and in the critical awareness of historicity to which their ritualized disclosure as art works initiates us.

It has been argued that art works in and of themselves exist to *appear* in the world rather than appearing incidentally to their existence in the world, that they are the image of historical existence rather than part of it, and hence necessarily experienced as historicity.[69] True as this may be, it is not an insight that circulates in the thoughts of people in their everyday lives; nor does it address the process by which non-mimetic objects such as baskets and Venetian glass become works of art and hence susceptible to investment with meaning. It is here that the museum intervenes, for by sequestering the objects of its collection from everyday life and arranging them in a way that underscores this rupture, the museum confers upon them the status of art and compels us to confront both their historicity and our own.

Making History

A straightforward discussion of this transformation, and of the value it might have for the construction of the citizenry, occurred in 1792, in the debates in the French National Assembly over the fate of monuments celebrating the Bourbon dynasty.[70] Predictably two different visions of art arose. One argued for the destruction of ancien régime monuments, seeing in them the persistent celebration of tyranny. The other, which would ultimately carry the day, contended that on the contrary, when viewed from the proper perspective, those same monuments could function as the epitaphs of despotism, as the enduring statement of its elimination. As a proponent of the latter view, one M. Duffaulx, argued, public structures such as the park at Versailles or the massive gate of Saint-Denis could serve as "simulacra of horror," reminding future generations of what had been, but was no more: they would enable posterity to say "for two thousand years despots burdened the world. The despots are no more."[71]

Duffaulx's logic is that when the material symbols of despotism are *considered as symbols*, that is as *signs* or *simulacra*, they logically exclude the presence of that to which they refer; the lived regime they embodied and occasioned becomes itself an object of reflection, relegated to the status of dead history. To segregate an object in a collection as a sign of past practices is in some measure to disable those practices: understood as the residue of history and culture, they are no longer natural.

Duffaulx's argument is a version of the early modern strategy for recuperating self-determination through systematic thought, but he transposes this strategy into historical terms. He suggests that by grasping the traditions that determine us *over* time as being themselves located *in* a certain time, we can free ourselves of their grip. Seeing laws and traditions as contingent historical incidents, and not parts of a natural order, forces us to acknowledge their obsolescence and opens them to the endless re-evaluations of history as retrospection. Like rationalism and critique, this move appropriates the logic of authority of the body of practice it wishes to annul: despotism grounded its authority on historical precedent, saying that because things had been done in certain ways in the past, they must be done in that way in the present. Duffaulx rephrases the power of accumulation into a logic of supersession: because such institutions could not be the same as they *formerly* were, they clearly no longer enjoyed the same authority. As part of the past, they no longer ruled the present.

This move has become second nature to our postmodern sensibility, but it was an important piece in both the fight for museums and the emergence of Cultural logic as an official doctrine. The originality of the museum consisted in the way it initiated the subject to an awareness of historicity and how it is produced. As Duffaulx's colleague Cambon pointed out, there is no better way to insure that there will be no return to despotism than by constructing new monuments to freedom and collecting all of the old ones in a museum. Detached from their location and meaning within the material fabric of everyday life, museum exhibits acquire a special aura: exemplary tokens of the world they point to, they beg interpretation and analysis. Signifiers of a bygone era that we invest with meaning through our study of them, they both trigger the production of knowledge and continually remind us that not only history, but truth, meaning and identity are products of social practice.

Thus in the very gesture the museum elevates objects to the

status of Cultural treasure, it cancels their prior symbolic value and makes of them signs of the dialectic of history.[72] Severed from the skein of uses that defined them as living practice, they become signifiers of both the loss and the recapture of the past, of both the past as irremediably past and of the apprehending gesture in the present that grasps the past as such and recuperates it as knowledge by writing it into history.

In this sense, what the museum really puts on display is Culture as a dialectic of meaning formation. While the objects it exhibits may be less meaningful because they no longer are embedded in the practices that previously gave them value and defined their use, they are also more so by virtue of the domain of knowledge and mode of being they now open to the viewer. They foreclose on one version of authenticity, since the world towards which they gesture can be understood but no longer experienced in its integrity. However, they compensate for this loss with the cognitive purchase on history they provide. This metamorphosis of living history into historical knowledge has a positive value for the state – and not just because it renders objectionable practices obsolete: it also constitutes the individual as an active agent in the production of history and reconciles him or her to its lessons.

In other words, by emptying its objects of their value and enlisting us in their resurrection as history, the museum initiates us into the mechanism of Cultural interpretation and the historical agency it provides. Extending the reach of discourse to the most apparently non-discursive things – material objects – the museum shows us that they are, like *all* objects one chooses to consider as cultural, the products of discursive constructions. It may seem that severing objects from their social and moral context and isolating them in a neutral sanctuary where they can no longer be used in everyday life, but only gazed at, would serve to underline their materiality. In fact, the converse obtains. The object is purged of its original living function so that it can be displayed as a pure vehicle of meaning and invested with a new sense, which is conferred by the rhetoric of display, the critical gaze, and the analytic thought of the viewer. Those who respond to the invitation and strive actively to endow the objects with significance, accede to an active role in the writing of cultural history.

The lesson is actually double. It consists in the apprehension of the object's historical meaning on the one hand, and, on the other, of our role in the manifestation of that meaning. Framing objects within a space and ritual explicitly consecrated to the formation of meaning forces us to confront our own activity, our role in the engine of cultural value. Using contemporary language, we might say that the museum denaturalizes objects the better to compel us to apprehend them as semiotic entities; and by foregrounding and multiplying the sites and occasions of that process, it compels us to acknowledge our own investment and responsibility in the production of history.

What museums teach us is that culture is the product of Culture – and vice versa: that what we perceive to be components of our cultural heritage, sources for the way we think and feel, are always also the products of subjective apprehension, objects whose meanings are always to some extent inflected by our understanding of them even as they shape our sense of ourselves.

It is by inducing us to perceive simultaneously our determination *by* history and our agency in the determination *of* history – that the museum transforms us into Cultural subjects properly speaking. Summoned to acknowledge the traditions that make us who we are, we find ourselves – and witness others – investing the objects that embody that tradition with meaning. Even as we acquiesce to indoctrination, we acquire a sense of autonomy, understanding that the identity of objects is conferred on them by the uses that are made of them and meanings that are attributed to them. The Revolutionary proponents of the museum understood this: they knew that the same "sacred instinct" which drives us to create works of art also "enflames the generous and sensitive person with the desire to be free," and that this desire can find exercise in imaginative *critical* discourse as well as artist creation per se.[73]

Putting Culture on Display

If the early theoreticians of the museum were keenly aware of its effect, they did not all agree on its desirability. Quatremère was perhaps its most vocal critic, primarily because he did not feel the revelation of historicity compensated for the loss of direct moral intuition. Nostalgic for an ideal age when art enlarged the scope of reality without the mediation of critical analysis or conscious reasoning, he correctly perceived that museums substituted for this direct moral infusion an operation of abstract analysis, which could only yield historical value. Rather than feeling and living the work of art, the museum viewer analyzed and understood it as an historical artifact, an example of craft and technique. As Quatremère lamented, the museum makes art a piece of history, and not even that, an epitaph.[74]

Yet with hindsight we know that Quatremère was only half right: the moral, religious dimension of art has not entirely disappeared; what has changed is the religion. Museums, too, are temples: to culture, high and low. And modernity venerates and believes in the existence of culture much as the ancients believed in their gods: we think of it as what made and makes our world the way it is, the framework of interdictions and encouragements, destinies and possibilities, within which our strivings take place.

The museum displays for our beholding this fabric of determination and intention even as it stirs us to critical judgment and self-expression; but the object of our beholding is no longer divine intention. It is history, exhibited as the dialectic of self-conscious endeavors through which individuals and groups construct their identity (Culture) and the sediments of practice, belief, and values which frame those endeavors and precipitate from them (culture).

At the most obvious concrete level, museums foreground this dialectic by staging the production of future art from that of the past. Their fundamental function at the origin was to provide facilities for the training of future generations of artists and thus ensure the ongoing enrichment of the patrimony. The museum building and its collections constituted a dedicated space where artists could develop their own styles by copying those of previous generations. However, by opening this spectacle to the public, the museum purveyed a lesson for its visitors on how the art and traditions of the future emerge out of the apprehension of the past *as past*. Numerous paintings depicting a painter painting a painting in a gallery, surrounded by visitors, testify to the success of this lesson: the museum was seen from the outset as deeply involved not just in the preservation of art, but in the display of its own role in the production of history.

Of course the same dialectic of historical progression applies to the critical knowledge of art that museums sponsor: they invite us to behold, but in beholding to think, and in thinking to revise, advance or contribute, however minimally, to the meaning of the objects we behold – and thus to modify their value. Like the copy of the masterpiece, every assessment one formulates of a work of art constitutes an adjustment to the repository of collective experience within which it occurs and hence to the work's identity for members of that culture. This dialectic between subjective experience and the identity and meaning of the object has animated the logic of the museum from the beginning. While the initial selection, disposition, and classification of the objects displayed in the museum was determined by professional functionaries, the people themselves were always intended to develop a sense of taste and an appreciation of the difference between the various works – and, of course, to furnish future generations of artists and curators. Indeed, David and his fellow deputy Grégoire assumed that the public would eventually take over the task of selecting works for inclusion in the national collection, since the museum's displays would not only inspire future artists but engender aesthetic discrimination in the broader public as well.

The material configuration of the museum ensures that this process of Cultural reproduction will not go unnoticed, that it can in fact become part of the lesson about history the museum delivers. Museums assemble and display people as well as objects. They convoke them into a limited space purged of any material function and channel their self-expression into well-defined discursive rituals. While the exact protocols of visiting the art collection took some time to establish, they have steadily evolved in the direction of repressing material contact with the works of art and limiting bodily expression.[75] Entering the art museum, we enter a Cultural arena where we are invited to exercise certain kinds of discourse to the exclusion of others. We are to situate, evaluate and appreciate the objects on display in measured tones and according to sanctioned historical and aesthetic criteria, but not to applaud them, touch them, burst into tears, break out in anger, or engage in loud, contentious arguments. When we display our proficiency in the codes of aesthetic judgment, we not only confirm our enclosure by culture, but gain a sense of Cultural mastery that allows us to gauge ourselves with respect to our peers. At the same time, by engaging in these rituals, museumgoers act out the spectacle of cultural reproduction. When we publicly identify and talk about objects *as cultural objects*, we exemplify and display in our own living practice the process of Cultural production they embody.

Museums put culture on exhibit in the objects they display; they exhibit Culture in the endeavors at self-expression they provision. Taken collectively, the latter provide an ongoing spectacle of the mechanism of Cultural production through which the community articulates its aesthetic values and historical identity. The museum's ideal subjects cannot help but see that the Culture they venerate is in part the product of their lives – including their acts of veneration. For museums confront us with both our culture and our Culture: both the fabric of uses, meanings, and accounts that constitute our history and heritage, and the process, continually reiterated in the semiosis of the exhibits, out of which that fabric is woven – the ongoing initiatives at understanding we undertake in visiting the museum.

In the final analysis, then, we do not have to choose between the discursive critique of history which Quatremère disparages or the intuition of virtue he exalts. For each is born of the other in the experience of the museum. Even as it compels its user to confront historicity, the museum embodies and stages a disclosure of transcendental value in which the subject can believe: that of Culture. Through its ongoing display of the dialectic of history, its exhibition of tens of thousands of people all over the world flocking to admire and talk about the products of other cultures and Cultures, the museum fosters a veneration for Culture. This may be different by virtue of its historical structure from the social forms of the Greeks, but it cements society together just as surely, binding the individual to the rules of social growth. Museum-goers believe in the value of their cultural heritage and in their role in defining it, and that belief welds them to their culture.

Staging Culture and culture, and bringing people to believe in their importance as mediations of identity, may well be the museum's greatest achievement. It is difficult to assess to what extent national collections actually succeeded in forming the national identity – certainly the Louvre was less instrumental in uniting the French than the long series of conquests which provided many of its early acquisitions. What is clear is that to the extent the museum did succeed in consolidating the people, it did so through the mediation of the new category of Culture, the operations and authority of which it made manifest. In so doing, the museum prepared the emergence in the latter half of the nineteenth century of the anthropological formulation of culture as the complex totality of relations, values, beliefs, and practices characterizing a people. By identifying, assembling, sequestering, and classifying the nation's patrimony (and eventually that of others as well), it made tangible the idea of a collective identity that accrues over time through the sedimentation of practice.

However, the museum also inscribed a new paradigm of subjectivity into the public conscience. In ritualizing Culture as the retrieval and constitution of historical identity, it situated the subject in a dialectic between present and past, autonomy and heteronomy. Elicited by and directed at an object that was neither entirely past nor present, the property of everyone and no one, constantly changing in its sameness, the subject was unanchored from the present, its acts of self-assertion deflected away from the actual, the material, the particular, towards a realm and practice of dialectical becoming. In positing a past that was to be reconstructed as knowledge, the museum suspended the subject in the aesthetic state of prolepsis, historically expressed: permanently gesturing towards a future moment of achieved comprehension in which one's history would be fully recuperated and one would be truly "cultured."

As with all Cultural endeavors the political implications of this shift are ambiguous at best. While the historico-aesthetic position may lead to an ethical "readiness" preparatory to social critique, it could also be surmised as diverting us from action in the world, by drawing us into a project which holds out the promise of authentic historical understanding and cultural identity, on condition that we not demand closure in the form of immediate material consequences.[76] The museum "displaces" social subjectivity in particularly concrete ways. It situates us in a controlled environment that is both saturated with sociality yet emptied of normal social interactions and rigorously monitored for conformity to administrative rules. In this space, self-expression occurs only in terms of the aesthetic, where the exclusion of closure minimizes open conflict and the risk of social or political disturbance: in issues aesthetic, no one can finally be right or wrong. Asserting ourselves in the museum, we have less need to do so in the streets, both because we have become more like one another by virtue of assuming the same heritage and historical vocabulary, and because we have partially assuaged our craving for freedom and agency. Both in theory and in practice, our delight or deception at the Vermeer exhibit, our judgment of Jasper Johns, does not cause us to rush out into the streets and rise up against the government.

Of course Culture *does* mobilize our competitive energies, but only to displace them to the struggle for a new form of status that is theoretically attainable by all persons willing to study and cultivate themselves. That part of Culture involves ranking and comparison is something the museum makes perfectly clear. An essential component of its ritual is the requirement that we experience art in public, in the presence of the community – and more precisely, shoulder to shoulder with the group we most closely compete with in the real world: our class peers. We cannot escape noticing the differences between our reactions, as we can when reading or even attending a movie. At the same time, the rigidity of the museum's protocols of presentation make it difficult to assign differences of reaction to outside agency: we are compelled to acknowledge them as differences among ourselves, and hence among our capabilities for appreciating art.

The Museum, the Novel, and Social Triage

The aesthetic theories of Baumgarten and Schiller adumbrate the correlation of aesthetic response to social status, and beyond that, to administrative responsibility in the state. Two centuries later the principle is deeply embedded in our society. It has been rigorously theorized in Pierre Bourdieu's work on the production, transmission, and accumulation of "cultural capital."[77] Short of engaging in the extensive sociological analysis of the type Bourdieu undertook in his seminal work *Distinction*, it is difficult to assess the effectiveness of museums in distributing Culture: one might well ask whether they actually fulfill their theoretical promise by indoctrinating large segments of the public in the dialectic of Culture, or merely serve as arenas for the display and reinforcement of class differences. The answer to that question depends to a large extent on the country and period under question.

However, what we can say is that art museums make us particularly aware of differences in our level of Culture. By convoking us into a common space and involving us in a meticulously regularized ritual of aesthetic judgment, they make our varying capabilities glaringly apparent. Just as they stage Culture, they foreground the social triage it operates. Here again, the simultaneous stimulation of conformity and differentiation that typifies cultural logic is apparent. Through the strictures on behavior it imposes, the ritual of the museum visit inculcates rules of conduct and solidifies class identity; but this very regularity in the protocols of contemplation accentuates variations of reaction. Judging art, we display our differences and rank ourselves.

But perhaps this is the point: art exhibits not only sort us out but *make us aware* they do so. They *demonstrate* to us that our relative inclination to discourse, our variable ability to assimilate cognitive etiquettes and express our individuality through them, can usefully serve as principles of social differentiation. Convinced that Culture helps us find our proper place, we acquiesce all the more readily to our own social classification. This could explain why the great bulk of the museum's public comes from the bourgeoisie: that is precisely the class that aspires to the administrative competence its operations are intended to specify.

The fact that not all people are willing to accept the viability of Culture as a mechanism of social, and especially economic, apportionment does not disqualify the museum as an instrument of hierarchization; on the contrary, it confirms its efficiency. It is self-evident that the museum has always operated exclusions, in spite of its pretensions to universal accessibility. It invites all of the people into its arena precisely so it can perform its triage, precisely so that they can experience for themselves, and thus come to accept as a decision they participate in, their relative fitness or unsuitability for service in the administrative classes. Should they decline to participate, they tacitly disqualify themselves from the aspirations of the bourgeoisie.

It has become increasingly fashionable in recent years to focus on the museum's exclusionary mechanisms, its brutal social triage, as evidence of its collusion with the most conservative social forces. However, the logic it deploys has long since been implemented self-consciously at all levels of society, in a multitude of professions and institutions which initiate and exclude according to similar mechanisms and in view of securing adherents to their particular forms of economic, political, and social activity. The drag race and the software convention perform triage as powerfully as the museum, and in the same way. They have their own venues, codes of expression, technologies, rituals of self-assertion, forms of dress, specialized lexicons, modes of social interaction, strategies of evaluation. And they exclude just as brutally – as most professors of Cultural Studies who have had extensive interactions with auto mechanics or industrial welders are well aware. The status the museum distributes, the qualifications it procures, may seem exceptionally desirable to the academic (who accordingly feels their exclusionary force as that much more objectionable), but they are of little consequence to those who have been interpellated by, and found fulfillment in, other arenas. The example of professional sports has made this painfully clear. There exist institutionalized forms of behavior and discourse indifferent to high Culture that are far less accessible and procure far greater economic benefit and social status – not to mention a sense of self: directors of internationally famous museums are no doubt pleased with themselves, but hardly more than the rap star or sports hero.

This generalization and dissemination throughout society of a mechanism of self-conscious identity formation, triage and status assignment, marks the ascendancy of Culture, rather than its collapse. It is not that these systems for sorting people out did not exist prior to the modern era, nor even that there were not similarly self-conscious reifications of their practices, or formalizations of their inclusions and exclusions: the clergy, aristocracy, and guild system obviously functioned analogously. What has changed is simply that this logic of identity consolidation has become universal, and universally self-conscious. And becoming universal, it has acquired a name and conceptual properties. That is why we can as easily speak of "drug culture," "biker culture," or "corporate culture," as of high Culture. Any form of behavior, from the sociopathic to the altruistic, can and does now conceive of itself as authorized by and productive of a script of values and practices that, precisely because it surpasses any individual's purview, acquires transcendent value, and justifies the range of acts it oversees – including the triage of potential newcomers to the culture. Thinking of oneself as part of a culture, taking pride in that fact, and actively striving to fill an active role in the perpetuation and enlargement of its legacy through the aesthetic appreciation of its material residues, have become universal reflexes of vastly disparate groups, from Star Trekkies to Harley riders. Exemplified and disseminated by the museum, the ethic of Culture has become a paradigm of subjectivity so foundational that we no longer even question its finality.

Of course, within this general paradigm, art museums valorize one particular dialectic of individual and collective identity – the one that frames the coming to terms with historicity in terms of the arts per se. They also inculcate a wide range of particular values that vary over time and according to reigning ideology. Just as the divide between Culture and culture in our everyday usage marks our sense of the difference between self-conscious, deliberate constructions of identity and those we inherit or absorb in spite of our selves, there is a less overt kind of triage and identity formation that occurs at the subconscious level through the internalization of such material. It is instructive in this regard to recall the way novels work in contrast to the museum.

That museums and literature construct subjectivity differently is obvious, and was already so two hundred years ago, when the private nature of fiction reading was often noted by the novel's critics, and the public nature of the museum formed the keystone of its utility as a means of forming civic identity. Considered contrastively, the two institutions can be thought of as devised to address the "cultural" fracturing of identity in the modern era into two dimensions, individual and collective, and two imperatives of self-realization: autonomy and conformity. They reflect as well the two domains of activity that become associated with each: the public and the private.

The museum was designed to implement the dialectic of identity within the public, social arena which the novel cannot penetrate. Museums constrain physical, social behavior; the novel cannot. In itself, the museum is nothing but a space with rules: it offers something up for contemplation, subject to certain rules of behavior. It is available for use only at certain times, by certain groups of people, at a certain price. Literature, considered at the institutional level, exercises no such hold on us. By the very nature of its private consumption, it cannot enforce norms of usage: we can do virtually anything we wish with a book, from reading it badly, intermittently, or in the bathroom, to crossing out portions of it, sitting on it, or lining the bird cage with it. Not so with the works of art in the museum. An entire range of objectionable behavior, solitary or collective, is proscribed by their enshrinement in a secure sanctuary, and one accepts those proscriptions once one enters the sanctuary. One can elaborate on the disciplinary implications of this difference, but to get at the more subterranean ways novels and museums sort us out, we have to compare the difference in the way we apprehend a narrative and an *exhibit*. Any effects beyond the general disciplinary effect of the museum are really effects of particular exhibits and the philosophies of hanging, types of content, pedagogical strategies, or narrative supplements they elect. The message one takes away from a museum visit is just that: the lesson of the *visit*.

This is important because at least since Lessing, much has been made of the difference between pictorial and verbal representation, generally focusing on the representation of successive events in time versus that of bodies in space. However, both the museum visit and the reading of a novel occur in time and are built up in the mind of the reader out of a succession of perceptions or pseudo perceptions. The more pertinent distinctions have to do with the transpositions of this experience into a discursive proposition, and with the different affect our imagination takes from each experience.

To the extent that all Cultural experience culminates in discourse, the visual work of art is obviously handicapped. The painted image can show us beauty but not give us the words to express it; it can show us how to behave but not how to formulate its moral discursively; it can depict an historical event or period, but cannot name it. Only textual accompaniments can do that. Lessing noted that the poet cannot really depict beauty, but only refer to it. This may be true, but literature has the ability, beyond stimulating us to imagine scenes and events, of articulating explicit propositions about them.

A painting cannot state a proposition and because of that, it makes us conscious of the propositions we formulate at its behest.

That paintings cannot speak does not mean we do not formulate propositions at the art exhibit – we necessarily do so as part of the aesthetic contract – but that we do so *self-consciously*: whether they are suggested by the pedagogical paraphernalia of the exhibition or result from our own reflection, we perceive them as coming from without the represented world. And to the extent we articulate them consciously, we sense them as our own. This is what makes the dialectic of Culture and history so manifest in the museum, and makes the museum so different from the novel. Museums compel us to acknowledge our own involvement in the Cultural project and to acknowledge as well the necessary culmination of that project in interpretative historical propositions.

The propositions we assimilate from reading a novel do not necessarily stimulate an awareness of Culture's dialectic, because they do not necessarily carry the aura of a second-level reflection. They can appear to emerge directly from the reality portrayed – as conclusions we "draw" from the story, rather than judgments we impose on it. We can grasp this in the impression of causality we infer from the consecuity of the plot: events that follow other events appear to follow *from* them. Simply by unfolding in time, they generate an implicit proposition: "x" occurs because of "y." Even explicit propositions advanced within a novel – such as the philosophical interventions of a narrator or character – enter our consciousness as components of a plot that unfolds over time; they are correlatives of a fictional world, expressions of its laws, not the fruit of our self-conscious attempt to abstract a message from an image, much less a second-hand lesson copied from a blatantly pedagogical guide (although they of course can be that as well).

Just as the strength and value of the museum visit lies in the way it makes us aware of the dialectic of Culture and history, and our role in it, so conversely, the value of the novel lies in the elegance with which it conceals this dialectic, insinuating the ideological microscripts of our culture into our mind.

The effectiveness of this operation has a lot to do with the affective charge of our imaginative reconstructions. As George-Marie Raymond pointed out in his study of the effects of painting, we cannot *not* see a painting that catches our eye. Yet even as it demands to be looked at, the painting places strict limits on what we see. Speaking to us directly through the intermediary of the senses, it leaves little room in its formal specifics for the imagination to see things it does not depict. Literature, on the other hand, Raymond continues, works by stimulating the imagination of the reader, who is in that sense the real poet: the poetic object "receives its features and character from the imagination and genius of the listener . . . The poet produces great effects, but less through what he says himself than through what he makes the person listening to him think of. . . . The latter is the real artist."[78]

Raymond is speaking of recited poetry, but his remarks apply to literature in general, and particularly the novel. As in the case of the proposition, the point is not that paintings cannot stimulate the imagination, but that when they do so, we are *aware* of it. Not so with the world the reader of a novel concretizes. It never attains the formal givenness of the image in the sense that it is never beyond revision; it is continually being built up out of components of the reader's experience. And because it constantly readjusts to new information or changes in our perception, our imagination of a literary event or character can never be wrong. Nor can it be unfamiliar, since we construct it out of pieces of past perceptions, events, places.

Because it is personally linked to us in this way, the fictional world we adumbrate is personally compelling in a way the painted scene is not assured of being. It does not need to be internalized, because it is already inside. This is what enables the literary work to speak to such a wide range of people. Each of us is free to imagine according to the limits of his or her particular experience – free even to forget large parts of the text that find no correlate in our experience, such as words we do not know. This mode of production ensures that whatever critical reflections the work occasions will be articulated with confidence: we can be certain that at the level of immediate "appearances" our apprehension of the literary object is correct, even if we are the only ones that can perceive it in just that way. (Hence the elaborate procedures of textual citation and analysis we learn for adjudicating critical disagreement – and the tangible difference between the undergraduate literature class and that of art history.)

There is a final difference that concerns the process of autotriage in literature and art. Among the propositions literature delivers are those implicitly or explicitly concerned with different kinds of reading and different levels of Cultural interpretation. The content of most eighteenth- and many nineteenth-century novels is explicitly concerned with understanding social practice and articulating cultural law, and many of the same works explicitly consider the effect of reading – especially novel reading – on the construction of identity. Paintings can of course also valorize different strategies of self-construction and social representation, but as recent works in art history demonstrate, they require exceptionally subtle assistance from the critic to formulate their message in a way the broader public can understand. While the museum is unparalleled at foregrounding the general paradigm of Culture, novels are unequaled in the varieties of apprehension to which they can initiate the reader. The novel can appropriate to its own advantage the constantly expanding array of subcultural discourses spawned by modernity – which are themselves the result of the generalization of the ethic of self-conscious Culture.

No doubt this explains the enduring power of literature as the preeminent Cultural institution (the cinema, its obvious rival, is in fact a subset of literature, and specifically of narrative fiction): it can keep up with Culture, offering each new "culture" works that incorporate its distinctive linguistic innovations, modes of analysis, bodies of expertise, and rituals of sociality. For the uninitiated, it provides a simulacrum of membership in the communities that define themselves through those discourses; for members of those "cultures," it procures the pleasure of recognition and a sense of expertise. And it associates all the forms of self-conscious Cultural formation with the pleasures of knowledge, membership, and growth.

To consider but one example: the realist novel of the nineteenth century taught its readers to take pleasure in the experience of authority that comes with the analysis of social and economic reality, political power, technology, even bureaucracy. That Dickens could transform the deadening legal bureaucracy of the Chancery into an object of aesthetic pleasure, that Balzac could devote large sections of *Eugénie Grandet* to the technicalities of bankruptcy, testifies to the fact that the eudaemonics of fiction reading had evolved by the nineteenth century far beyond identifying with characters.

This incorporation of material reality conforms in its logic to Schiller's paradigm of the aesthetic – since the novel approaches its vast collection of data not with an eye to their historical specificity, but under the guise of appreciating them as forms. Dickens may disavow the noxious effects of the lawsuit, Balzac the avarice of his protagonist, but they transform both into compelling and fascinating aesthetic forms, to be appreciated for their purity of self-interest, complexity of structure, refinement of tactic, and, especially, their implacability. The same phenomenon persists unabated today: novels continue to entrance readers as an access into the realm of the specialized, parasitizing every form of technical discourse, from the legal system, or the world of government surveillance, to computer encryption.

As it evolves into realism in the nineteenth century, the novel not only expands its compass, offering its reader the privilege of ranging at will throughout reality – of transforming anything and anyone into an object to be observed – it also invites that reader to assume, through the process of objectification and critical analysis, a position of superiority with respect to the object. The reading public of the nineteenth century oversees society in its entirety from the privileged perspective of one for whom anything can be the object of interest and pleasure, and, more importantly, the occasion for formulating laws. In the virtual polity of the novel, individual readers can make laws (of behavior) at their pleasure.

What made – indeed, still makes – the cultivation of this critical detachment so attractive is its tacit correlation with a superior destiny. Unlike museums, novels can explicitly correlate the operations of Cultural apprehension to particular social classes and vocations. The nineteenth-century novel's plots of social ascendancy, for instance, associated analytical detachment with the acquisition of status, wealth, and power. This was of course something which other institutions, such as the university and the museum, could and did do more obliquely. However, fiction was not limited to arguing the privilege of the Cultured like the university, or staging it like the museum. It could disclose and discuss particular scenarios of social ascendancy which readers could realize according to various logics of causation and universalize to a greater or lesser degree, applying them to themselves or not. Realist fiction always presents its social codes as the product of an ongoing collusion between reader and text. In this sense, the social "laws" which readers extracted from realist fiction were, like the laws of Schiller's ideal State, always the "clearer expression" of a reader's "inner legislation." That they emerge in particular clarity in certain cases underlines, in addition to the predilections and interpretive choices of the author, those of the reader.

Thus if fiction cannot stage the dialectic of Culture as a public ritual, like the museum, it subsidizes the ideology of high Culture nonetheless. It does not operate social stratification in public, but covertly enables it. Providing by virtue of its relative accessibility a terrain on which all classes could commingle, the novel also provided through its multiplication of reading protocols and strategies of decipherment a means for differentiating those readers – or more properly a means by which they could differentiate themselves. While it cannot make us as aware of our involvement with social norms, cultural legacy, and status allocation as the museum, it can involve far more of us in the process, subsidizing our conviction of individuality and autonomy with as much vigor as the museum persuades us of our enclosure in a collective tradition.

In the final analysis, narrative fiction achieves the dissemination of a version of aesthetic experience throughout the entire social fabric. The last limitation on this paradigm's generalization – literacy – having been overcome by the cinema, the entire population can be formed by example and convoked into finding their places in society. Movies may not seem part of high Culture, but they hail most of us into interpretive initiative with more insistence than Dutch landscapes – and they hail far more of us as well. The fact that they do not demand that one talk about them (although nearly everyone does, to some degree) may appear to be a dilution of the Cultural program Schiller had in mind, but it is a logical and necessary step in the universalization of cultural logic. As Matthew Arnold conceded, unless "free creative activity" could be linked to activities other than making great works of art, it could not possibly be advanced as a the "highest function of man," since that would disqualify the greater part of humanity from fulfillment.[79]

The imposition of the aesthetic as a general ideology of human conduct and a means for determining eligibility to govern, required its preliminary debasement: it had to be made accessible to a wide range of people, activities, and localities, and linked to a more general program of identity formation and social triage. This was the goal of the museum and the achievement of the novel.

4

Culture, Critique, and Community

In the modern era the ways of imagining the social economy that I have been charting finally coalesce in the term "culture," which becomes an explicit category of appeal that can be invoked not just as a way of thinking about individual and society, but as a principle of identity and analysis, a moral and political value as well as a commercial one – and this by a wide range of constituencies: the state and its educational apparatuses, the new social scientific disciplines, the bourgeois intelligentsia, the various artistic and commercial enterprises of the "art world," political parties left and right, the vast ensemble of technologies and industries we call the "media," and, increasingly, by a bewildering array of subcommunities and dissident forms of self-assertion, as well as those who wish to monitor or expunge them.

There are no doubt political and economic reasons why the processes under consideration should become explicit and pervasive in the nineteenth century. Industrialization, with its corrosive effect on traditional rural economies and its need for a generally literate, highly mobile and relatively malleable population, made materially manifest the economic imbrication of the individual within a system endowed with an agency and logic of its own. By the time "culture" gives a name to the authority of systematic practice, the power of the nascent capitalist world-economy has been making itself felt for two centuries.[1] At the same time, the French and American revolutions made abundantly apparent the extent to which material, social, and political reality could be directly shaped through shared discourse. The Revolutionaries' self-conscious, deliberate, and highly publicized debates on how to "make" history by articulating a radically new culture – and cultivating a new citizen – made it difficult to escape a sense of reality as genuinely historical, as the product of human endeavor unfolding within a system of consciously negotiated rules and historically accumulating habits.

The intensification and spread of public discourse was in turn accelerated by the development of cheap paper and the industrialization of the print economy. The mass press and popular literature of the nineteenth century constructed a synchronous collective consciousness unparalleled in earlier times; but they are dwarfed by the modern era's use of voice and image in radio, film, popular music, and television to fashion values even in the absence of literacy. The internet is the most dramatically "systematic" of these new media: it allows one to fabricate an identity, affective as well as economic, political, and social, through engagement with a discursive system that is purely systematic in that it substitutes involvement with protocols, disembodied discourse, and standardized iconic representations for encounters and exchanges with people and objects in the material world.

Whatever the reasons for its appearance, culture's emergence as a category of concern in the nineteenth century confirms that its mechanisms and authority had become foregone conclusions. Just as the early modern preoccupation with customary practice, or the eighteenth-century obsession with prejudice and public opinion, reflected an apprehension with respect to economies of authority that were perceived to regulate human freedom, so too the modern concern with culture and Culture testifies to their preponderance in our imaginations as systems that determine our identity.

The most telling evidence of such apprehension can be found in the programmatic simplifications of culture which are deployed as a means of bringing its slippery dialectic under control. For no sooner is culture theorized as a dialectic between individual discursive initiative and the law of collective practice, than attempts to reformulate it in more manageable terms begin to proliferate. We are familiar with the two dominant strategies in this trend, for they give rise to the two divergent (reductive) concepts of culture that continue to resonate in our usage today: the idea of "high" Culture and the anthropological concept of culture.

Getting a Handle on Culture

One way of gaining control over culture is to construe it as a voluntary activity: a program of reflective analytic inquiry undertaken by individuals in an effort to overcome their baser inclinations and attain truth, social harmony, and self-satisfaction. As we have seen, this idea appears already in the late eighteenth century in the writings of authors such as Schiller and Fichte, but it is most frequently identified in Anglo-Saxon thought with Matthew Arnold's 1869 *Culture and Anarchy*. For Arnold, in a celebrated formulation, Culture consists in the "pursuit of our total perfection by means of getting to know, on all the matters which most concern us, the best which has been thought and said in the world."[2]

While this concept retains much of the Enlightenment notion of getting beyond prejudice and habit through critique – Arnold goes on to mention that it is designed to turn "a stream of fresh and free thought upon our stock notions and habits, which we now follow staunchly but mechanically, vainly imagining that there is a virtue in following them staunchly which makes up for the mischief of following them mechanically" – its predication of an absolute pre-existing "best which has been thought and said in the world" dissociates the efforts of the individual from the actual production of change. Culture becomes a reaffirmation of what has already been said, the cultivated person the custodian and transmitter of universal values. Correlatively, those values are located by this formulation in a set of canonic artifacts, the professional administration of which is conferred upon that expanded division of the academy loosely associated with the humanistic studies, with the new discipline of literary study taking a preeminent role.[3]

An even more radical severing of the dialectical production of cultural law from its statutory force can be found in the social scientific definition of culture as a structure of relations, practices, values, and beliefs. This anthropological concept of culture finds incipient formulation in the writings of Helvétius, Montesquieu, Herder and Rousseau, but its most celebrated inaugural formulation is generally attributed to Edward Tylor. In the opening lines of his 1871 *Primitive Culture*, he defined culture as an overarching structure of practices: the "knowledge, belief, art, morals, law, custom, and any other capabilities and habits acquired by man as a member of society."[4] This definition sees culture not as a process of individual, or even collective, self-improvement, but as a structure that exists and can be understood independently of the individual acts that precipitate it. The Revolutionary notion of public opinion, by contrast, was expressly understood to be not only the product of, but constantly vulnerable to, individual discursive initiatives.

Like the Arnoldian formulation, Tylor's approach separates the rules of society from the processes of their formation, although it is an historical self-evidence of a sort that the idea of culture as an impersonal system of practices should arise in conjunction with the cult of the individual; for the idea of individual personality only makes sense against the backdrop of a set of normative practices against which individuals define themselves. It is thus not surprising that in novels of the period the two notions are frequently reciprocal: protagonists typically confirm their mastery over the social world by mapping it into codes – one thinks of Balzac's characters, or Stendhal's, for instance.

The social scientific structure of culture is more formidable and frightening than precursor notions such as custom, since it encompasses virtually all the components of social life, which, as Lionel Trilling notes, "are connected in secret as well as overt ways with the practical arrangements of a society and which, because they are not brought to consciousness, are unopposed in their influence over men's minds."[5] Still, by reducing culture to an analyzable structure, the social scientist can bring it within the purview of knowledge and eventual control. Laying bare the rules we have unconsciously internalized can free us from culture's tyranny. This was the plan of one of the precursors of sociology, Auguste Comte, who thought his work could free society from the shackles of unconscious habit by "directing the complete regeneration of our ideas and mores," and the same logic resonates nearly a century later in Emile Durkheim's objective "to extend scientific rationalism to human behavior, by showing that past behavior can be reduced to relationships of cause and effect and then transformed, by an equally logical operation, into rules of action for the future."[6] Like high Culture, social science aims to enlighten, but rather than guiding the individuals whose behavior deposits practice, it seeks to understand that practice as a structure within which social being is formed.

The purest version of this analytic impulse is found in ethnography, which also outlines a particular methodology for securing knowledge about such structures. As with Arnold, ethnography retains from the dialectical logic of culture a commitment to the critique of one's own culture, but it performs this critique indirectly, through the implicit comparison with another society. Like all enactments of cultural logic, ethnography "includes, minimally, translating experience into textual forms."[7] However, rather than articulating cultural law as a dialectic between the normative and the particular, or the present and the past, ethnography finds it in the difference of one society from another.

The ethnographer scrutinizes an *other* culture from the position of a privileged outsider who is not a member of the community under observation and thus is partially exempted from its practices. James Clifford characterizes the method as "a continuous tacking between the 'inside' and 'outside' of events; on the one hand grasping the sense of specific occurrences and gestures empathetically, on the other stepping back to situate these meanings in wider contexts."[8] The ethnographer is like the individual engaged in Cultural critique in that his or her authority is secured by experience in the culture under study: not only familiarity with the language and customs, but actual residence and life within its framework of practices.[9] However, that immersion is never complete: though ethnographers in the field are in a sense immersed in the culture they describe, they remain exempt from its laws. Their position – reminiscent of the journalist or novelist – is that of an observer whose neutrality is guaranteed by the impersonal protocols of scientific analysis. All of the variations on classic "participant observation" ethnography which Clifford describes assume that one achieves a grasp on the authority of a culture only to the extent one can avoid or extract oneself from the position of the monological subject enmeshed within it.[10] Ethnographic writing in this sense might be thought of as an intersocial variation on the cultural logic of historical self-awareness: it extracts itself from its own unconscious social reflexes, but does so by moving outside of them, rather than looking back at them in time. Ethnography acquires a perspective on its own culture by getting partially inside another.

This is just one variation of the more general social scientific strategy of hypostatizing the dialectic of culture in regular structures and processes. Interestingly though, this strategy becomes incorporated into the dialectic it wants to arrest, since over time the social scientific protocols of inquiry aggravate and intensify the processes of historical change which their taxonomic logic annuls. For as social science has refined and redoubled its efforts to understand and optimize social practice, it has spawned a proliferation of further structures, laws, categories, and forms of practice, all of which themselves complicate the fabric under scrutiny – and need to be analyzed and managed. From macroeconomics to cultural capital and gender theory, each new concept or economy of transactions found lurking under reflexive practice requires a further theory, a new domain of expertise and a professional bureaucracy for its deployment. Contrary to what one might expect – and to the logic behind many research grants – the tabulation and systematization of social practice does not reduce its complexity or make its production more predictable; rather it triggers a proliferation of more social forms in need of monitoring and management. Beneath its promise of statistical certainty and closure, social science, like the humanities, opens on to an infinite economy of historical production.

Still, the social sciences differ from the aesthetic-critical disciplines in that, as their name implies, they purport, like the natural sciences, to study phenomena that largely preexist and function independently of their structures of cognition. Rather than leveraging their investigations into a claim of autonomy or absolute (aesthetic) value, they propose an analytic program that exonerates them from responsibility for the current state of affairs but implicates them for the future. Aesthetic interpretation, conversely, encourages us to think we have a role in the articulation of our society's *legacy*, but not that we can effect material practice in the present. Social science proposes no absolute values, but impels those who claim to understand social practice to assume responsibility for its future shape. Precisely because economists claim to understand the laws of economics, we look to them to ensure a healthy economy through the "policies" they propose to our governments. We do not blame psychologists for the traumas they posit to exist, but we expect them to provide "therapy" for the people they determine are so afflicted.

If the social scientific attempt to catalogue the forms of culture only propagates more cultural forms, the high Cultural strategy of maintaining cultural values triggers, for its part, a proliferation of new value formations. By identifying culture with a relatively stable set of special objects and procedures of aesthetic judgment, high Culture as Arnold conceived of it aimed to stabilize society by identifying enduring values and reinvigorating society with their truths. But aesthetic interpretation cannot insure the transmission of particular values or meanings. This may have been difficult to understand at the time of Matthew Arnold, when the discipline of literary studies was in its infancy and the canon seemed a self-evident thing, but a century and a half of tradition have shown us that both the works making up the canon and the meanings attributed to them are continually shifting.

Training students to identify and explicate the universal values embedded in great works may sound like a conservative program on the face of it; but the demand of originality and significance (as in "a significant and original contribution to the scholarship on . . .") gives the lie to that belief. Literary study demands change and revision as much as continuity, and the persistent imperative lurking behind it – as behind all other Cultural endeavors – to reassess received values and assumptions, disqualifies it from the univocal conservative function it is often assumed to serve. Aesthetic value is born of the individual aesthetic experience, in the moment of sublation that Schiller theorized as the achievement of full subjectivity; this moment is not consonant with the simple transmission of doctrine. We all know this intuitively: who thinks of artists or literature students as models of conformity?

Of course within the larger dialectic of culture the canon functions to certify and give material substance to the history and legacy of the community. But the ethic of self-cultivation does not merely transmit or reaffirm that legacy: it continually subjects it to critique. There are, as we shall see, many other objects and transactions that construct identity in a similar manner. The thousands of pilgrims that flock every day to get a glimpse of the (heavily restored) Mona Lisa behind its Plexiglas barrier are achieving a goal in their mind, but their sense of themselves and of their relationship to tradition and practice is probably more acute during the thirty seconds they are negotiating the purchase of their ticket in a foreign language. Conversely, those people who stand and converse reflectively for twenty minutes in front of an etching by Rembrandt could find something to reflect upon at Disneyland as well. If people familiar with the canon enact the processes of self-realization with more complexity than some of their peers, this only proves that high Culture is an effective motor of social triage, as we discussed in the previous chapter. It does not make it a uniquely privileged instrument for inculcating specific values, as it is frequently assumed to be.

This is not to downplay the necessity within a society for a common set of cultural reference points similar to what E. D. Hirsch argued for in *Cultural Literacy*, but merely to point out that the processes of self-realization involved in the dialectic of culture act themselves out with respect to a broad range of practices and continually expand the set of objects which they treat as aesthetic.[11] The canon is as much a process of value formation as a fixed body of masterpieces; it is in its production that Culture occurs.

We see the political correlate of this splitting of culture into two reductive versions – the high Cultural and the anthropological – in the antagonism between liberalism and communitarianism that has structured modernity. The primacy of the social scientific cultural matrix resonates in the communitarian idea that individual subjects find the resources for their identity in the history, tradition, values, and practices of the culture into which they are born. Conversely, for the liberal this cultural matrix is not only not primordial in the formation of political, social, and economic subjectivity, it can actually hamper that development by constraining the individual's free pursuit of self-expression – much as the Revolutionaries saw ancien régime prejudices thwarting the development of the free citizen.[12] From this perspective, equal rights for all can only be assured if justice is conceptualized and institutionalized independently of the notions of the good which specific cultures may uphold.

The paradox of this ideological schism lies in the fact that the so-called communitarians' insistence on the primacy of the cultural matrix leads them to militate not for a communitarian political system, but rather for one that respects the particular cultural identities of all the diverse constituencies of today's multicultural society. Conversely, liberalism's insistence on individual choice is necessarily grounded in a belief in universal principles and values, since only such principles could frame a truly impartial political and economic order.

This partition of culture into two distinct and distinctly different concepts has been attributed to particular social and material conditions in nineteenth-century Britain, such as growing economic specialization or the Victorian fear of uncontained desire.[13] However, from the perspective of this study these are simply two inaugural instances of a long history of attempts to reduce culture's dialectic into more ideologically docile forms. Both are born of the perception that one's life and identity are ineluctably mediated by shared forms and the consequent felt need to overcome that mediation – to get beyond culture's grip by arresting its mechanism in a structure (the anthropological strategy) or making it a function of deliberate value formation (the aesthetic ethic).

It is important to understand that such endeavors do not run counter to culture's operations, but are rather inscribed within its logic. This is something the Revolutionaries and Rousseau knew: by making the mechanisms of cultural determination explicit, they instigated the compulsion in their subjects to overcome its strictures, or at least to understand them.

This is perhaps the most self-evident, yet also the most subtle and paradoxical dimension of cultural logic. The more oppressively culture weighs on us and the more acutely we feel its effects, the greater our initiative to bring it under control through intensified regimes of assessment, theorization, and self-awareness. The more elaborate these reactions become, the greater their precipitate of further cultural forms to be excavated and appraised. The analysis of culture renders its imperatives and values explicit and implants them in our consciousness, even as it deposits new forms of individual and collective practice (those deployed in the analysis of culture) and new forms of identity.

The motor of this process lies in the practice of critique which cultural logic instills in us as an ethical imperative. Critique is a way of resisting the habits of practice, but it also embeds us more deeply in the logic of culture, both by increasing our respect for systematic rules and increasing our commitment to self-perfection through understanding. Using the personifying language we so frequently employ when talking about behaviors we take for granted, we might say that culture insinuates and perpetuates itself by challenging us to resist it. By this very token, however, "it" is neither a permanent structure nor just a process of understanding, but rather a law of being that hovers, like the word "being" itself, between identity and change, permanence and becoming.

Culture as Critique

What all of the diverse parties invoking culture over the past two centuries have in common, whether they see culture as an oppressive strategy of the hegemony, as the reservoir of law and order, as the site of absolute value, or simply as the ground of social truth, and whatever their apparent strategies for getting a grip on its machinery, is a fundamental commitment to the value of critique. They all assume that by turning their analytic gaze on collective practice and exposing its implicit assumptions and semiotic mechanisms, they can secure an augmented control over their identity and destiny. We might call this the tacit ideology of cultural logic: it is the script behind all of our various construals of culture, and it is a script that implies us as its actors: to the extent that we take our distance from our world and habits of thought, we accede to the higher ethical community of the "cultured."

If it seems disputable that we share this universal belief in critique, it is simply because we prefer to see those opposing our views as lacking just such distance. For the Left, conservative advocates of tradition are by definition unwilling to question their received values. For the Right, the same unwillingness to question received doctrine is exactly what characterizes the Left's dogmatism. But the fact that we all disparage those unwilling to question their habits of thought testifies to a universal commitment to critique, just as does, from another perspective, the distaste with which most writers on culture consider the present: whether they are lamenting the loss of tradition or calling for its overthrow, they all concur that the present situation is compromised.

The practice of critique to which we are all tacitly committed does not inhere in particular institutions or objects, but in the interrogation of current assumptions. Rather than a body of set values it bespeaks a process of endless revision and improvement; and it encompasses all people, not just those conversant with a canon. It is an economy of continual production that has as its end no definitive structure, no precise set of values, no single class or universal truth, but rather and only the dissemination of its own logic, which by entangling us ever more deeply in self-awareness, drives a process of social coalescence and global convergence.

Although it is easy to assert the primacy of critique as such, it is more difficult to illustrate, since critique always manifests itself within, and thus risks becoming confused with, particulars. Just as the social scientific study of social practice necessarily elaborates itself around and within some specific society, so too the deployment of critique is always directed at and imbricated in a particular cultural formation. The difference between the general ethic of critique that is intrinsic to the logic of culture and the specific works of cultural critique which draw on that logic is analogous to the difference between the structure of the museum, which specifies that its exhibits have meaning and incites us to determine that meaning, and the message of a particular exhibition or show, which constructs a definite reading of a particular period, artist, genre, and induces us to sanction it.

And just as the assignment of a specific meaning to a work of art in one sense goes against its nature *as* work of art, so too, the historical judgments leveled at the behest of critique inevitably compromise its commitment to continual change by settling for a particular, historically situated, ideologically inflected conclusion. Such reductions are inevitable moments in the dialectic of culture, however, since they furnish the backdrop of received assumptions against which future critical disclosures can elaborate themselves.

Nineteenth-century Britain, for instance, reduced culture to a principle of order to which one could appeal in opposition to an impending sense of social disarray. This occurred in the terms of the anthropological notion of culture as a complex whole grammar, but also in the terms of high Cultural pursuits. With respect to the former case, Christopher Herbert has shown how, intent on limiting the unbounded desire they saw menacing human society, the Victorians found in the anthropological notion of culture a countervailing principle of social restraint.[14] With respect to the latter, Arnold's *Culture and Anarchy* is exemplary. It proposes the universal pursuit of knowledge, beauty and "right reason" as "a principle of authority, to counteract the tendency to anarchy" which Arnold saw looming in the rampant assertion of personal liberty.[15]

In the early twentieth century, one appeals to Culture as a countervailing principle of distinction and a natural mechanism of social stratification. The threat here, as expressed for instance in José Ortega y Gasset's 1929 polemic *The Revolt of the Masses*, or F. R. Leavis's 1930 *Mass Civilization and Minority Culture*, is the loss of discrimination and tradition, and hence of value, brought about by the growing political dominance of the masses and the dissolving effect of mass culture.[16] What the Cultured minority provide for Leavis is nothing less than discriminating capabilities necessary to progress; they are "the consciousness of the race" that insures society has the "power of profiting by the finest human experience of the past."[17] But it is also clear that part of the value of Culture lies in the natural social stratification this exaltation of a particular sensibility and practice brings.

T. S. Eliot, writing in 1948, will underscore this role of Culture in creating different classes, which he sees as both natural and positive, since "class and region, by dividing the inhabitants of a country into two different kinds of groups, lead to a conflict favourable to creativeness and progress."[18] However, by the late fifties, the attributes of Culture will have changed again, as its implicit linkage to dominant traditions becomes a subject of dispute. In this period, as Lionel Trilling would note, the class formerly assumed to be the custodians of Culture increasingly promote an antagonistic or adversarial stance towards its effects, explicitly dissociating the ethic of historical critique from the body of traditions and values that have grown up around it in the past century.[19] History, more than ever in the post-war world of international capitalism, becomes something to resist, and to the extent Culture is reduced to a body of traditions that perpetuates past practice, it is itself brought into question. At the same time, and in reaction to this move, a conservative ideology appeals to Culture precisely in the name of those traditions and the force of social order they represent.

These two postures persist in an intensified form in the present day along the doubled axes of domination/subordination and tradition/critique. The self-conscious assertion of values that is demonized as the dominant class's principle weapon of oppression is exalted as a strategy of resistance for dominated minorities. Reiterating the gesture we identified at the origins of cultural logic, people today – majorities as well as minorities – establish their identity more than ever by appropriating to their own ends the economy of authority that intimidates them. Acknowledging the contingency of their identity on collective practice, they make the elaboration of their own counter-practice an ongoing priority, selectively appropriating its components from competing cultures. Identity has become a self-conscious construct of intersocial *bricolage*, culture a global menu of practices within which the self can scavenge, Culture the constant assimilation of new elements into one's "own" properties and a new collective practice.

That culture should lend itself to so many ideologically charged projects is a natural correlate of its assumptions: to the extent it associates the production of history with human initiative, it invites and authorizes the identification of history with a *particular* initiative. One meaning of ideology is that of a naturalizing discourse that disavows the self-interest of particular historical determinations by identifying them with natural processes of human development. Ideology in this sense found an invaluable tool in the idea of culture (it is probably no coincidence that the two terms emerged in roughly the same period). Calling something "cultural" was – and is – a way of asserting its widespread acceptance and gradual genesis as a natural way of life, and denying its subordination to any single historical incident or narrow interest. After all, whatever our attitudes towards culture, we intuitively think of it as the precipitate of time and shared practice – not the triumph of the moment or the will of the individual. Culture's rule has been ratified by tradition. This makes it irresistible to those intent on justifying specific practices: identified with culture, any project takes on the patent of history and consecrated practice. Culture can thus become a fearsome weapon as well as a path of redemption.

The myriad ideological reductions to which "culture" is subject have been analyzed extensively, first in Raymond Williams's classic *Culture and Society*, and subsequently in a number of excellent studies focusing primarily on the Anglo-Saxon world.[20] These accounts, which it is beyond the scope of this essay to examine in their specifics, typically assign the divergent dimensions of culture to different parties and moments, recuperating in a drama of historical succession or a structure of opposition the closure and wholeness, the full values and immediate feelings with which the dialectic as such can never rest. Precisely because such accounts are committed to specific agendas, no single one of them can convey the constant that frames all expressions of social history, and which I would locate in the imperative of critique.

In the sense of a universal ethic that I am proposing here, critique can neither be reduced to the particulars of material history nor to the disdain for that history with which Culture is frequently reproached. Critique specifies rather an ongoing interrogation of particulars that refuses to settle for any definitive conclusion. Uncovering and analyzing specific practices, testing and contesting its own assumptions, critique always leaves new ones in its wake. Its exposure of cultural rules spawns more cultural rules, the validity of which we are committed to in advance by virtue of having articulated them. Whatever new position it carves out (which from a future point will of course turn out to be itself embedded in assumptions from which it needs to be rescued), that position will always seem to be both the product of individual initiative and the revelation of a social law. The result of critique is thus a greater belief in the law of shared practice *and* in our agency in its production.

One can understand how this works by examining the way critique simultaneously operates historical continuity and change. To this end, it is useful to break it down into stages or moments.

The first move in freeing us from social reflexes is to bring them to the fore and clarify their law. However, this also brings those reflexes into existence for others who may not have been aware of them; and it endows them with the authority of fact. Raising unconscious habits to the level of consciousness within a community makes them available for judgment and displacement, but it also consolidates them as a structure of history in our minds. This is why even the most willfully subversive critique never succeeds in disrupting the continuity of history or the production of culture: to rigorously contest dominant practices one must first make their dominance apparent, endowing them

with a consistency and authority that justifies their subversion –
but also bestows upon them the aura of historical inevitability,
making them a place through which all must pass.

Still, even as this process consolidates the law as history, it
transforms that law into an object of our analytic judgment,
thereby loosening its hold on us. Critique transforms practice
from being the framework of our knowledge to being its object.
Once subject to our critical scrutiny, our habits are opened to
revision. This is the emancipatory effect of Culture. Having
become aware of the things we do, we can no longer do them
unthinkingly.

At a third level, however, the analytic work that makes the
laws of practice available for conscious assessment always precipitates further cultural formations, both in its revelations or
conclusions and in the values and principles of inquiry upon
which it relies. The latter are left in its wake as new habits of
procedure. The former are foregrounded and invested with the
aura of truth that rectifications of error always enjoy. In fact, they
are doubly persuasive, partaking both of the heightened awareness of historical perspective and of the patent of self-evidence
which they acquire by virtue of being *our* conclusions. Whether
or not the disclosures of critique are more rational than the habits
they displace, they are always more compelling. This is why
Culture is so effective at folding us into the law: it makes both
the laws of history we uncover through our critical analysis and
the more rational practices we put in their place seem to be the
consequence of our initiative, an expression of our convictions.
Critique recruits us into expressing social law as *our* conclusion.

Yet, critique also has the long-term effect of reinforcing the
impersonal authority of shared practice. Whether or not it displaces or neutralizes any particular habits or values, it always
foregrounds the prestige and authority of social practice in general
as a law to be reckoned with. The more attention we focus on the
critical annulment of a particular practice, the greater our awareness of the enduring primacy of collective practice in general. We
can sense this augmentation in the steadily increasing prestige of
"culture," as a foundational category in the modern era. If we
now assume it to be the very ground of identity, that is because
we have been in the grip of its ethic for so long.

This dialectic of annulment and reinstatement affords us the sensation of autonomy even as it reveals the systematicity of truth, since it makes the disclosure of the overarching system the confirmation of our successful analysis. At the same time, the logic of culture insulates us from the stasis of closure, since we know that however vigorously we defend them, our conclusions are always provisional: the procedures we unconsciously adopt to lay bare our habits will always deposit more "laws" which will require scrutiny and historicization, lest they too degenerate into unexamined habit and prejudice. The logic of culture thus commits us to a project of critical analysis that prolongs itself into the future as the attempt to comprehend its own (past) practice.

As a process of social self-awareness and historical understanding, Culture-as-critique no longer belongs to a single class, group, or historical moment. Rather, it has become the primary framework by means of which a broad range of societies can conceptualize class formations, communities, and social behavior as historical phenomena subject to modification. It demands not that one adopt a particular set of national values or unvarying principles, but, on the contrary, that one continually interrogate traditions, habits, and social laws – that one call into question precisely that which goes without saying.

Of course one can argue that this demand itself derives from a cultural formation serving particular interests, as indeed do all ethical imperatives. What makes the Cultural imperative of critique different, and gives it its ethical appeal, is that it acknowledges the unavoidability of partiality and local interest – even its own – and demands that we strive to expose and move beyond it. Its only unvarying doctrine is that we accept no unvarying doctrine; which is perhaps why the people most committed to Culture devote so much of their energy to attacking its foundations.

There are several logical correlates to the notion of Culture as an ethic of critique that I am advancing. The most obvious, perhaps, is that culture is not a property: nothing is *a priori* cultural or noncultural. Any object can become a cultural object by being identified as having meaning and force of rule within a particular community – as being a sign of collective practice. To claim that some things are inherently cultural (or not) is to invert the logic of culture: things enter the realm of culture when they are understood to have a significance or value for members of the community above and beyond their material incarnations. I believe Terry Eagleton somewhere uses drainpipes as an example of things that are not Cultural, but drainpipes can be as Cultural as poetry if they are singled out self-consciously by the members of a community as significant expressions of their affiliation to a body of values and practices – as is indeed the case in my part of the world, where people proudly display signs on the front of their houses saying "I have disconnected my down spouts" (to avoid overloading the sewers with rainwater) as a badge of ecological enlightenment.

By the same logic, the redemptive patent of Culture cannot be assimilated to a particular class or institution. While the deliberate enactment of that ethic – which I have been designating with an uppercase – has frequently relied on the arts, there is no *a priori* reason why the same process cannot be located in other domains, and be administered by different personnel. The classic justification for identifying the arts with Culture is that they express universal values, in the name of which Culture interpellates the individual. This may well be, but it neglects the fact that the arts can only do this when they have been identified *as* art by some other framing practices or discourses. Moreover, the values attributed to art are always *attributed* to it by historically situated non-artists, using propositional language. And these values are hardly universal or permanent; they vary markedly from generation to generation, as anyone following feminist studies or the New Historicism hardly needs to be told.

Art is an effective conduit for Culture in the modern era simply because Culture has designated it as such, much as Culture has spawned museums celebrating every conceivable form of practice, from lead mining (there are in fact *many* museums devoted to lead mining: in Wanlockhead and Dumfries, in Scotland, and in Joplin, Missouri, for instance) to being a stuntman (the Hollywood Stuntmen's Hall of Fame is in Moab, Utah). We can make any kind of object into a reservoir of cultural value, and if we have decided by convention that certain kinds of expression by definition call for the explicit interrogation of history and the specification of their meaning, it is merely because we require an identifiable pool of such objects for our ongoing cultural work. That decision is a correlate and consequence of Cultural logic, not its origin, as we can see in the fact that the Fine Arts and Literature were invented as special domains of ethical and cognitive recreation only after the Enlightenment. (Previously "literature" simply meant anything that had been written, from alchemical treatises or military histories to the lives of saints, and art had a far broader connotation, covering almost any form of human ingenuity.) Art and those who explain it are identified with Culture not because they embody specific values, but because they incite us to ascertain value ourselves, and guide us in that process.

Perhaps a more difficult point to accept is that Culture's ethical claim is not grounded in any particular content – although it necessarily finds expression in particular content and the values associated with it. Rather, it consists entirely in the practice of historical critique as such. Critique has moral value because it is a form of resistance to habit, a refusal to accept without question the practices that define one, seeking instead to assess the right way at every juncture. The roots of this ethic can be found in the forms of resistance to traditional church authority out of which cultural logic emerged: the Reformation and the New Science, but also the Enlightenment demonization of "prejudice." It persists and diversifies in the modern era, from F. R. Leavis's exhortation to resist mass culture in the 1920s, or Guy Debord's attempt to inflict damage on the society of spectacle in the 1960s, to postmodernism's infatuation with repudiating the traditions from which it derives its voice.

Simply put, critique's only enduring ethical claim is that it emancipates us from error. It locates identity and virtue in the acknowledgment of a flawed present – not in the identification of a precise future. The world it opens up to us will, one hopes, be free of our current delusions, but that can only occur if we maintain our distance from our assumptions. Selecting and pursuing a particular future will not get us there, precisely because it will not free us of our current prejudices and mistakes – but merely project them into the future.

The debates over Cultural programs in the French Revolution put this into relief. One reason they achieved consensus with respect to the *Muséum national* and the natural history collections of the Jardin des Plantes (which had no precedents and therefore were not easily linked to specific future results) but could not agree on the organization of national education was that in the latter's case, the future consequences of the various proposals were all too apparent. The repudiation of the past could engender consensus by pointing out the abuses to which previous practice had led; but when precise future results were specified, consensus tended to break down, as potentials for class domination became clearer. The critique of past practice necessarily evokes shared history and, in that minimal way at least, builds community. Imagining specific futures can draw more tightly together some members of the community, but it also risks excluding others. It is the moment when particular interests enter the scene – the political effect of culture that, flowing from the moment of critique, sets aside its feigned disinterest in material reality to specify a precise shape for change.

Another way of getting at this issue is to say that Cultural critique conceives of objectivity in terms of historical remove, not spatial. Contrary to ethnography, it specifies truth to derive from the scrutiny and critique of one's own habits, and not from the observation of others. The subject who critiques can only critique his or her own past, not that of others, for it is the very immersion within prejudice which guarantees our authority to describe it and makes its overcoming through an effort of historical critique so meritorious.

But can one achieve any kind of perspective on a culture from within it? For some, the loss of a transcendent position of universal value – precisely what ideologies of culture such as Arnold's promised, but which history has made difficult to believe in – makes cultural criticism impossible.[21] But cultural critique as such cannot come from the outside. It is grounded in the intimate acquaintance with a set of practices and the determination not to be determined by them, rather than in the assertion of an outsider's neutral perspective. *Criticism* can come from the outside, but it involves a different mode of authority, based on the appeal to universal or external values, rather than on the insider's natural understanding of his or her culture; it is further compromised by its determination by its own culture – which is why adjudication of conflicts between different cultures within a single society is so difficult.

From the perspective of critique, there is no point outside of culture – and Culture never promised to deliver one. Because our cultivation is a dialectical process, the critical power, as even Arnold acknowledged, is always necessarily provisional; it is historically and culturally embedded and all it can offer us is "an order of ideas, if not absolutely true, yet true by comparison with that which it displaces."[22] We can demonstrate our mastery over our reflexes of social practice only if they are *our* reflexes. This seems intuitively obvious for those who have internalized the logic of culture (most readers of this book): Andrew Sullivan's critique of the gay rights movement or Jesse Jackson's critique of the African American community carry an ethical charge that Jesse Helms's criticism cannot.

Still, the insiders' moral leverage hinges on their readiness to question the structures of identity grounding their authority. Which is why we see a strange dance between celebration or affirmation and dissent or repudiation in much contemporary cultural critique. For instance, the *mestiza* writer Gloria Anzaldúa does not hesitate to invoke the "indian women's tradition of resistance" in the cause of her very untraditional lesbianism, claiming her heritage even as she dissents from its strictures. If she feels she can do both, it is because she is so deeply embedded in her world: "I feel perfectly free to rebel and to rail against my culture. . . . because, unlike Chicanas and other women of color who grew up white or who have only recently returned to their native cultural roots, I was totally immersed in mine."[23]

This idea that the immersion in a tradition authorizes one to contest it would have seemed strange to a medieval Christian, but it has become nearly universal with the spread of the logic of culture. Indeed, as Lionel Trilling noted nearly thirty-five years ago, its propagation has become one of the central preoccupations of the modern academy. We are still very much caught up in the project of universalizing the logic of culture that so exercised the French Revolutionaries, but our emphasis has shifted from the inculcation of common values through analysis to the universalization of the practice of critique. The result is the proliferation of what Trilling aptly called the "adversarial" attitude toward culture.

Resisting Culture

Trilling identifies the adversarial attitude with modernity, but it would have been familiar to anyone in the late eighteenth century. It consists of trying to get beyond one's own environing culture, contesting its value and its grip:

> Any historian of the literature of the modern age will take virtually for granted the adversary intention, the actually subversive intention, that characterizes modern writing – he will perceive its clear purpose of detaching the reader from the habits of thought and feeling that the larger culture imposes, of giving him a ground and vantage point from which to judge and condemn, and perhaps revise, the culture that produced him.[24]

Resonant of the journalism we earlier encountered, this is an exemplary articulation of the imperative to critique – indeed, one could gloss the "adversarial attitude" as simply another way of designating the oppositional energy of critique. It describes not only the Revolutionary attempt to get beyond ancien régime values, but the vantage point from which Arnold spoke in 1869; and to the extent literature actually provokes this questioning, it performs exactly the reform which F. R. Leavis and Denys Thompson prescribed in 1959 as an antidote to the cultural impoverishment of the contemporary world: "we are committed to more consciousness; that way, if any, lies salvation. We cannot, as we might in a healthy state of culture, leave the citizen to be formed unconsciously by his environment; if anything like a worthy idea of satisfactory living is to be saved, he must be trained to discriminate and resist."[25]

It is worth dwelling on this exhortation briefly, and on the project of which it is a part. Like the Revolutionary journalists, Leavis and Thompson aim to reinvigorate the historical awareness of the people by training them to read the mass media critically – advertisements, especially. However, unlike the Revolutionaries, Leavis and Thompson can invoke Culture as an ethic. Two features of their program make it exemplary of such appeals. First, the authors theorize culture (as unconscious practice) in terms of a lost fullness for which only Culture (as conscious critique) can compensate. Second, their remedy reproduces and accelerates the very process of dispersion and dilution they seek to arrest. Leavis's and Thompson's language situates them squarely within the adversarial tradition that Trilling noticed. If "salvation" is needed, it is because we are in a post-lapsarian state with respect to an earlier age of richer culture. In their call to arms, Leavis and Thompson, like so many others, associate the culture that has been lost with the pre-industrial organic community and its rooted way of life.

In fact, *whenever* Culture (or culture) is invoked, absence or loss are never far behind. As a state of a society or an index of a general level of human development, culture is present mostly in its absence, most notable in its decline. This loss is typically figured in terms of a disintegration attributable to human intervention: the organic community whose passing Leavis attributes to mass culture and industrial modernity is lamented two hundred years earlier by Rousseau, who lays the demise of simplicity at the feet of culture and its vain obsession with refinement. Two hundred years before Rousseau, Bartolomé de las Casas and Alonso de Zorita lamented the passing of the Aztecs' way of life, at the hands of the Spaniards' missionary zeal.

For Matthew Arnold the idea of culture is similarly inseparable from that of decline and loss – that of the Western Classical tradition that was being overwhelmed by the philistine materialism of the British middle class. Remarkably, sixty years later, that tradition is still disappearing, when Leavis first voices his alarm in 1930 – and twenty years and one world war after that, when T. S. Eliot voices his. It is disappearing in Spain in the 1920s for Ortega y Gasset, in America in the 1960s for Lionel Trilling, and still disappearing in the 1980s, for Alan Bloom and E. D. Hirsch. In the 1990s its disappearance attains apocalyptic intensity in the writing of Robert Bork, even as, at the same time and most curiously, those dissident subcultures who *call* for its demise, protest their suffocation in its proliferating hegemonic folds.

Such recurrences suggest that the organic community's demise is less an historical phenomenon than a precipitate of an unchanging logic and analysis – and the anxiety it provokes. I would argue that the organic community is an ideal that gradually coalesces in conjunction with, and as the obverse of, the recognition that identity is culturally mediated. Like the coherent imago with which the infant in Lacan's mirror stage identifies and yearns to be, it is the vision of coherence and wholeness which the constitution of our identity in the *béance* of Culture, with its deferrals and displacements, precipitates. The fantasy of the whole life is a symptom of our yearning to overcome the mediations that we have come to understand construct us.

And, consistent with the logic we have inherited from our early modern forebearers, we seek the alleviation of our anxiety by appropriating the mechanism that inspires it. Acknowledging the supremacy of a system of authority is the first step in its disablement, since it allows us to have unlimited confidence in that system's economies when we appropriate them to our own ends. Thus the Revolutionaries' awe before the power of public opinion incited them to choose it as the foundation of their Republic. One could cite numerous instances of the same tactic today. Preoccupied with the power of discourse, Foucault constructs a new, powerful form of discourse; theorizing culture's mechanisms of interpellation, Cultural Studies interpellates subjects into its disablement.

However, these strategies in no way arrest the proliferation of cultural logic, much less set boundaries to the forms of practice it engenders. They simply, like all instances of critique, reconfigure the laws of collective practice as the products of our individual mentation, bringing us into the dialectic of culture. We can see this in Leavis's and Thompson's project.

To counteract the mediations of mass culture they propose their own therapeutic mediation. Like the Revolutionaries, they are unwilling to leave "the citizen to be formed unconsciously by his environment," helpless and bereft of the habits of critique. People "must be trained to discriminate and resist." Accordingly, they outline a program of critical exegesis which takes as its objective the demystification of the rhetoric of advertising. Prompting the student to ask questions such as " 'what response does the text want to evoke?'; 'What kind of persons can you imagine as responding to such an appeal as this last? What acquaintance would you expect them to have of Shakespeare's work and what capacity for appreciating it?' "; they guide the student toward identifying the public which different advertisements address and the strategies used to that end.[26]

Remarkably, this program accelerates exactly the process

Leavis and Thompson bemoan, by relocating the educational enterprise and the dialectic of identity formation away from an appreciation of the finer things, towards the engagement with mass culture. Its net effect is to demonstrate that a medium considered by people like themselves to be incapable of stimulating cultural critique – a medium that does not merely "give" the people what they want, as Leavis lamented in 1930, but "shows" them what they want, a medium that involves "surrender, under conditions of hypnotic receptivity, to the cheapest emotional appeals" – can in spite of its shortcomings provide an occasion for historical critique and ethical formation.[27] Far from reasserting the value of the canon, Leavis and Thompson expand and disperse it, by providing a new venue and mode of analysis for constructing identity. Henceforth, their students will not be limited to Shakespeare in the realization of their identity: they can choose instead to engage advertisements critically, scouring their rhetoric for signs of the social work they do, the subgroups they presuppose, the behaviors they promote.

What is at stake here is more than just the integrity of the canon. When Leavis and Thompson demonstrate that autonomy and identity can be nurtured in even as degraded a transaction as the advertisement, they confirm that Culture is fully compatible with the economic developments they decry. The products of the mass market are as viable as any other cultural form as an object of critique. In fact, they are in some senses better, since by their very ubiquity and vulgarity mass productions foster the resistance and self-distancing which cultural logic counts on: it is difficult *not* to acknowledge and take one's distance from commercial culture's crude mechanisms of consensus and taste formation.

By expanding the range of objects and situations in which ethical critique can take place, Leavis and Thompson not only prefigure the rise of "popular" culture as an object of serious study, they open the way to an expanded economy of community formation. In keeping with the imperative – consistent since the eighteenth century and no more so than today among those committed to resisting hegemonic Culture – of universalizing the logic of culture by involving *all* people and peoples in it, their program shows how identity can be won through the critique of material and economic forms as well as those of high Culture.

This is something Trilling seemed to intimate when he

remarked that as the adversarial ethic became more widespread and entrenched, it formed a new class of the enlightened that tended "to aggrandize and perpetuate itself" in much the same way as the dominant culture it opposed: "it generates its own assumptions and preconceptions, and contrives its own sanctions to protect them."[28] What this suggests is that critique leverages us out of history not so much at the level of discourse by disabling the structures of authority we contest – since we reaffirm their deeper logic in the gesture of critique itself – as at the level of material life, by incorporating new communities around topics of resistance.

It remains quite literally debatable whether we recover some measure of self-determination and control over history by appropriating the mechanism of authority that defines us and using it to grasp the specifics of our fabrication; or whether, as the more recent examples of the social sciences and Cultural Studies suggest, we simply accelerate the proliferation and penetration of culture's rule by attempting to master it. Whatever one concludes – and of course the whole point of Culture is that one is free to conclude whatever one wishes, provided one follows a few rules – there is one clear effect of all attempts to grasp culture: they foster community formation.

The Proliferation of "Cultures"

The process Trilling notices is one with which we are all familiar today, because it has penetrated into virtually all domains of social life, where it functions to secure identity for individuals and groups, and continually reconfigures the community in the process. In the preceding chapter I discussed in some detail how the novel and the museum, each in their way, allow their users to differentiate themselves according to their taste, modalities of reaction, and level of self-consciousness. To a significant extent, the same processes are invested by the "mass culture" which Leavis decried in 1930. As his own subsequent analysis suggests, even commodified forms such as the cinema, the popular romance, television, or advertising, can occasion critique and Cultural awareness. Of course the critique of commercial (and political and ideological) representation has been steadily growing ever since Roland Barthes's *Mythologies*. As the rapidly changing organization of literature departments attests, the pursuit and certification of Culture, even at the level of the Ph.D., need no longer involve the classics.

There is no reason to think that non-academics cannot use the materials of the mass media in similar ways or, more to the point, that the mass media do not stimulate in the broader public a similar enterprise of identity formation. One could, for instance, show how films such as *Silence of the Lambs* or *Titanic* build into their structure appeals to divergent constituencies – different tastes, classes, ideologies, gender politics – that are not necessarily reconcilable but allow the film to be "appropriated" by various publics and cultures in the terms of their own aspirations and values.

Such forms of "popular culture" function in much the same way as the more traditional institutions of social triage: they encourage people to sort themselves into categories and classes on the basis of their tastes and types of response. Those forms which invite aesthetic interpretation – the museum, literature, the cinema, music, the theater – are the most effective, since they induce us to speak and to become aware that when we do so we distribute ourselves into groups, if only through the expression of our tastes. But we also are increasingly encouraged to express our values and identity through all of the things on which we expend our money and time, whether those be material acquisitions such as clothes or intangibles such as travel. This kind of self-classification organizes the social body, even as it provides the individual with a simulacrum of freedom in the exercise of choice.

From the point of view of the state and society, the cost of this freedom is reduced control over the content and meaning of the lesson. The advantages, however, are multiple. First, the state – or in the contemporary context, the hemisphere or indeed the world – secures a certain uniformity of disposition and behavior without coercive intervention. Second, the enterprise of self-expression is melded into the economy. To the extent that this process has the potential of recruiting *everybody* into it at the level of material acquisitions, the economic inflection of the Cultural ethic insures a continual production and exchange of value. Third, this expanded model of identity formation induces a far wider range of people into forming their own laws: articulating norms and construing their identity in terms of those norms – to which they are necessarily committed in advance. This logic of self-inscription may not necessarily result in a homogeneous community, since many subgroups will coalesce around values and practices antithetical to those of the larger community, but it will imbue *all* the people with the habit of self-inscription, rather than just those who pursue formal education.

This way of stimulating identity formation seems paradoxical in that it constructs a coherent social body by universalizing the process of differentiation. But this is the logic of Culture in general, and it is even more apparent in the notion of education. People generally assume that pursuing a blatantly normalizing education will help them realize their individuality and discover their particular destiny. A diluted version of the same logic animates all of the less obviously Cultural undertakings through which we develop ourselves, from choral groups or continuing education courses, to hobbies, sports leagues, and ecotourism. All of these derive from and reinforce the assumption that mastering new practices, accumulating expertise, and engaging in collective rule-bound activities will both help us express our individuality and procure us membership in a subcommunity.

This logic of self-realization has colonized the entire social body and all of its practices. It encourages us to elaborate our identity by elaborating shared codes of practice with other like-minded individuals, forming subcultures that assert their difference from the more general framing culture by countering, contesting, or simply extending the boundaries of the latter. Subcultures accomplish this in the same way Culture does: by elaborating new forms of aesthetic expression, identifying a patrimony, inventing new forms of speech and dress, and codifying new rituals of self-affirmation, all of which are made available to members of the subculture as their own distinctive legacy. Subcultures are born of the desire to construct a distinctive identity, to be different within a range of sameness, but they are all governed by and reproduce the deeper logic and protocols of Culture. They specify their origins in certain historical conjunctions, select the objects that will be part of the sacred legacy, collect and enshrine these in special places, and invite adherents to participate in the ongoing definition and assessment of the community's heritage and values by engaging in informed, discipline-bound historical reconstructions or interpretations of its history and sacred objects.

The classic symbol of American culture, baseball, furnishes a straightforward example of all these practices. It has a rich and well-documented history, dramatized and consecrated by a critically acclaimed documentary; a museum; a Hall of Fame and procedures for induction; a hierarchy of officers; extensive records of past games; standardized protocols of statistical assessment for comparing careers; a rich collection of heraldic paraphernalia (pennants, caps, colors, mascots); commodified tokens of affiliation, such as autographed baseballs, baseball cards, World Series programs, and so forth; and complex, locally variable grammars of behavior, governing the comportment of players (who wear mustaches and spit copiously) and spectators (who reverse their hats at key moments, rise and sit at particular junctures, consume particular foods, emit collective sounds). And, like all professional sports, baseball insures that critique remains firmly at the center of its structure, by articulating itself in terms of past history and the endless process of retrospective assessment and self-positioning.

What is interesting is that people feel their participation in such rituals (which some would see as mass narcotization) as confirmation of their particularity. They are of course no different in this than readers of this book, most of whom are either deeply embedded in, or attempting to insert themselves into, a "culture" of ritualized practices that similarly holds forth the promise of individual distinction – and steady employment. Some people (increasingly fewer these days) believe that being an ardent Cubs fan and having memorized the statistics of every player for the past twenty years is less likely to procure a sense of status than getting a Ph.D. in English, but at one level the endeavors are quite similar in their logic and objectives: they seek distinction in the mastery of rules and the construction of historical awareness, and they express identity in the ritualized display of expertise.

The Cultured, popular and otherwise, are united by their belief in originality; they find a common ground in their espousal of distinction. What binds us together at the national, and increasingly at the international, level, is our shared commitment to individual self-realization and our belief that this ideal is most easily achieved through competitive involvement in highly formalized, rule-bound practices – practices which by that token are necessarily normative and impersonal. In fact, the more formalized, impersonal, and complex the rules, the greater the sense of individual distinction their mastery affords, since as the deposit of a history of collective practice, rather than of the actions of a single agent or interested party, they are less likely to detract from the sense of autonomous self-expression they afford. The limiting end of this spectrum is occupied by natural language, the confident and original use of which, in rap as in politics, secures prestige and fortune, but it is also exemplified in the concept of the game, which is defined by its pure formality, the explicitness of its rules, and their rigorous impersonality.

I have purposely chosen an extreme example of subcultural formation in baseball to underscore that even the most anodyne mass forms of leisure subscribe to and continually reiterate the deep grammar of Culture. Obviously, one could find similar components of systematic differentiation and identity construction in more properly "cultural" formations: religious or ethnic communities, political organizations, regional groups, educational institutions, or even professions. That the paradigm has penetrated and aligned itself with even the most commodified forms of recreation illustrates the extent to which, in our commitment to differentiation as a principle of identity, we are all indentured to a similar underlying framework of assumptions. The effect of this commitment is a social homogeneity that is grounded in a uniform cultivation of difference. Like Culture, subcultures integrate us into the normative. Their dogged pursuit of distinction aligns them with each other and with the larger community – increasingly a global community – that is secured by and grounded in this logic.

The global penetration of this paradigm, as evident in postcolonial theory as in French rap music, is inseparable from its economic dimensions.

The Culture of Commodity

If sports, rock music, rap, and skateboarding perform a version of the same work of cultural coalescence and individuation as do the opera and the museum, they are also more blatantly and intimately linked to the processes of free-market capitalism. They generate vast amounts of wealth, most of which, as ever, will accrue to the property owners (although the property in question can include one's perfectly tuned body or the resolutely anti-bourgeois rap song). And they clearly disseminate their own regimes of discipline, their own ideologies of aspiration that recruit and enclose the subject in a teleology of permanently deferred self-realization (ask any Cubs fan). For some, "popular" culture does not qualify as Culture at all, precisely because it is not conscientious enough in disavowing its economic interest. However it typically compensates for this lapse of protocol by its more consistent repudiation of the state's (and bourgeois society's) norms: the ritual desecration of established values by grunge and rap, or the extravagantly differential forms of appearance and address adopted by skateboarders, sports fans and advocates of body piercing, stand as parodic reductions of the ethic of critique.

Because most penetrating analyses of Culture have been Marxist, we are accustomed to understanding the processes at issue here as the consequences of an economic system and material history, rather than what enables it. (Although Althusser provides a partial corrective to this assumption by showing that the ideological state apparatuses of Culture are necessary to the production of the means of production – the mind sets of the compliant worker.) However, from the perspective of this analysis it is apparent that the mobile, adaptable, self-enrolling, alienated, pseudo-autonomous subject upon which capitalism depends cannot be envisioned or produced in the absence of cultural logic. It is no coincidence that the accelerating globalization of the open market has occurred in conjunction with the dissemination to the developing world of the logic of systematic identity formation – or that that logic was, and is, purveyed by the Cultural institutions of the developed countries. It is also no coincidence that many of these developing countries increasingly turn to fundamentalist religious belief as a form of resistance to globalization. With its depreciation of individual inquiry in favor of faith, religion is one of the few forms of modern consciousness that is resistant to colonization by the logic of culture.

That the pervasive subcultural genre of identity acquisition has become linked to material acquisition and the market is clear. Indeed, that is what allows it to penetrate different societies throughout the world and endow identity with the portability that the world's increasingly mobile population (or the expansion of global capitalism, depending on your point of view) requires. But the fact that a form of practice is purveyed in large quantities to a disparate population at profitable prices, and that they seem to gain little by it in the eyes of their more cultivated peers, no more disqualifies it from a role in instigating awareness than do the Louvre's prices of admission, its huge multinational clientele, and the superficiality of most tours disqualify its art from a similar function. The dominant mass cultural forms – television, radio, cinema, music, sports – can obviously provide loci of community formation that cross linguistic barriers. But so can the acquisition of material products or the use of new tools and technologies, as the internet attests.

Take what is surely the most minimal or degraded form of identity construction: shopping. While it may not be as productive of self-awareness as literary theory (a point some of my colleagues would dispute), it is something anyone can do anywhere, and it procures a sense of integration into the community by involving two parties in a pattern of negotiation and exchange – hence its universal appeal for tourists. For those who yearn for the rooted organic community, this is the obvious defect of commodified culture: because it fits in anywhere, it cannot procure a sense of belonging anywhere in particular.

However, that is the whole point of commodified Culture: it provides a means of differentiating among communities on a different basis than just geographical location, race, or even religion, by broadening the spectrum of shared knowledge and ways of doing things that gives communities something in common and is explicitly acknowledged as doing so. For some it is no doubt less comforting to think of rural Bangladeshis using cell phones than to imagine them sharing the experiences of the day at the hearth with their families. But the fact that the rural communities in developing nations can and do use cell technology brings them just that much closer to their "developed" counterparts. Not in the sense of having more technology at their disposal, but in the sense of thinking about communicating with people in similar ways, of being accustomed to maintaining relationships over distances, of acting on one's desire to talk at the moment one has it, of possessing the confidence and the technology to project one's needs and desires towards disembodied authorities and remote friends when one needs to.

For those in the grip of cultural logic, there is no innocent social practice. Every new tool opens on to new behaviors and questions about the values that behavior might entail. Every modification in the way we do things provokes self-awareness and an interrogation of the way one has done things up to now. Telecommunication has changed the meaning of community and friendship; it makes possible collaboration with people one has never met, the contracting of obligations with entities one cannot comprehend, the construction of multiple virtual identities – and the obligation to deal with them.

This is perhaps a trivial example but it is meant to illustrate the extent to which the deliberate adoption of practices – and hence the awareness of one's embeddedness in and determination by practices – has expanded with the market. Whether the logic of culture facilitated the rise of capitalism or was elaborated in its service, both emerged roughly contemporaneously, with the development of world-economies in the early modern period, and both are complementary. From a liberal economic perspective the imperative of self-cultivation provides infinite opportunities for cultural capitalization and thus for a continual production of wealth. Tourism is one of the largest components of the GNP of France, but the same can be said of the Galapagos Islands or South Africa. Any locale, community or practice can be marketed as an object for cultural acquisition, provided it can be made to seem significant and worthy of understanding. From the Kalihari desert or the Museum of the Tomato on Guernsey to the daily exodus of the short-tailed brown bats in Austin, people flock to sites from which they think they can learn or experience something new. Wherever they stop, they spend money to acquire experience, which, rendered into narrative accounts or social critiques, becomes cultural capital, certifying for others their commitment to new knowledge and the self-improvement it brings. The discourse of cultural experience enhances one's social status and can even make money.

Clearly, the logic of seeking distinction in conformity is highly congenial to industrial modes of production and global trade, but so is the compulsion of critique to identify and shed old habits. The market inflects this need towards material acquisition; it purveys activities that promise us change even as they inscribe us in shared practices. The most debased forms of this kind of Culture do not involve discourse on one's practice, merely its continual, self-conscious increment. Dress, food, music, travel, sports, tools, appliances, technology, specialized terminology: anything that can be readily acquired and self-consciously displayed as an expression of one's cosmopolitanism and/or modernity can theoretically become a badge of cultivation and distinction. In a sense the nineteenth century's expansion of the term "culture" to encompass the totality of a community's life finds its logical extension here: if everything a community does can be considered culture, and not just its self-consciously symbolic representations, then Culture as an ethic can construct self-awareness around any and all social practices.

The intrusion of the economic in modern versions of self-realization is undeniable. Still one ought not simply assume the latter process to be an effect of material history. If capitalism has been able to penetrate every corner of the globe and create an unquenchable thirst for merchandise and new cultural forms, it is in part because cultural logic has penetrated every corner of the globe too, saturating humanity with the assumption that identity and a full life hinges on self-realization and that such self-realization requires an awareness and updating of the practices that define one.

The logic of culture globalizes identity by impelling us to engage in discourse about practice. Through the market, travel, the school, and the chatroom, it inscribes us in an ongoing dialogue with members of our own culture and of other cultures, and urges us to consider alternatives to our current habits. Whether or not we achieve accord with respect to specific values and practices, the simple fact of pursuing the exchange of ideas aligns us within a further overarching set of practices and protocols of discussion, communication and information organization. Economic globalization depends on this communality of procedures and the incipient communality of values and interests it precipitates. In this sense, the spread of the logic of culture underlies the globalization of the market. Thus to conclude from the failed attempts at containing its dialectic that the main consequence of Culture is the perpetuation and proliferation of cultural logic, is not to suggest that it has no economic or political consequences.

It is perhaps worth underlining that even at this global level, the paradoxical logic of culture persists. It draws us all together within the shared commitment to articulating our difference from others – which we do by affiliating ourselves with collective trends. The chic of golf, the infatuation with the sport utility vehicle, the proliferation of pocket organizers have less to do with intrinsic utility than with the acquisition of a "lifestyle." Nor can this phenomenon be reduced to one of Americanization. Sushi, salsa, and baguettes are not American; nor are lattes, Afro-pop, or curry. If the West has been simplified into an image of the modern, the developing countries have become the home of the real, the authentic; and each seeks to enhance itself by acquiring the accoutrements of the other.

The pursuit of authenticity in the attributes of the other constitutes a degraded form of critique. Its fundamental predicate – as convenient for the marketing executive as it is for the travel agent – is that we question and modify our own practices and seek authenticity in those of others. There is of course a certain colonial (and counter-colonial) dimension to this trend, since it configures distinction in terms of appropriating and making a part of one's effortless postmodern *sprezzatura* the culture on which the Other stakes his or her identity. Thus the West African youth makes his adaptation of Parisian fashion part of his coming into manhood; the affluent white American adolescent dons baggy jeans and listens to rap.

The market thus provides an apparent shortcut to the social integration which the earliest theorists of Culture sought. The basic assumption is still that one "expresses oneself" and secures distinction by identifying and mastering systems of practice. However, in place of the discursive models catalogued by the Humanists as a means of acquiring distinction and a fuller life, today's global subject selects from the field of *all* practices – and demonstrates "mastery" simply by appropriating a practice or technology to his or her own ends. Whether or not the Microsoft employee and the Parisian fishmonger actually have anything in common philosophically (but they will, eventually), they will by the logic of global capitalism not go to war as long as both are more intent on selecting a scooter for their children than on contesting the spiritual values of the other.

Of course the stronger discursive kind of self-awareness persists and has indeed intensified in the modern era. The adversarial disposition Trilling noted is stronger today than ever before, and – in keeping with the tradition we have charted since the Renaissance – directs itself at the systematic economy that seems to determine our lives: that of the untrammeled free market. Thus in response to the Multilateral Agreement on Investments the multinational World Social Forum is born. This raises the prospect, for those who are repelled by the penetration of capital into every corner of the globe, that the saturation of reality by market forces may produce a consoling countereffect by engendering a communality of practice against which a shared critique and identity might articulate itself.

There is of course a darker version of this story, that sees all of the processes I have described as part of a larger scenario of alienation. Culture is part of this plot in that its logic incites us to think that self-realization can only be procured by engaging in heavily mediated forms of discourse, that we must in fact seek fulfillment in mediation. It draws us into talking and listening in certain ways and with certain equipment. It persuades us that we can only regain some measure of autonomy in a world held hostage to impersonal systems by committing ourselves wholeheartedly to those systems – making them the conduit of our identity, an effect of our volition rather than our predicament. Locating our identity in impersonal technologies of discourse exchange, we submit to the protocols of communication and ways of being they entail. We are told we must "express ourselves," and we are channeled towards certain ways of doing so.

From this perspective, the proliferation and complication of technologies of representation, from the novel and the press of the eighteenth century, through the school and museum of the nineteenth, to the film, radio, television, telephone and internet of the twentieth, systematically compromises all social interactions. Rather than talking to friends in the neighborhood or at the pub, we listen to reassuringly familiar faces talking at us on a screen. Instead of saying hello to the person next to us on the bus, we say hello to our cell phone and a friend across town. Rather than making new friends where we work, we chat daily with old ones by email. Even the already degraded form of self-expression that is shopping finds itself subjected to the imperatives of the "information age": rather than browsing at the bookstore, we browse on the net, substituting for the tactile pleasures of leafing through a volume and rubbing elbows with other people the more abstract satisfaction of being recognized by Amazon.com's database. It is a telling commentary that a significant factor in the sales of a book like this one is the presence or absence of its cover *image* on the web page. Authenticity and the real, as both enthusiasts and detractors of postmodernism like to remind us, have been overwritten by economies of simulacra that are driven by mindless technocracies.

It is probably no consolation to note that we are all ourselves the agents of economic globalization – unless there is someone reading this who has never eaten a banana, used sugar, driven to work, seen an Kung-Fu movie, used a computer, or bought any clothes made offshore. However, it is worth reminding ourselves – that human relations have *always* been mediated, by language, of course, but also by everything language can underwrite: systems of authority and belief, forms of government, traditions, economic systems, and previous technologies, all of which in the past tied people to particular places, ranks, tasks, and masters. The industrialization of representation in the modern era indeed makes it easier than ever to regulate the habits of an ever greater number of people; but it also increases the access of people to other lives and identities, by pre-aligning their habits with those of similar people all over the world. The trade-off for a shallow-rooted life of diminished sociability is almost limitless mobility. Once everybody's life is accessible to Big Brother, and it will soon be, given the enthusiasm which we are feeding our particulars into databases, it will no longer matter where one is or what one is doing. We will be ourselves anywhere.

If this suggests that it is increasingly more difficult to change identities simply by changing places, it also makes changing places easier. This is one of the benefits of global culture that no doubt accounts for the enthusiasm with which it is embraced by those in politically or economically stressed locations. It is easy enough to forget, when rhapsodizing in Princeton or Berkeley about rootedness in a community or the importance of the family, that there are communities and families one would just as soon not be part of. The uniform mediations of global culture make it easier to leave them.

The commodification of self-formation triggers common practices among people dispersed throughout the world. The positive consequence of this is that at some minimal level we are all members of a community. When this sharing becomes extensive enough, as it does at the level of formal education and the higher technologies, people become highly mobile – not just physically, but culturally and economically. It is this kind of mobility that allows, for instance, India to furnish the computing industry a lion's share of professional programmers. And while for some the idea of a Bombay resident telecommuting to Redmond, Washington may constitute a regrettable loss of Indian rootedness and organic wholeness, it is a choice that most prefer to make for themselves, and which greatly increases the flow of value, people, and practices between the two countries (the two cultures), reducing, among other things, the likelihood of conflict.

What all this suggests is that if the institutionalized forms of Culture at the outset served to protect class interests and property, the logic of culture that has persisted in the wake of high Culture's decline has become a means of class and property *formation*. It endures and proliferates not as a set of narrowly defined high Cultural institutions, but in the form of an infectious logic that recruits subjects to regimes of self-differentiation and community affiliation, which it links to the acquisition of "properties" that are potentially convertible not just into an accrued sense of self-awareness or augmented social prestige, but into cold cash. Culture is tied to class interests, but not just in the sense of protecting the property of the entrenched bourgeois: it engenders new classes and recruits members for them, creating a world in which community consists less in topographical proximity than in shared interests, expertise, and values.

This may seem a rather fangless story for those accustomed to more bracing accounts of culture as evil incarnate or paradise lost. Admittedly, the benefits of these economies of subcultural identity formation do not rise to the level of "salvation." Nor, I would contend, do they constitute the pernicious opiate they are frequently accused of being. Or if they are an opiate, it is a universal one to which we all are addicted. It takes a curious kind of self-blindness to one's own institutional, political, and economic imbrication to think that *other* people's involvement in commodified practices could not be reaping benefits of self-awareness. Or maybe it is not so curious, since that is precisely the kind of self-blindness that Culture promotes: the kind that lets academic speculation feel it has a better grip on reality than the dupes of mass culture – and lets the dupes of mass culture feel the same way about academics. In any case, one should hardly need to argue after Althusser that high Cultural institutions, and especially educators, are as deeply involved in the perpetuation of the capitalist system as are Microsoft and Shell.

Those who lament the failure of Culture to deliver on its promise of a better world frequently point to the persistence of conflict, racism, and oppression, and the recent resurgence of "tribalism" in areas such as the Balkans. There are several observations one can make with respect to these points. First, the mere fact that people throughout the world know and care what is happening in Kosovo or Rwanda or East Timor, and that they formulate their concern in similar terms of basic human rights and democratic process, testifies to the inexorable process of universalization.

Secondly, and along the same lines, many conflicts that are cited as evidence of Culture's failure are just as clearly evidence of resistance to its success. Especially in areas where the globalization of social forms comes into conflict with religious practices and values, or where its scenarios of communality through standardized forms of production and consumption are not readily implemented and therefore cannot compensate for the practices they displace, one can expect that the program of commodified self-realization will be met with aggressive resistance.

Thirdly, the intensification of ethnic and racial strife, especially in Europe, is in one sense a consequence of the success of culture in creating a mobile, self-defining world populace and hence of increasing drastically the tensions which mass migration inevitably brings. Armed with a common notion of how to define and assert themselves, if not the material means to do so, and confronted with borders that this universal logic – among other things – has rendered increasingly porous, the world's population will flow towards the most congenial environments. And they will not always be greeted with open arms. That we are all increasingly like each other does not mean we like competition, or each other: on the contrary, if we fear the unfamiliar, we only truly hate what we know.

Finally, the global anomie that many associate with the failure of Culture as a universal set of values may be the clearest evidence of its triumph as a dialectical practice: if we cannot agree on a single set of values, it is because everybody everywhere has become aware of the importance of culture and equally proficient in constructing their own. Our shared commitment to the logic of culture compels us to assert our difference. This is what accounts for the rise in identity politics over the past few decades and for the demand for recognition on the part of an ever-expanding array of subcommunities within the larger national cultures.

The nearly universal demand on the part of minorities that their particular values and practices be acknowledged and respected as part of their claim to dignity confirms the extent to which we all assume not just that individual identity is bound up in collective practice, but that it hinges on the *articulation and assertion* of one's difference. The underlying assumption of multiculturalism is not simply that our lives draw part of their meaning from their immersion in shared practices, but that the full expression of our identity can only be achieved through the deliberate conceptualization and affirmation of the distinctiveness of those practices. As we all become more alike, this imperative becomes more pressing.

Dealing with Difference

A fundamental assumption of multiculturalism is that the recognition of a culture should not be contingent on its consonance with the dominant culture, much less some set of universal criteria. It is enough that a culture means something to the community whose identity it secures, particularly since people outside of that culture have no way of knowing exactly what its components mean, much less how they acquire their meaning. What is all too often forgotten in such assertions is that "a culture" is not an unchanging body of traditions or materials, but rather a constantly shifting sense of collective identity which a community, whose membership is itself constantly changing, forges out of continual reassessment of its legacy and values.

The relationship of minority to dominant culture is similarly in flux, continually readjusting itself to the demands of the community – although with a time lag that frequently seems intolerable. In countries peopled by immigration, in particular, today's ethnic majorities are often yesterday's minorities, today's minorities tomorrow's majorities. Minority culture, like all culture, is continually becoming aware of itself, and constituting itself in that awareness; and what constitutes the minority is constantly changing. The logic of identity that underwrites demands for recognition on the part of minority and majority cultures alike also argues against the fetishization – or facile dismissal – of any particular practice. Many of the cultural materials that are scorned today as relics of dead white male supremacy were themselves important tools of cultural formation in the past. Tolstoy – to take a celebrated instance – may have become the emblem of hegemonic arrogance for certain proponents of multiculturalism today, but he no doubt represented something quite different to the millions of Slavic immigrants in the latter part of the nineteenth century – and who were themselves struggling to overcome discrimination in their new country. The fact that such former minorities have since become part of the majority no more argues against the enduring value of their cultural materials than does the fact that Hispanics will soon be the majority ethnicity in much of the American West mean that their cultural heritage must suddenly transmute from being the voice of a silenced minority to being the oppressive voice of domination and intolerance.

What the logic of culture tells us is that while there will always be minorities and majorities, they will not always be the same, and that clinging to one's current status is as antithetical to the construction of identity – for majority and minority alike – as is the deprivation of one's legacy of traditions. It is not in one's self-interest to reject other cultural practices out of hand, because it can only represent an impoverishment and petrification of one's identity and sense of self. Similarly, to expect that the materials taught in schools reflect the precise status and proportion of majorities and minorities at any given moment is naive, not only because it does not take full account of the fact that liberal democracy is, as Charles Taylor aptly put it, a "fighting creed" with values of its own to defend (and the majority has the same right to defend those values as the minority has to promote its own), but also because it is blind to the historic structure of culture as a continual dialectic of community formation. What is important is the *act of constructing a legacy* which is behind the demand for the inclusion of minority cultural materials in the curriculum; the actual incorporation of those materials into the canon marks a *fait accompli* and is less important as a catalyst of future cultural identity, than as a monument of achieved recognition.

Since culture is by definition always a work in progress, what people are defending when they speak up for "their" culture is nothing more or less than the construction of identity they are in the process of acting out at that very instant. No body of materials, no tradition, has the ability to endow anyone with identity or a sense of self; only that person's *awareness of* such a tradition can do that, and that awareness, while contingent on the traditions with which it is familiar at any moment, is not *a priori* limited to any specific set.

In his analysis of the modern notion of individual identity Charles Taylor stresses its dialogical dimension: "we define our identity always in dialogue with, sometimes in struggle against, the things our significant others want to see in us."[29] However, there is an important *impersonal* dimension to the dialectic of identity as well. The whole point of the concept of culture (and one of the reasons people so frequently argue about cultural *materials* in the schools) is that it allows us to conceive of the dialectic of identity in *impersonal* terms, as an accommodation of subject to *system* and vice versa. It is the impersonal nature of the system – the fact that it does not reflect any particular interests – that allows us to engage it and adjust our desires, tastes, and aspirations according to its rules. As a system, it by definition represents the whole economy of practices rather than any particular competing interest. We can accept its authority without subordinating our identity to that of some other individual.

That is perhaps why particular doctrines have proven so much less effective than the market in promoting cultural conciliation. Not only is it more difficult to locate and oppose systems of value when they insinuate themselves through a myriad of objects and styles than through moral imperatives or coercion, it is also difficult to understand that the object one has purchased as an expression of one's distinction and in consequence of one's own desires, might have gained a significant cultural purchase on one's identity. The pure systematicity of capitalism, its commitment to a process of endless increase that is more concerned with incorporating people into its economy than with the cultural particulars of those people or their identity as individuals, make it an especially effective vehicle of cultural merger.

But what are the implications of cultural logic and the ethic of critique for the politics of identity which saturate the postmodern world? One can perhaps start to answer that question by isolating some moves that are inconsistent with cultural logic.

First and foremost, it seems obvious that to the extent identity is constituted in a dialectic between individual act and systematic norm, it cannot be hypostatized in any particular set of practices or any unchanging group. Nor can the ethical edge of critique be permanently claimed by – or granted to – any individual or community. The liberal tendency to exalt the minority community simply because it is a minority is as aberrant as the conservative tendency to claim virtue for one's own practices. Eulogizing the Other may allow us to feel we have acceded to a position of critical atonement – one which is unavailable even to the members of the Other culture – but it does not secure the moral patent of critique, which requires that we interrogate and *change* our *own* practices.

The conservative counterpart of this move similarly locates the ideal of pure virtue "elsewhere," but aligns it with one's own culture's lost fullness. Like liberals, conservatives attribute a deeper authenticity to a particular group, but the group they typically exalt are the elites which gave the past its resplendent sense of purpose (Ortega y Gasset is unparalleled in this regard, but T. S. Eliot is close behind).

Cultural logic argues against any such assignments of virtue. Virtue is a function of the dialectic of critique, and cannot be permanently acquired as a property. No community can lay permanent claim to the moral high ground, even if it owes its sense of self to an inaugural moment of repression or persecution. However understandable it may be, allowing oneself to be taken over by a permanent rehearsal of felt injustice or moral indignation arrests the dialectic of self-realization and imprisons us in an identity that is by definition intolerable. This does not mean that we cannot recall our origins or celebrate our traditions; merely that we must constantly interrogate them and contest their usefulness to our present needs, our changing status, our evolving identity within the larger social picture.

The traditional "high" Cultural strategy for doing this was through the mediation of aesthetic judgments, occasioned by the discursive forms which were the "mass media" of their day. These forms are still highly effective – especially the press and the written word – but they are seconded by more volatile modes of discourse that spectacularly dramatize social practices and divisions. These do not hesitate to indulge the open expression of antagonisms – witness the televised spectacles of domestic discord, incest, sexual deviation and the like that are popular in America, such as the Jerry Springer show – but they also perform a continual archeology and recentering of social and institutional practice. This is especially evident in the racial mixing and realignment of gender roles which such "confrontation" shows stage. Whatever their aesthetic shortcoming, these spectacles bring to light, and thus open to both critique and celebration the values, procedures, and habits of thought of a society.

When, instead of such interrogation, critique congeals into a claim of moral primacy, the play between individual and collective which grounds identity begins to break down; rather than a force of cohesion, the assertion of identity in such terms (which are no longer those of culture and hence predictably dysfunctional as a means of community formation) becomes a force of social disintegration. This is most visible in those areas of the world where religion supersedes culture as the grounding framework of identity. But incipient versions of the same breakdown occur whenever one (sub)culture becomes fixed on its irreducible difference from – and moral superiority to – competing cultures. This no more leads to warm feelings of communality and tolerance than does the none too convincing repudiation of the dominant culture by its accredited representatives. Both moves are exclusionist in their moral logic and thus undercut their oft-reiterated commitment to openness.

However, as Nazism and the Balkan conflict showed us, both of these reductions pale in comparison with the destructive force unleashed when the ethical claims of Culture are further disfigured, and its contestatory or repudiating moment directed not at one's own practices or past, but at another community. The uncritical celebration of one's own community in conjunction with the desire to liquidate another, is not an instance of culture in anything but the most distorted use of the word, no more than the Great Leap Forward is a progressive moment by virtue of its name. Frequently when people talk of "Culture's" failure to bring about world harmony, they seem to be referring to a canonical set of western works and traditions of liberal thought. But the whole point of the canon as Culture conceives it is that it does not have any single meaning and can thus always be put to evil uses. It may in fact be the case that nineteenth-century theories of Culture as absolute national unity contributed to the twisted ideology of the Nazis; however, this does not disqualify other concepts of culture and the endeavors such concepts sponsor from being potentially valuable instruments for advancing the welfare of humanity, any more than the horrors of Stalinism disqualify socialist theory from a useful future. Most horrors find a way to justify themselves, and they typically borrow their language from accredited theories and discourse. It is precisely Culture's tremendous potential as a way to social consolidation and the moral leverage it extracts from that potential that makes it so susceptible to misuse. The canon insures that we all can understand each other, not that we all will agree.

When the rule of critique degenerates into narcissism, when the interrogation of one's assumptions turns into their celebration, when instead of scrutinizing one's own motivations one passes judgment on all others, then society runs amok. This may happen regularly, and it may borrow the vocabulary of cultural logic (what other vocabulary could it borrow, since we are immersed in and defined by that of culture?), but it should not be confused with culture, either as a process of identity formation or as an ethical commitment to that process.

Culture fosters social cohesion by aligning people within a similar ethic of critique and engaging them in discursive networks that inevitably coalesce into communities. Cultured subjects do not celebrate themselves or their beliefs because they are never fully self-coincident, but always in the process of realizing their identity between the ephemeral fullness of felt truth and the alienated, discursively mediated re-cognition of their framing assumptions. The ethic of constant self-interrogation implicit in

this model is incommensurate with the glorification of any particular identity, national, ethnic, or individual, since it contains as
one of its crucial moments the stepping back from habitual
practice, the *contestation of everything that goes without saying.*

If there is an underlying universal ideology of Culture – a tacit
scenario of "natural" behavior that draws on the deep logic of
culture – it would simply be this: that we contest all of our
unexamined assumptions, and especially those that we rely upon
when we engage in Cultural critique and arrogate its claim to
truth. The moment that one steps back from one's own practices
and assumes a position of greater wisdom is the moment of
greatest susceptibility to error, if only because, convinced of one's
averted perspective, one is less likely to question one's conclusions. Culture demands that we resist such convictions, and to
that extent, that we resist *its authority*.

Another way of saying this is that if culture has somehow
survived as a category of appeal in spite of its susceptibility to
ideological critique it is simply because it incorporates such
critique into its ideology. Culture prescribes dissent to its claims.
Positioning us within a dialectic of continual revision, it demands
that we not only remain vigilant with respect to our customary
reflexes, but that we continually interrogate the underlying ideological affiliations of that gesture of emancipation. To be truly
Cultured is to strive to see beyond the occluded self-interest and
partiality of the systems of inquiry that the Cultured deploy.

The same logic accounts for the persistent wariness with which
the Cultured regard the Cultural tradition within which they
work – or the diligence with which proponents of Cultural Studies
call into question those institutions and practices from which their
authority flows. For it is also clear that in terms of its commitment
to critique Cultural Studies is eminently Cultural. This evaluation
may raise the hackles of some of its practitioners who see a
certain institutional kind of Culture as antithetical to a better
imagining of social life, since it seems (but only seems) to situate
them squarely within the ideology they decry. However, if as I
am arguing, the deep logic of Culture extracts moral and historical authority from the willingness to contest the foundations of
authority, then Cultural Studies is not only Cultural in its logic
and practice, but quintessentially so. Taking its distance from
unexamined "natural" practices, it unmasks their complicity with

particular interests and neutralizes them with a demystifying
critique. This, as everyone from Talleyrand to Leavis or Guy
Debord confirms, is the redemptive strategy of the modern subject, and it is the gesture out of which the whole notion of Culture
grew.

Cultural Studies also exemplifies the political dimension of
Culture. While its practitioners frequently distance themselves
from the "disinterested aesthetic reflection" traditionally identified with Arnoldian high Culture, their own political commitment
confirms that the deeper logic of culture is not antithetical to
politics: Culture merely specifies that political work can also be
done under the guise of abstract interpretive discourse – which is
a pretty good description of Cultural Studies.

Further, as a practice of theorizing politics and politicizing
theory (to cite one of its self-characterizations), Cultural Studies
implicitly debunks the myth of unmediated subjectivity and
argues the redemptive value of Cultural mediation. For one can
scarcely imagine a more mediated form of political intervention,
a discourse more saturated with allusions to existing conceptual
frameworks, and more likely to produce new ones. Constructing
its deconstruction of tradition *within* a tradition, disseminating
its arguments *against* Culture through channels and institutions
accredited *by* Culture, Cultural Studies exemplifies the logic of
culture as a motor of change: it appropriates the mechanisms of
the very economy of authority it wishes to resist, appropriating
its mechanisms and rhetoric as a means of eluding their control.

We have seen confirmations of this process, from the republican
rhetoric of the French Revolution to the demystification of advertising undertaken by Leavis and Thompson. That such deliberate
attempts to shape collective discourse have since their inaugur-
ation two centuries ago changed the material, social, and political
conditions under which we live – and in most cases changed them
for the better – is self-evident. That proponents of Cultural Studies
refuse to be satisfied with such progress is both commendable
and, again, evidence of their profound commitment to the ideology of Culture. Their recurrent analysis and repudiation of enduring, unexamined (and hence by definition, prejudicial) institutions
in the name of a more enlightened future is the very hallmark of
the ideal Cultural subject, who, as we remember, is permanently

motivated by the anticipation of an achievement that will (like the abolition of social evil) never be fully realized.

There is a final aspect of cultural logic that Cultural Studies makes apparent. This concerns the commitment to universalizing critique as a practice of identity formation. We remember that a key feature of the developments that led to the emergence of the notion of culture was the Enlightenment generalization of the privilege and operations of self-awareness to *all* people. This impulse persists stronger than ever today. As a tacit ideology, critique demands first and foremost that everyone adopt its ethic. If it endorses no particular social content, it *does* recruit us into the practice of systematizing social behavior as a basis for our identity.

Ideally, in a world totally saturated with cultural logic, everyone would be constantly involved in critique. To the extent we were all possessed of, and constantly reshaping, a distinct identity, there would be no excluded minorities in such a world, no "culturally deprived." Everyone would find their place through their own effort. This is where the universalizing thrust of culture expresses itself. It is not a question of formulating universal truths to which everyone must agree, but of demonstrating that by means of Culture anyone anywhere can find their own truths. Culture's objective is to incorporate the world into its framework of identity and self-realization. And it is the nagging awareness of this requirement that drives the most committed of its agents – the intellectuals who are the most self-conscious about their practices – to promote, foster, and celebrate the consolidation of identity in any group they perceive to constitute a possible exception.

As we noted earlier, constructing one's identity as a distinct culture against the specifics of a dominant culture is not transgressive with respect to Culture, even when that is done in a spirit of contestation or subversion. Culture thrives on resistance, since resistance is what precipitates self-awareness and new forms of practice. What would be transgressive from Culture's point of view would be proving that some people simply cannot achieve any sense of self through the critique of practice and the elaboration of shared rules. It is to foreclose on such a possibility that the liberal components of society who believe most deeply in

Culture, and who have the most to lose should the deep logic of Culture ever be discredited, work so hard to invigorate and put in evidence the identity-building efforts of minorities and the marginalized. This compulsion to recruit all of the excluded portions of the larger community into the satisfactions of self-realization explains the otherwise baffling celebration of value-free diversity. What is really being argued is not diversity *per se*, since there are many diverse forms of unacceptable behavior with which we do not wish to enrich the fabric of society, but rather the inclusiveness of Culture, its ability to accommodate even those versions of identity elaborated in opposition to what are perceived to be its dominant values.

The hailing of diversity is, finally, an adaptive move for the dominant cultures as well as the minorities. Becoming aware of how and why communities form, and differ, and believe the things they do, is a coping mechanism even more essential in the age of global migration and telecommunication than it was in the age of exploration. Already in 1930, F. R. Leavis lamented that "the modern is exposed to a concourse of signals so bewildering in their variety and number that . . . he can hardly begin to discriminate. . . . the distinctions and dividing lines have blurred away, the boundaries are gone, and the arts and literatures of different countries and periods have flowed together."[30] Today it is not just the arts and literatures, but the economies, populations, and technologies that are circulating freely. It is no longer feasible to think of one's identity as anchored in a single community, when one's work, social relations, eating habits, and leisure pursuits intersect multiple regions, social classes, languages, national interests, and religious affiliations. In such a context reflecting on how such formations are created and why we might want to – or have to – incorporate them into our identity is not a luxury but an indispensable component of survival.

Notes

Preface

1. Christopher Herbert, *Culture and Anomie: Ethnographic Imagination in the Nineteenth Century* (Chicago: University of Chicago Press, 1991), p. 1.

Introduction

1. Armand-Guy Kersaint, *Discours sur les monuments publics, prononcé au conseil du département de Paris, le 15 décembre 1791* (Paris: P. Didot l'Aîné, 1792), p. 10.
2. Christopher Herbert, *Culture and Anomie: Ethnographic Imagination in the Nineteenth Century* (Chicago: University of Chicago Press, 1991), p. 2.
3. For analyses of the term's genesis and various meanings: Raymond Williams, *Keywords*, revised and expanded edition (London: Fontana, 1988); Zygmunt Bauman, *Intimations of Postmodernity* (London: Routledge, 1992); Robert J. C. Young, *Colonial Desire* (London: Routledge, 1995). For ideological analyses of culture: Raymond Williams, *Culture and Society 1780–1950* [1958] (New York: Columbia University Press, 1983), and *Marxism and Literature* (Oxford: Oxford University Press, 1977), pp. 128–35; Terry Eagleton, *The Idea of Culture* (Oxford: Blackwell, 2000); Ian Hunter, *Culture and Government: the Emergence of Literary Education* (London: Macmillan, 1988); David Lloyd and Paul Thomas, *Culture and the State* (London: Routledge, 1998). For interpretations of the anthropological notion of culture: Herbert, *Culture and Anomie*; Roy Wagner, *The Invention of Culture*, revised and expanded edition (Chicago: University of Chicago Press, 1981); Clifford Geertz, *The Interpretation of Cultures* (New York: Basic Books, 1973); James Clifford, *The Predicament of Culture* (Harvard: Harvard University Press, 1988).

4. Classic discussions of culture from a specific historical point of view include: Matthew Arnold, *Culture and Anarchy* [1869], ed. S. Collini (Cambridge: Cambridge University Press, 1993); José Ortega y Gasset, *The Revolt of the Masses* [1929] (New York: W. W. Norton & Co., 1994); F. R. Leavis, *Mass Civilisation and Minority Culture* (Cambridge: Minority Press, 1930); T. S. Eliot, *Notes towards a Definition of Culture* (London: Faber and Faber, Limited, 1948); F. R. Leavis and Denys Thompson, *Culture and Environment: the Training of Critical Awareness* (London: Chatto & Windus, 1959); Lionel Trilling, *Beyond Culture* (New York: The Viking Press, 1965). Noteworthy contemporary examples include Alain Finkielkraut, *The Defeat of the Mind*, trans. Judith Friedlander (New York: Columbia University Press, 1995), Geoffrey Hartman, *The Fateful Question of Culture* (New York: Columbia University Press, 1997); Charles Taylor, *Multiculturalism: examining the politics of recognition*, ed. and introduced by Amy Gutman (Princeton: Princeton University Press, 1994); Michel Wieviorka, *La Différence* (Paris: Balland, 2001).

5. "Civilization and its Discontents," in *Standard Edition of Complete Psychological Works*, trans. James Strachey (London: Hogarth Press, 1961), Vol. XXI, p. 96.

6. Geoffrey H. Hartman, *The Fateful Question of Culture*, p. 210.

1   The Roots of Cultural Logic

1. Bartolomé de Las Casas, *Apologetic History of the Indies*, in *Introduction to Contemporary Civilization in the West* (New York: Columbia University Press, 1946), p. 35.

2. Montaigne, "On Cannibals," in *Essays*, trans. J. M. Cohen (London: Penguin, 1958), pp. 108–9.

3. Lionel Trilling, *Sincerity and Authenticity* (London: Oxford University Press, 1972), pp. 20–6.

4. Pascal, *Pensées*, trans. A. J. Krailsheimer (London: Penguin Books, 1966), p. 46.

5. See Benedict Anderson, *Imagined Communities: Reflections on the Origin and Spread of Nationalism* (London: Verso, 1983).

6. Francis Bacon, *Thoughts and Conclusions*, in Benjamin Farrington, *The Philosophy of Francis Bacon* (Liverpool: Liverpool University Press, 1964), p. 95.

7. Bacon, *Thoughts*, pp. 76, 92.

8. René Descartes, *Discourse on Method and Meditations on First Philosophy*, trans. Donald A. Cress (Indianapolis: Hackett, 1993), p. 2.

9. Descartes, *Discourse on Method*, p. 6.
10. Ernest Gellner, *Reason and Culture* (Oxford: Basil Blackwell, 1992), p. 28.
11. Descartes, *Discourse on Method*, p. 3.
12. Descartes, *Discourse on Method*, p. 1.
13. Friedrich Schiller, *On the Aesthetic Education of Man. In a Series of Letters*, translated with an introduction by Reginald Snell (New York: Frederick Ungar, 1965 [originally published London: Routledge and Kegan Paul, 1954]), pp. 26–7 (Second Letter).
14. Hobbes, *Leviathan*, ed. Richard Tuck (Cambridge: Cambridge University Press, 1991), p. 35.
15. Reinhart Koselleck, *Critique and Crisis: Enlightenment and the Pathogenesis of Modern Society* (Cambridge, MA: MIT Press, 1988 [originally *Kritik und Krise*, Freiburg/München: Verlage Karl Alber, 1959]).
16. Koselleck, *Critique and Crisis*, p. 57.
17. Bacon, *Thoughts*, pp. 100, 99.
18. Descartes, *Discourse on Method*, p. 8.
19. Descartes, *Discourse on Method*, p. 9.
20. Descartes, *Discourse on Method*, pp. 9–10.
21. Baldesar Castiglione, *The Book of the Courtier*, trans. George Bull (London: Penguin, 1967, revised ed. 1976), p. 298.

2   Inventing Culture

1. Johann Gottlieb Fichte, *Gespräche über die Bestimmung des Gelehrters* [1794] in *Sämmtliche Werke*, 8 vols. (Berlin: herausgegaben Immanuel Hermann Fichte, 1845–6), 6:290–449, p. 324.
2. Fichte, *Gespräche*, p. 298.
3. *The Structural Transformation of the Public Sphere: an Inquiry into a Category of Bourgeois Society*, trans. Thomas Burger, with the assistance of Frederick Lawrence (Cambridge, MA: MIT Press, 1991 [originally: *Strukturwandel der Öffentlichkeit*, Hermann Luctherhand Verlag, Darmstadt und Neuwied, 1962]).
4. François Xavier Lanthenas, *Motifs de faire du 10 août un jubilé fraternel* (n.p. [Paris]: Convention Nationale, 1793), p. 7.
5. "De la perfectibilité de l'espèce humaine", in *Ecrits politiques* (Paris: Gallimard, 1997), pp. 700–20, esp. pp. 716, 719.
6. Jeremy Popkin, *Revolutionary News, the Press in France 1789–99* (Durham, NC: Duke University Press, 1990), pp. 9–10, notes that the collections of the Bibliothèque Nationale alone contain more than thirteen hundred periodicals from the period 1789 to 1799.

7. Claude Labrosse et Pierre Rétat, *L'Instrument périodique: la fonction de la presse au XVIIIe siècle* (Lyon: Presses Universitaires de Lyon, 1985); Jack R. Censer and Jeremy Popkin, eds., *Press and Politics in Pre-Revolutionary France* (Berkeley: University of California Press, 1987); Jeremy Popkin, *News and Politics in the Age of Revolution: Jean Luzac's "Gazette de Leyde"* (Ithaca: Cornell University Press, 1989).

8. Popkin, *Revolutionary News*, p. 5.

9. Popkin, *Revolutionary News*, p. 5.

10. *Le Patriote Français*, first prospectus (March 16, 1789), p. 4. All translations are my own.

11. *Patriote Français*, first prospectus, pp. 1–2.

12. Prospectus for *Instruction publique, Journal d'instruction sociale, par les citoyens Condorcet, Sièyes et Duhamel*, in *Gazette national ou Le Moniteur universel*, 16: 442 (Thursday, May 23, 1793).

13. Prospectus for *Instruction publique*, 16: 442.

14. Stanislas Louis Marie Fréron, *Convention Nationale: Opinion sur la liberté de la Presse, et sur d'autres objets de législation; suivie d'un projet de décret, par Fréron, Représentant du Peuple, député de Paris à la Convention nationale. Prononcé dans la séance du 9 fructidor* (Paris: 1794), p. 12.

15. Fréron, *Opinion sur la liberté de la presse*, p. 12.

16. In their book published subsequently to my writing of this chapter, David Lloyd and Paul Thomas provide an elegant global reading of cultural ideology in terms of the concept of representation; *Culture and the State* (London: Routledge, 1998) .

17. *Révolutions de France et de Brabant*, No. 8 (January 16, 1790), p. 361.

18. *L'Ami du Peuple*, September 23, 1789, cited in Claude Bellanger et al., *Histoire générale de la presse française*, 5 vols. (Paris: PUF, 1969), 1:455.

19. *Révolutions de France et de Brabant* No. 5 (December 26, 1789), p. 235.

20. *Révolutions de France et de Brabant*, prospectus, p. 3.

21. *L'Orateur du Peuple*, Vol. VII, No. 3 (29 Fructidor An II), p. 24.

22. *L'Orateur du Peuple*, Vol. VII, No. 3 (29 Fructidor An II), pp. 17–18.

23. *L'Orateur du Peuple*, Vol. I, No. 7, pp. 50–1.

24. *Lettres de Robespierre à ses commettans*, No. 1, p. 40.

25. *Lettres de Robespierre à ses commettans*, No. 1, p. 15.

26. *Lettres de Robespierre à ses commettans*, No. 3, p. 131.

27. *Journal Politique-National*, No. 1 (July, 1789), p. 8.

28. *Lettres de Robespierre à ses commettans*, No. 1, p. 2.

29. *Introduction aux Révolutions de Paris*, p. 29.
30. *L'Observateur françois, ou le Publiciste véridique et impartial* (L. P. Couret, Imprimeur) No. 1 (1790), p. 8.
31. Joseph Antoine Joachim Cerutti, *La Feuille Villageoise* (Paris: Chez Desenne, Libraire, au Palais-Royal, No. 1 et 4), (1790), prospectus, p. 5.
32. *La Feuille Villageoise* prospectus, pp. 5–6.
33. Talleyrand-Périgord, *Rapport sur l'instruction publique* (Paris: L'Imprimerie Nationale, 1791), p. 93.
34. *Feuille Villageoise*, seconde année, No. 27 (March 29, 1792), 4:29.
35. *Feuille Villageoise*, seconde année, No. 38 (June 14, 1792), 4:269. See also No. 1 (September 30, 1790).
36. *Feuille Villageoise*, prospectus, p. 4.
37. *Feuille Villageoise*, seconde année, No. 38 (June 14, 1792), 4:269 [emphasis added].
38. *Feuille Villageoise*, seconde année, No. 51 (September 27, 1792), 4:580.
39. Matthew Arnold, *Culture and Anarchy* [1869], ed. Collini (Cambrige: Cambridge University Press, 1993), esp. pp. 94, 97, 151.
40. Louis-Sébastien Mercier, *De J. J. Rousseau, considéré comme l'un des premiers auteurs de la révolution*, 2 vols. (Paris: Buisson, 1791), 1:108.
41. J. G. Herder, "Ideas for a Philosophy of History," in *J. G. Herder on Social and Political Culture*, translated, edited and with an introduction by F. M. Barnard (Cambridge: Cambridge University Press, 1969), p. 264.
42. J. G. Herder "Yet Another Philosophy of History," in *J. G. Herder on Social and Political Culture*," p. 184.
43. Herder, "Yet Another Philosophy of History," p. 184.
44. Herder, "Ideas for a Philosophy of History," p. 284.
45. Herder, "Yet Another Philosophy of History," p. 216.
46. Herder, "Ideas for a Philosophy of History," p. 313.
47. Georg Simmel, "The Conflict in Modern Culture," in *The Conflict in Modern Culture and Other Essays*, translated, with an introduction by K. Peter Etzkorn (New York: Teachers College Press, 1968), p. 11.
48. Fichte, *Gespräche*, p. 299.
49. Arnold, *Culture and Anarchy*, p. 62.
50. Immanuel Kant, "What is Enlightenment," in *The Portable Enlightenment Reader*, ed. Isaac Kramnick (New York: Penguin Books, 1995), p. 3.
51. For one interesting discussion of authorship and identity, see Peggy Kamuf, *Signature Pieces* (Ithaca: Cornell University Press, 1988).

52. Léonard Bourdon de la Crosnière, *Mémoire sur l'instruction et sur l'éducation nationale* (Paris: De l'imprimerie Cailleau, An second de la liberté), p. 42.

53. Reinhart Koselleck, *Critique and Crisis: Enlightenment and the Pathogenesis of Modern Society* (Cambridge, MA: MIT Press, 1988 [originally *Kritik und Krise*, Freiburg/München: Verlage Karl Alber, 1959]), p. 147.

54. The promotion of literacy and call for universal public instruction arrive at different times in different social settings across Europe. See Thomas Munck's recent survey of literacy and education trends across Europe: *The Enlightenment: a Comparative Social History, 1721–1794* (New York: Oxford University Press, 2000), esp. pp. 46–59.

55. J.-P. Rabaut Saint-Etienne, *Projet d'éducation nationale* (n.p. [Paris]: De l'imprimerie nationale, n.d. [December 21, 1792]), reprinted in *Procès-verbaux du comité d'instruction publique de la convention nationale*, 6 vols, publiés et annotés par M. J. Guillaume (*Collection de documents inédits sur l'histoire de France* publiés par les soins du ministre de l'instruction publique, vols. 192–7) (Paris: Imprimerie Nationale, 1891), 1:231.

56. Helvétius, *De l'homme, de ses facultés intellectuelles et de son éducation; ouvrage posthume de M. Helvétius* [1772], 2 vols. (Londres: Chez la Société Typographique, 1773), 1:451, 457.

57. Lanthenas, *Motifs*, pp. 22–3.

58. *Opinion de Fourcroy, député du département de Paris, sur le projet d'éducation nationale de Michel Le Pelletier*, Prononcée dans la séance du 30 juillet 1793, p. 3.

59. *Rapport fait à la Convention Nationale au nom du comité d'instruction publique*, le 1er nivôse an 3 [December 22, 1794] (n.p. [Paris]: Convention Nationale, 1794), p. 5.

60. *Motifs*, p. 28.

61. Jean François Ducos, *Sur l'instruction publique et spécialement sur les écoles primaires*, (n.p. [Paris] L'Imprimerie nationale: n.d.), in *Procès-verbaux*, 1:187.

62. François Xavier Lanthenas, *Censure publique* (Paris: Imprimerie nationale, 1793), p. 10.

63. Ducos, *Sur l'instruction publique*, 1:187.

64. Talleyrand, *Rapport*, p. 93.

65. Talleyrand, *Rapport*, p. 12.

66. Joseph Garat, *Rapport sur l'établissement des écoles normales (*), par Lakanal. Séance du 3 brumaire, l'an III de la république* (De l'Imprimerie nationale, Brumaire, l'an iii), reprinted in *Procès-verbaux*, 5:155–6.

67. L. F. A. Arbogast, *Rapport et projet de décret sur la composition des livres élémentaires destinés à l'Instruction publique, présentés à la Convention Nationale, au nom du comité d'instruction publique* (n.p., n.d. [Paris: 1792]), p. 10.

68. Jean Debry, *Discours sur les fondemens de la morale publique prononcé le 2 vendémaire l'an troisième* [September 23, 1794] (n.p. [Paris]: Convention nationale, n.d. [1794]), p. 10.

69. Michel Pelletier [Le Peletier de Saint-Fargeau], *Plan d'éducation nationale, présenté à la Convention par Maximilien Robespierre, au nom de la commission d'instruction publique, le 26 juin 1793* (n.p., n.d., [Paris, 1793]), p. 10.

70. Le Peletier, *Plan*, p. 15.

71. Debry, *Discours*, pp. 2, 14, 17.

72. Le Peletier, *Plan*, p. 22.

73. G. F. W. Hegel, *Reason in History*, trans. Robert S. Hartman (New York: The Liberal Arts Press, 1953), p. 50.

74. Arbogast, *Rapport sur la composition des livres*, p. 10.

75. Garat, *Rapport*, 5:156.

76. Claude-Laurent-Louis Masuyer, *Discours sur l'organisation de l'instruction publique et de l'éducation nationale en France. Examen et réfutation du système proposé par les citoyens Condorcet et G. Rome* (n.p., n.d. [Paris: 1792]), p. 23.

77. Henri Bancal, *Discours et Projet de décret sur l'éducation nationale, prononcés à la convention nationale, le 24 Décembre 1792* (Paris: Imprimerie Nationale, 1792), p. 9.

78. Fourcroy, *Opinion*, p. 3.

79. Fichte, *Gespräche*, pp. 324–5.

3 Instituting Culture

1. Three accounts of particular interest and influence: Ian Watt, *The Rise of the Novel* (London: Chatto & Windus, 1957); Michael McKeon, *Origins of the English Novel 1600–1740* (Baltimore: Johns Hopkins University Press, 1987); Georges May, *Le Dilemme du roman au XVIIIe siècle* (New Haven: Yale University Press, 1963).

2. Henry Fielding *Joseph Andrews*, ed. R. F. Brissenden (Penguin Books, 1977), p. 185.

3. *Joseph Andrews*, p. 185.

4. Jean-Jacques Rousseau, *Œuvres complètes* (Paris: Gallimard, Bibliothèque de la Pléiade, 1964), 2:23.

5. Rousseau, *Œuvres complètes* 2:23.

6. Charles-Joseph Panckoucke to Rousseau [c. 10 February 1761], in R. A. Leigh, *Correspondance complète de Jean-Jacques Rousseau* (Genève: Institut et Musée Voltaire and Madison: University of Wisconsin Press, 1969), 8:77–9.

7. See my "Reading Women: Fiction, Culture and Gender in Rousseau," *Eighteenth-Century Studies* 27, No. 3 (Spring 1994): 421–47.

8. For an extensive analysis of this move and its implications see Terry Eagleton, *Ideology of the Aesthetic* (Oxford: Basil Blackwell, 1990).

9. Eagleton, *Ideology of the Aesthetic*, and *The Idea of Culture*; David Lloyd and Paul Thomas, *Culture and the State* (New York and London: Routledge, 1998); Ian Hunter, "Aesthetics and Cultural Studies," in Lawrence Grossberg, Cary Nelson, and Paula Treichler, eds., *Cultural Studies* (New York: Routledge, 1992), pp. 347–72.

10. The original series of letters making up the collection was written in 1793 from Schiller to the Danish prince Friedrich Christian of Schleswig-Holstein. They were subsequently revised and added to, and published in the short-lived review *The Graces*, which Schiller edited. For a brief introduction see Friedrich Schiller, *On the Aesthetic Education of Man. In a Series of Letters*, trans. Reginald Snell (London: Routledge & Kegan Paul, 1954). For an extensive historical introduction, analysis, commentary, and summary of the essay's reception: Friedrich Schiller, *On the Aesthetic Education of Man in a Series of Letters*, trans. Elizabeth M. Wilkinson and L. A. Willoughby (Oxford: Clarendon Press, 1967). The translations are based for the most part on the more readable Snell translation, with emendations based on Wilkinson and Willoughby, where it is more accurate; in all cases I give page references to both editions, the Wilkinson and Willoughby after the slash.

11. Schiller, *Aesthetic Education*, p. 62/75 (Eleventh Letter).

12. Schiller, *Aesthetic Education*, p. 74/97 (Fourteenth Letter).

13. Schiller, *Aesthetic Education*, p. 73/94 (Fourteenth Letter).

14. Schiller, *Aesthetic Education*, p. 72/91 (Thirteenth Letter).

15. Schiller, *Aesthetic Education*, p. 74/96 (Fourteenth Letter).

16. Schiller, *Aesthetic Education*, p. 32/19 (Fourth Letter).

17. Hegel, G. W. F. *Vorlesung über die Äesthetik*, in *Werke*, 20 vols., (Frankfurt am Main: Suhrkamp, 1970), 13: 90–1; all subsequent citations are from this edition.

18. Schiller, *Aesthetic Education*, p. 74/97 (Fourteenth Letter).

19. Schiller, *Aesthetic Education*, p. 76/101 (Fifteenth Letter) [emphasis added].

20. Schiller, *Aesthetic Education*, p. 78/105 (Fifteenth Letter).

21. Schiller, *Aesthetic Education*, p. 81/109 (Fifteenth Letter).

22. Schiller, *Aesthetic Education*, p. 88/123 (Eighteenth Letter).

23. Schiller, *Aesthetic Education*, p. 89/125 (Eighteenth Letter).
24. Schiller, *Aesthetic Education*, p. 90/125 (Eighteenth Letter).
25. Schiller, *Aesthetic Education*, p. 33/21 (Fourth Letter).
26. Schiller, *Aesthetic Education*, p. 97/139 (Twentieth Letter).
27. Schiller, *Aesthetic Education*, p. 101/147 (Twenty-first Letter).
28. Schiller, *Aesthetic Education*, p. 99/141 (Twentieth Letter).
29. Schiller, *Aesthetic Education*, p. 81/111 (Sixteenth Letter).
30. Hunter, "Aesthetics and Cultural Studies"; Lloyd and Thomas, *Culture and the State*.
31. Schiller, *Aesthetic Education*, p. 28/11 (Third Letter).
32. Schiller, *Aesthetic Education*, pp. 27–8/11 (Third Letter).
33. Hegel, *Vorlesung*, pp. 27–8.
34. Hegel, *Vorlesung*, p. 74.
35. Schiller, Aesthetic Education, pp. 119/183 (Twenty-fifth Letter).
36. Hegel, *Vorlesung*, pp. 25–6.
37. Schiller, *Aesthetic Education*, p. 101/147 (Twenty-first Letter).
38. Schiller, *Aesthetic Education*, p. 101/147 (Twenty-first Letter).
39. Immanuel Kant, *Critique of Judgement*, translated with an Introduction, by J. H. Bernard (New York: Hafner Press, 1951), p. 124.
40. Hegel *Vorlesung*, p. 27.
41. Schiller, *Aesthetic Education*, p. 102/147 (Twenty-first Letter).
42. Schiller, *Aesthetic Education*, p. 102/147 (Twenty-first Letter).
43. Antoine-L. Lavoisier, *Réflexions sur l'instruction publique*, présentées à la Convention Nationale par le Bureau de Consultations des Arts et Métiers (n.p. [Paris], n.d.), p. 14.
44. Jeanbon Saint-André, *Sur l'éducation nationale* (L'imprimerie nationale, n.d. [December, 1792]), reprinted in *Procès-verbaux*, 192:278. See also Claude-Laurent-Louis Masuyer, *Discours sur l'organisation de l'instruction publique et de l'education nationale en France. Examen et réfutation du système proposé par les citoyens Condorcet et G. Rome* (n.p., n.d. [Paris: 1792]).
45. Schiller, *Aesthetic Education*, p. 51/55 (Ninth Letter).
46. Daniel J. Sherman, *Worthy Monuments: Art Museums and the Politics of Culture in Nineteenth-Century France* (Cambridge, MA: Harvard University Press, 1989), pp. 16, 193.
47. Lloyd and Thomas, *Culture and the State*, pursue this analysis in great detail.
48. Antoine Chrysostôme Quatremère de Quincy, *Suite aux Considérations sur les arts du dessin en France* (Paris: Desenne, 1791), pp. 18–20.
49. François Antoine Boissy d'Anglas, *Quelques idées sur les arts* (Paris: Convention Nationale, 1794), pp. 8–9.
50. Schiller, *Aesthetic Education*, pp. 52–3/58–9 (Ninth Letter).

51. Reinhart Koselleck, *Critique and Crisis: Englightenment and the pathogenesis of Modern Society* (Cambridge, MA: MIT Press, 1988 [originally *Kritik und Krise*, Freiburg/München: Verlage Karl Alber, 1959]), pp. 98–157, esp. 152.

52. Ian Hunter, "Aesthetics and Cultural Studies," pp. 354, 362.

53. Antoine Chrysostome Quatremère de Quincy, *Considérations morales sur la destination des ouvrages de l'art* (Paris: Crapelet, 1815), esp. pp. 66, 79.

54. In addition to works previously cited, see Tony Bennett, *The Birth of the Museum: History, Theory, Politics* (New York and London: Routledge, 1995); Didier Maleuvre, *Museum Memories: History, Technology, Art* (Stanford: Stanford University Press, 1999); Eilean Hooper-Greenhill, *Museums and the Shaping of Knowledge* (London: Routledge, 1992); Andrew McClellan, *Inventing the Louvre: Art, Politics, and the Origins of the Modern Museum in Eighteenth-Century Paris* (Berkeley: University of California Press, 1994); Edouard Pommier, *L'Art de la liberté: doctrines et débats de la révolution française* (Paris: Gallimard, 1991) and "Idéologie et musée à l'époque révolutionnaire," in *Les Images de la révolution française*, ed. Michel Vovelle (Paris: Publications de la Sorbonne, 1988); Daniel J. Sherman and Irit Rogoff, eds., *Museum Culture: Histories, Discourses, Spectacles* (Minneapolis: University of Minnesota Press, 1994).

55. Krzysztof Pomian, *Collectionneurs, amateurs et curieux: Paris-Venise, XVIe–XVIIIe siècle* (Paris: Gallimard, 1987); Bennet, *Birth of the Museum.*

56. Extensive discussions of these shifts can be found in Pomian, *Collectionneurs, amateurs et curieux*; Bennett, *Birth of the Museum*; and Hooper-Greenhill, *Museums and the Shaping of Knowledge.*

57. Concise summaries of the origins of museums can be found in Roland Schaer, *L'Invention des musées* (Paris: Gallimard/Réunion des Musées Nationaux, 1993), and *The Genesis of the Art Museum in the 18th Century*, ed. Per Bjurström (Stockholm: Nationalmuseum, 1993).

58. Cited in Schaer, *Invention des Musées*, p. 78.

59. *Second rapport sur la nécessité de la suppression de la commission du muséum, fait au nom des comités d'instruction publique et des finances, par David, député du département de Paris, dans la séance du 27 nivôse, l'an II de la République française* (n.p. [Paris]: De l'imprimerie nationale, n.d.), pp. 4–5.

60. Boissy d'Anglas, *Quelques idées sur les arts*, p. 36.

61. Quatremère de Quincy, *Considérations*, pp. 52, 64.

62. See especially Bennet, *Birth of the Museum*; Hooper-Greenhill,

Museums and the shaping of knowledge; McClellan, *Inventing the Louvre*; and Maleuvre, *Museum Memories*.

63. Quatremère de Quincy, *Considérations*, p. 65.

64. Quatremère de Quincy, *Considérations*, pp. 57–8.

65. McClellan, *Inventing the Louvre*, p. 34.

66. George-Marie Raymond, *De la peinture considérée dans ses effects sur les hommes de toutes les classes, et de son influence sur les mœurs et le gouvernement des peuples*, seconde édition (Paris: Charles Pougens, 1804), p. 152.

67. McClellan, *Inventing the Louvre*, esp. pp. 99–114.

68. Sherman, *Worthy Monuments*, pp. 216–17.

69. Maleuvre, *Museum Memories*, esp. pp. 56–71.

70. For a synopsis of the debate see Edouard Pommier "Idéologie et musée."

71. *Moniteur universel*, No. 237, Friday, August 24, 1792.

72. Edouard Pommier, postface to Jean-Baptiste Le Brun, *Réflexions sur le Muséum national* (Paris: Réunion des musées nationaux, 1992), p. 66.

73. Boissy d'Anglas, *Quelques idées sur les arts*, pp. 6–7.

74. A particularly stimulating consideration of these issues can be found in Maleuvre, *Museum Memories*.

75. See Sherman, *Worthy Monuments*, for an overview of administrative policy in French provincial musuems. Brandon Taylor, "From Penitentiary to 'Temple of Art': Early Metaphors of Improvement at the Millbank Tate," in *Art Apart: Art Institutions and Ideology across England and North America*, ed. Marcia Pointon (Manchester: Manchester University Press, 1994), pp. 9–32, examines the Tate's function as an embodiment of bourgeois regimes of order and reform.

76. The notion of ethical readiness is from Hunter, "Aesthetics and Cultural Studies"; Terry Eagleton provides a mordant critique of this idea of a "general activating capacity" in *The Idea of Culture*, pp. 18–19, as do Lloyd and Thomas, *Culture and the State*.

77. Pierre Bourdieu, "Capital symbolique et classes sociales," *L'Arc* 72 (1978): 13–19; *La Distinction* (Paris: Editions de Minuit, 1979).

78. Raymond, *De la peinture*, pp. 101–2.

79. Matthew Arnold, "The Function of Criticism," in *Culture and Anarchy and other writings*, ed. Stefan Collini (Cambridge: Cambridge University Press, 1993), p. 28.

4 Culture, Critique, and Community

1. Immanuel, Wallerstein, *The Politics of the World-Economy* (Cambridge and Paris: Cambridge University Press and Editions de la Maison des Sciences de l'Homme, 1984); Fernand Braudel, *La Dynamique du capitalisme* (Paris: Arthaud, 1985).
2. Preface to Matthew Arnold, Culture and Anarchy [1869], ed. Stefan Collini (Cambridge: Cambridge University Press, 1993), p. 190.
3. For an extensive analysis of this development see Ian Hunter, *Culture and Government: the Emergence of Literary Education* (London: Macmillan, 1988).
4. Edward Tylor, *Primitive Culture* [1871], 2 vols. (New York: Henry Holt, 1889), 1:1.
5. Lionel Trilling, *Sincerity and Authenticity* (London: Oxford University Press, 1972), p. 125.
6. Auguste Comte, *Système de politique positive ou traité de sociologie*, 4 vols. (Osnabrück: Otto Zellner, 1967; reprint of 1851–81 edition), 1:3; Emile Durkheim, *Les Règles de la méthode sociologique* [1937], 5th ed. (Paris: Quadrige/Presses Universitaires de France, 1990), Préface de la première édition, p. ix.
7. James Clifford, *The Predicament of Culture* (Harvard: Harvard University Press, 1988), p. 25.
8. Clifford, *The Predicament of Culture*, p. 34.
9. As Roy Wagner aptly notes, "an 'anthropology' which . . . disdains to invest its imagination in a world of experience, must always remain more an ideology than a science"; *The Invention of Culture*, revised and expanded edition (Chicago: University of Chicago Press, 1981), p. 3.
10. Clifford, *The Predicament of Culture*, pp. 21–54. In addition to Clifford's work, the reader might consult: Christopher Herbert, *Culture and Anomie: Ethnographic Imagination in the Nineteenth Century* (Chicago: University of Chicago Press, 1991), and Clifford Geertz, *The Interpretation of Cultures* (New York: Basic Books, 1973).
11. E. D. Hirsch, Jr., *Cultural Literacy: What Every American Needs to Know* (Boston: Houghton Mifflin, 1987).
12. My discussion here is informed throughout by Michel Wieviorka, *La Différence* (Paris: Balland, 2001), esp. pp. 54–8.
13. Steven Connor, *Theory and Cultural Value* (Oxford: Blackwell, 1992), pp. 234–5, and Herbert *Culture and Anomie*. The nostalgia for a world undivided emerges with most intensity subsequent to the explicit conceptualization of culture in its opposed anthropolog-

ical and aesthetic senses, as Connor rightly points out, but it is not a consequence of that split – it can be found in Rousseau and even earlier.

14. This is the overarching thesis of *Culture and Anomie*.
15. Arnold, *Culture and Anarchy*, p. 89.
16. José Ortega y Gasset, *The Revolt of the Masses* [1929] (New York: W. W. Norton & Co., 1994); F. R. Leavis, *Mass Civilisation and Minority Culture* (Cambridge: Minority Press, 1930).
17. Leavis, *Mass Civilisation*, p. 5.
18. T. S. Eliot, *Notes towards a Definition of Culture* (London: Faber and Faber, Limited, 1948) p. 59.
19. Lionel Trilling, *Beyond Culture* (New York: The Viking Press, 1965).
20. See footnotes 4 and 5, Introduction, *supra*.
21. Geoffrey Hartman, *The Fateful Question of Culture* (New York: Columbia University Press, 1997), pp. 225–8.
22. Arnold, "The Function of Criticism," in *Culture and Anarchy*, p. 29.
23. *Borderlands/La Frontera* (San Francisco: Spinsters, 1987), p. 21.
24. Trilling, *Beyond Culture*, pp. xii–xiii.
25. F. R. Leavis and Denys Thompson, *Culture and Environment: the Training of Critical Awareness* (London: Chatto & Windus, 1959), p. 5.
26. Leavis and Thompson, *Culture and Environment*, esp. pp. 20–51.
27. F. R. Leavis, *Mass Civilisation*, pp. 8–10.
28. Trilling, *Beyond Culture*, p. xvi
29. Charles Taylor, *Multiculturalism: examining the politics of recognition*, ed. and introduced by Amy Gutman (Princeton: Princeton University Press, 1994), pp. 32–3.
30. Leavis, *Mass Civilisation*, pp. 18–19.

Index